Understanding Central Asia

Since Soviet collapse, the independent republics of Kazakhstan, Kyrgyzstan, Tajikistan, Turkmenistan and Uzbekistan have faced tremendous political, economic, and security challenges. Focusing on these five republics, this textbook analyzes the contending understandings of the politics of the past, present and future transformations of Central Asia, including its place in international security and world politics.

Analysing the transformation that independence has brought and tracing the geography, history, culture, identity, institutions and economics of Central Asia, it locates 'the political' in the region.

A comprehensive examination of the politics of Central Asia, this insightful book is of interest both to undergraduate and graduate students of Asian Politics, Post-Communist Politics, Comparative Politics and International Relations, and to scholars and professionals in the region.

Sally N. Cummings teaches in the School of International Relations at the University of St Andrews, UK, where she is also Founding Director of the Institute of Middle Eastern, Central Asian and Caucasus Studies. Her publications include *Sovereignty After Empire* (co-ed., 2011); *Symbolism and Power in Central Asia* (ed., Routledge 2010); *Kazakhstan* (2005) and *Oil, Transition and Security in Central Asia* (ed., Routledge 2003).

"True to its title, this thought-provoking study offers a nuanced understanding of contemporary Central Asia that cuts through stereotypes and situates the region in broader social science and history debates. With its clear thematic structure it offers an incisive and accessible account of the principal influences on the political transformation of the Central Asian states. This is a book that should be read not only by advanced students of the new Eurasia, but all those interested in deepening their knowledge in this fascinating and increasingly diverse part of the world."

Roy Allison, University of Oxford, UK

"This book provides a clear and persuasive interpretation of political developments in the post-Soviet Central Asian states. The author deftly weaves together a broad range of factors that shaped the countries' recent evolution, including the legacy of the past, religion, national identity, economics, and international relations. She also situates her interpretation in the context of the scholarly literature on the subject. Her analysis is well informed and judicious. People seeking an introduction to contemporary Central Asia should start here. Those who are familiar with the subject will enjoy her engagement with the diverse body of scholarly opinion. This book deserves to be essential reading on Central Asia today."

Muriel Atkin, George Washington University, USA

"This is a superb guide to contemporary Central Asia by a leading scholar in the field. Dr Sally Cummings assesses the political transformation of the five former Soviet 'stans' since their emergence as independent states in 1991, as well as the economic, foreign policy, and security challenges facing each state. Concise yet comprehensive, *Understanding Central Asia* is an excellent introduction to the region for scholars, students, and professionals."

Adrienne Edgar, University of California, Santa Barbara, USA

"*Understanding Central Asia: Politics and Contested Transformations* is a masterful and encyclopedic work, and ever so timely, coming as it does at the twentieth anniversary of the collapse of the U.S.S.R. and the formation of these five countries. Seeking to merge social science theory with an area studies approach, Cummings' work touches on all the fundamental questions relating to state-building in the Central Asian region. In a cogently written fashion she makes the reader aware of the conflicting interpretations on how to understand the Central Asian region, both how it is constituted, what colonization brought to these territories, and whether years of Soviet rule were a further continuation of colonization or a different kind of political experience."

Martha Brill Olcott, Carnegie Endowment For International Peace, USA

"This book is both a major achievement and an important contribution to the field of Central Asian studies. Drawing upon a rich body of literature from across the social sciences and humanities, it offers the most comprehensive account of the region's political transformation since it was jolted into independence from Soviet rule in 1991."

Pauline Jones Luong, Brown University, USA

Understanding Central Asia

Politics and contested transformations

Sally N. Cummings

Routledge
Taylor & Francis Group

LONDON AND NEW YORK

First published 2012
by Routledge
2 Park Square, Milton Park, Abingdon, Oxon OX14 4RN

Simultaneously published in the USA and Canada
by Routledge
711 Third Avenue, New York, NY 10017

Routledge is an imprint of the Taylor & Francis Group, an informa business

British Library Cataloguing in Publication Data
A catalogue record for this book is available from the British Library

Library of Congress Cataloging in Publication Data
Cummings, Sally N.
 Understanding Central Asia : politics and contested transformations / Sally N. Cummings.
  p. cm.
 Includes bibliographical references and index.
 1. Asia, Central–Politics and government–Textbooks. I. Title.
 JQ1080.C86 2012
 320.958–dc23   2011038083

ISBN: 978-0-415-29702-8 (hbk)
ISBN: 978-0-415-29703-5 (pbk)
ISBN: 978-0-203-40314-3 (ebk)

Typeset in Times New Roman
by Cenveo Publisher Services

For Ashley and Liam

Contents

List of illustrations

Tables

Maps

Timelines

Acknowledgements

This book says a thank you to all those people who have made and continue to make the study of Central Asia a joy. My thanks therefore to the specialists, here acknowledged or unacknowledged, who continue to write such engaging work and without whom this volume could not have been written. Thanks therefore to my students, undergraduate and graduate, who generate a critical and vibrant interest in developments of the region. And, above all, my thanks to countless friends and colleagues in Central Asia: for their generous hospitality, their wisdom and their support over, now, a great many years. My thanks to those who kindly agreed to read parts or all of the manuscript: Roy Allison, Muriel Atkin, Adrienne Edgar, Matteo Fumagalli, Peter Golden, Pauline Jones Luong, Martha Brill Olcott, Wojtek Ostrowski, Johan Rasanayagam, Madeleine Reeves, John Roberts and John Schoeberlein; any errors of fact or interpretation are my own. My gratitude goes also to those who have helped make this book a possibility: to Craig Fowlie, Leanne Hinves, Jillian Morrison and Dorothea Schaefter at Routledge and also, in the very final stages, to Karen Angelosanto, Vicky Bruce, Olivia Maurier, Stewart Pether and, on the maps and tables, Ned Conway. And, of course, my loving thanks to my husband and also our two little ones, Ashley and Liam. Now just six and five, they have accompanied me in the writing of this book and also on my more recent travels and residence in Central Asia. It is to them, as a small token, that this book is dedicated.

Note on transliteration

Central Asia is a place of tremendous cultural, linguistic and historical variation; names, places and scholarly references have consequently both changed over time and are also variously transliterated. The transliteration system in this book is far from perfect, offering by no means the definitive answer. In the text, I have generally used more familiar English spellings for both Russian and Central Asian words. The Library of Congress system has generally been used for the transliteration of Russian words and names, although some exceptions have been made to retain familiarity. Again, because of familiarity in English, for Central Asian words and place names I generally transliterate from the Russified/Cyrillic spelling (using, for example, a 'k' rather than a 'q'). For the plural forms, I add 's'.

1   Introduction

> Interests of the most varied kind are bound up with those vast territories, hitherto so little known, which are comprised under the general denomination of Central Asia. The historian knows this to have been once the trysting-place of the numerous powerful hordes of nomadic races, who penetrated into the very heart of Europe, spreading ruin and devastation like a deluge; the geographer knows this region as the one that is still the most imperfectly represented on the map, where rivers, mountains, and cities can only be traced in vague outlines; the ethnologist recalls to his mind the group of Turanian peoples, together with indistinct ideas connected with them; and lastly, the politician perhaps looks forward to the collision that may take place between the two greatest powers on earth – the one by sea, and the other by land.
>
> (von Hellwald 1874: ix)

The self-referred 'Austrian military author' Friedrich von Hellwald's musings on Central Asia point simultaneously to the region's obscurity and importance. Historically and as a discrete geographic region, Central Asia has often disappeared, submerged into bigger political and geographic areas. In 1994, a historical study of Central Asia commissioned by UNESCO (Dani and Masson 1992: 19) acknowledged that 'the role and importance of the various peoples of Central Asia are often inadequately represented in university courses, to say nothing of school textbooks'. In another author's view, the area seemed to be simply receding out of view altogether until very recently, falling into a sort of geographical black hole 'between disciplinary cracks' (Gross 1992: 17). In the same year, André Gunder Frank (1992) was also to refer to the 'black hole' of Central Asia. As John Schoeberlein (2002: 4) writes, however, we do not need to be 'among those who hope for things to get worse so that others will recognize the importance of this region'.

The endurance of a romantic, dangerous and arcane image of Central Asia may stem partly from a phenomenon that Edward Said (2003: 55) noted of the Middle East, namely that people are 'not quite ignorant, not quite informed'. When informed, furthermore, their image is often reliant on popular media, which paints the region either as a place of swashbuckling heroes or terrorists, from the

Great Game to interesting plots for James Bond movies, the BBC Series *Spooks* or the 20th Century Fox Network Series *24* (Heathershaw and Megoran 2011), or even as a site of hilarity, including Turkmenistan's late President Saparmurat Niyazov and, most recently and importantly, Sasha Baron Cohen's invention of Borat (Saunders 2010). In Gunder Frank's (1992: 4) terms it 'makes no sense to regard "Central" (or "Inner") Asia and its many different peoples as somehow all different from the rest of the world then and now. There was and is unity in diversity, and Central Asia was not apart from but constituted the core of this reality of human history and existence'. This normalcy is juxtaposed to so many of the received wisdoms and stereotypes we have today. Seasoned travellers to Central Asia will remark, often somewhat incredulously, that there were no militant Islamic societies. There were no nomads of the bygone era. There were certainly no Borats.

This fluctuation in the region's prominence and sometimes its very existence is partly on account of the region's geography. As a landlocked region, Central Asia is open to the influence of its neighbours, particularly when those neighbours at various times have been empires or great powers. The Persians, Turks, Greeks, Arabs, Chinese and Russians have all encroached on and transformed this region. At the same time, the unique features of the steppe (Sinor 1990) and its position on a frontier with these great powers (Barfield 1989; Grousset 2005) has nevertheless facilitated, and even compelled, the rise of its own strong indigenous rulers, notably those associated with the great Turkic and Mongol empires. The most recent instance of Central Asia's reappearance has been after the collapse of communism in 1991.

This book addresses the contemporary period and it takes as its object of study the five ex-Soviet republics of Kazakhstan, Kyrgyzstan, Tajikistan, Turkmenistan and Uzbekistan. This is not everyone's idea of Central Asia. Many take Central Asia to be a far broader expanse that is more reflective of the area covered by a territory, often referred to in the English language as Inner Asia or Central Eurasia. Such a large expanse, therefore, would also take in Turkistan (east and west), Manchuria, Inner and Outer Mongolia and Tibet. A Central Eurasian perspective would also be likely to include parts of southern Siberia, northeastern Iran and northern Afghanistan. But still it can be argued that in contemporary usage the Central Asian, Russian and English understandings of the term more often than not refer to the five independent republics (Akiner 1998).

The post-Soviet focus in this book is further dictated by the author's own interests and background. While a diverse set of themes are studied, the book's focus is on the region's broader political transformation since 1991. To locate 'the political' in the region, the book traces its history, identity, institutions, economics and its wider place in the world. It does so not chronologically but thematically, and for each of these related themes it asks a set of questions that have dominated their discussion of late. The isolation of these five republics for a study of post-Soviet change is further justified by the enormous influence the 'intertwined Russian, Soviet, and Marxist transformations' continue to exert on these countries' early independence trajectories and how Soviet legacies go to the heart of the modern identity of various Central Asian peoples 'from the semi-desert environments of western Uzbekistan to the lush valleys of the Pamir Mountains shared by Tajiks and Kyrgyz, to say nothing of the cosmopolitan settings of Almaty and Tashkent' (Sahadeo and Zanca 2007: 9). Politically, the region has remained very much post-Soviet.

Russian influence on the region is, in historical terms, a recent phenomenon. This is, after all, 'a "Turko-Persian" cultural world' (Golden 2011). The term 'Turkmen' specifically referring to Turkic tribes in Central Asia who had converted to Islam, was first noted in the tenth century (Bartol'd 1968; Saray 1989; Edgar 2004). Similarly, the great Russian orientalist, academician Vasilij V. Bartol'd (1958) referred to how the word 'Tajik' was first recorded in the literature on Central Asia by the historian Bayhaqi who related how he had overheard a senior Iranian so describing his nationality in conversation with Mas'ud of Ghazni in 1039. The historical consensus appears that when invading Muslim Arabs and their Persian-speaking allies arrived in Central Asia by the seventh century AD they encountered nomads on the steppes north of the Syr, who, while then predominantly Turkic Darya became a mixed population 'using Eastern Iranian languages as the medium of cultural and official communication, and dominated successively by a mixed Sasanian, Hephthalite and Turkic aristocracy' (Bergne 2007: 5); in short, 'in the ancient period, the nomadic peoples of the steppe were predominantly Iranian' (Levi 2007: 18). The majority of Tajiks would come to speak a Western Iranian language (Persian, i.e. the language of Fars, a minority speaking Eastern Iranian languages of Yaghnob and the various Pamiri), the remaining Central Asians, Turkic languages.

After Islam had taken root, a dynasty of local governors, known as the Samanids, established a strong local political organization owing only nominal allegiance to the distant Abbasid caliphate of Baghdad. For the following thousand years the original Pre-Islamic Central Asian population would be either driven from the region or governed and gradually assimilated by a succession of invaders, including numerous Turkic peoples, such as those led by their dynasties, the Karakhanids (who overthrew the Samanids) and Seljuqs. Still other Turkic tribes arrived, intermingled and fought with the Mongol invaders in the thirteenth century (Morgan 1990) and, finally, arriving in the fifteenth and sixteenth centuries, as the confederation that became known as the Uzbeks (Allworth 1990). Russian traveller Khanykov noted that the Uzbeks by the middle of the nineteenth century were already the dominant group in the area. If Turkic speakers ethnically came to dominate, the use of Persian, partly as a result of surviving interaction with the main area of today's Iran, continued to survive in government and social life, especially in Samarkand and Bukhara (Bergne 2007).

Within this ethno-linguistic mix, the fate of the category 'Sart' is illuminating (Schoeberlein 1994). At the time of his research Bartol'd (1997) noted that 'Sart' had come to mean 'an Uzbekized urban Tajik'. But, as Alisher Ilkhamov (2004) notes, this traditional image did not accord with the Soviet ethnographic and socialist project, the relatively poorer rural Uzbeks conforming more neatly than the more prosperous urbanized Sarts. Sart was thus dropped in favour of Uzbek. Paul Bergne (2007: 9) elaborates how within 'this composite "Sart" nationality were as yet unassimilated representatives of both Turkic and Tajik groups. On the Turkic side were Kipchaks, "Turks", Kyrgyz and Kara Kyrgyz (up to the 20th century the Russian names for Kazakhs and Kyrgyz respectively), Karakalpaks, Turkmen people, Uzbeks, etc., many of whom still lived nomadic or semi-nomadic lives'. In the Soviets' further attempts to categorize ethno-linguistic groups, therefore, they were also faced with the challenge of differentiating between Kazakh and Kyrgyz. During the 1924–36 national territorial delimitation process, in which the five selected ethno-linguistic groups of the Kazakhs, Kyrgyz, Tajiks, Turkmen and Uzbeks were given their own national republics, a Soviet Central Asian space was born, and the borders of each of these Soviet Socialist Republics became those of the newly independent five '-stans'. Central Asia's 'catapult to independence' (Olcott 1992) serves as a pivotal event, a critical juncture for all sorts of related developments that now place the five countries as independent actors.

Contemporary Central Asia in historical and global perspective

Emerging from this Soviet obscurity, authors have asked, are the five '-stans' 'one or many?' (Gleason 1997). The answer is not simple because the five Central Asian countries share obvious commonalities as well as stark differences which push them as much apart (Bohr 2004; Suyunbaev 2010) as together (Gleason 1997; Tolipov 2006). The common historico-cultural threads just outlined, whose complexity and constant flux undermine regional stereotypes, can be as common in the degree of diversity as in their uniformity. At the same time Central Asia's still recent emergence from Soviet rule has also left a number of what might be termed specifically Soviet legacies in all five states (Rakowska-Harmstone 1994). These Soviet legacies include: initial international isolation (both from the capitalist (Kaser 1992) and Muslim worlds (Khalid 2007c)); a politicized 'strong-weak' state (McMann 2004); a largely resource-based and therefore skewed economic development (Kandiyoti 2007); environmental degradation (Sievers 2003) that had resulted from Soviet gargantuan projects of modernity involving, for example, nuclear testing (Semey, Kazakhstan), river diversion with the (desiccation of the Aral Sea (Weinthal 2002) and intensive crop irrigation (Virgin Lands, Kazakhstan)); despite intensive Russification and Slav settlement during the Soviet period the emergence also in early independence of cultural titular superior status in the context of multi-ethnic states (especially Kazakhstan (Dave 2007), Kyrgyz Republic (Huskey 1997), Tajikistan (Akbarzadeh 1996)) with often a large second ethnic group (e.g. Uzbeks (and Russians)) in the Kyrgyz Republic, Tajiks in Uzbekistan or Russians in Kazakhstan (Bremmer and Welt 1995); and, awkward, either porous or potentially irredentist borders (particularly the enclaves in the Ferghana Valley and the Russian-Kazakh border for the former).

Legacies, Soviet or preceding, create challenges in the independence period. These include: consolidating new statehood and civic identities, while allowing for the growth of national cultures that were formerly developed but also oppressed; navigating from a highly controlling political system in which the Communist Party monopolized both state and regime, to one that provides at a minimum a system seen to deliver on its promises in a transparent way regulated by a fair and accountable set of rules; diversifying the economy so as to reduce these countries' great power dependencies on global and volatile commodity prices while ensuring the continued livelihoods of those employed in agriculture and rural areas, with a view also to reducing overall poverty levels; and, establishing their independent foreign policies to reflect their worldview and pragmatic national interests. From an everyday perspective, in short, providing a new political container which enables the ordinary Central Asian to feel a sense of belonging and security, and lead a just and decent way of living is no easy matter when the various ethnic, cultural, religious and political priorities of each of the republics must be considered.

These challenges are not unique to Central Asia but the combination of pre-Soviet heritage, Soviet experience and geography offers a unique set of tools and a unique set of emerging outcomes. Specialists in political theory or comparative politics may enquire why Central Asia may provide an intriguing example alongside other regions. Those who already know the region need no persuading. While exciting, however, the beguiling and romantic nature of the region is not sufficient reason in itself for anyone to write thematically about it. Central Asia is particularly interesting as its evolution arises partly from its hugely diverse set of past and current influences. The compression of time and space that occurred again with Soviet collapse, when, almost by surprise (Yurchak 2006), peoples seemed to be again asked overnight to get used to a new set of rulers and ways of governing and existence means there is much to discuss that is interesting in political terms. In determining what makes this region what it is, it is necessary to consider, for example, that it still had a substantial nomadic population as recently as the beginning of the twentieth century and that the Soviet developmental project, that simultaneously aimed to sedentarize, collectivize and make literate the entire region in the fastest speed undertaken by any state modernization project to date. Attempting to further an in-depth understanding of any region is worthwhile, since it increases our critical faculties for assessing often Eurocentric methods and methodologies. Central Asia has and continues to be a laboratory for developmental projects; some gains have been made, but a great many have suffered and continue to suffer.

Various defining features of an early independent Central Asia are already emerging. The Soviet Union was called 'the Second World' and independent Central Asian republics continue to distinguish themselves from a Third World country (including in juxtaposition to their neighbour Afghanistan). But what does a cursory examination of the evidence suggest? Central Asian republics rank among the most corrupt nations of the world. They are also less free than other regions, comparable to some African countries (Freedom House Index 2011).

They do, however, rank generally higher on indexes of state capacity, than, say, African states (Beissinger and Crawford 2002), having emerged on independence, as we shall see, with a partial statehood developed under the constraints of Soviet federalism. Economically, they emerged from the Soviet era with colonial-type structures and lopsided development that made them primarily raw material producers, with some now sitting on enormous natural resource wealth. Societies emerging from Soviet rule were highly educated and literate. Economically their GDP per head income levels vary from those of mid- to lower-level income countries. According to the World Bank (2011), poverty levels vary significantly, the opposite poles being the poorest Tajikistan and the fastest growing economy of Kazakhstan which has registered a double digit growth rate since 2001 (Cummings 2005). But even in the latter, income levels among the population remain hugely varied. Overall, the indicators are mixed and do not slot the region comfortably into either the 'first' or 'third' worlds.

In terms of political regime, the five have flirted with liberalization but the landscape remains on the whole an authoritarian one. In terms of ethnicity and ethnic belonging, we have examples of distinctly multi-ethnic states juxtaposed with more mono-ethnic ones. With the important and tragic exceptions of Tajikistan (1992–7), Uzbekistan (2005) and the Kyrgyz Republic (2002, 2010), Central Asia has been relatively more stable than comparable post-colonial countries in the immediate aftermath of imperial collapse.

The book's themes and organization

Understanding why Central Asia has come to hold these political associations is the subject of this book. In the following chapters six key themes that have served to strengthen our understanding of newly independent Central Asia are discussed: its regional classifications; its past; its culture, beliefs and identity; its politics; its economic transformation; its security and wider international relations. These six areas help answer some of the political questions that independence has brought. For example, how has independence changed the way the region's borders are drawn and experienced? How has it changed the way leaders and societies evaluate their pasts? How has it changed the way societies are governed? How has the new political container changed the way economies are managed and accessed by the outside world? And how are these new entities being secured, both in providing positive sovereignty (the state providing sufficient goods and services) and negative sovereignty (the securing of borders to prevent penetration from the outside world)?

Chapter 2, devoted to a discussion of what we understand by the geography of Central Asia, shows how my study concerns the five post-Soviet Central Asian republics. I am mindful that this definition of Central Asia is subject to reshaping. That reshaping, it is argued later, is primarily concerned with security interests, particularly in light of the challenges of Afghanistan and the growing influence of the region's two great powers, China and Russia. But it is also a function of how actors, domestic and external, attribute meaning to their region. While in the

Table 1.1 General indicators

Country	Land area (sq km)	Population Estimates (millions)	Main ethnic groups	Urbanization	Exports/Sector
Kazakhstan	2,724,900	15.52	Kazakh 63.1%, Russian 23.7%, Uzbek 2.8%, Ukrainian 2.1%, Uighur 1.4%, Tatar 1.3%, German 1.1%, other 4.5% (2009 census)	59%	Oil and oil products; ferrous metals; chemicals; machinery; grain; wool; meat; coal
Kyrgyzstan	199,951	5.59	Kyrgyz 64.9%, Uzbek 13.8%, Russian 12.5%, Dungan 1.1%, Ukrainian 1%, Uighur 1%, other 5.7% (1999 census)	35%	Cotton; wool; meat; tobacco; gold; mercury; uranium; natural gas; hydropower; machinery; shoes
Tajikistan	143,100	7.63	Tajik 79.9%, Uzbek 15.3%, Russian 1.1%, Kyrgyz 1.1%, other 2.6% (2000 census)	26%	Aluminium; electricity; cotton; fruits; vegetable oil; textiles
Turkmenistan	488,100	5.00	Turkmen 85%, Uzbek 5%, Russian 4%, other 6% (2003)	50%	Gas; crude oil; petrochemicals; textiles; cotton fibre
Uzbekistan	447,400	28.13	Uzbek 80%, Russian 5.5%, Tajik 5%, Kazakh 3%, Karakalpak 2.5%, Tatar 1.5%, other 2.5% (1996 est.)	36%	Energy products; cotton; gold; mineral fertilizers; ferrous and non-ferrous metals; textiles; food products; machinery; automobiles

Source: Compiled from: Nations in Transit (2011); EIU Country Reports (2010 and 2011); National Census Results (2009); *The World Factbook*, Washington, DC: Central Intelligence Agency (2011) and CIA (2011).

Soviet period the five '-stans' had been known as 'Middle Asia and Kazakhstan', in 1993 leaders decided to rename themselves as Central Asia. This decision in itself is interesting. Rather than expressing a strong regional identity, it reflected an identity by default. The institutionalization of the region, or regionalism, has been largely absent from the Central Asian landscape. A larger 'geopolitical framework' (Banuazizi and Weiner 1994), in which contiguous states are included is also, in part, a response to the observation that Central Asian states have been better at co-operating when outside powers have been involved. The chapter also looks at the various debates that surround the term 'heartland' and the degree to which we may comfortably use this term.

As a bridge to Chapter 3, questions are asked about what point of history authors begin with when they try to understand Central Asia. Before the arrival of Islam, our knowledge and understanding of Central Asia came largely from archaeologists. Written texts date predominantly from the seventh century with the arrival of Islam (Soucek 2000). Most of the historical discussion in Chapter 3, however, is devoted to the Soviet period and, for the purposes of this book, with reason: as elsewhere in the Soviet Union Soviet border delimitation became congruent with the specific naming of categorized ethno-national groups. Chapter 3 draws on the exciting new archival evidence that gives a far fuller sense of how borders were drawn and chosen. Furthermore, modernization itself led to sedentarization and industrialization, settling nomads and reconceptualizing tribal attitudes to territory to the point where Olivier Roy (2007) links the kolkhoz to reconstituted identities. But challenging questions about this process remain, not least as to how far the ethnography project was a success. Did the employing of Soviet cartographers entail a reshaping of the identity, or was it an expression thereof? Given the extent to which ethnographers were employed, some now question the degree to which we can call the state borders arbitrary or not. Why did the Tajiks lose out so badly to the Uzbeks? And was imperfect state creation a legacy of Soviet rule? The chapter, in conclusion, assesses the nature of sovereignty that the republics of the Soviet era bequeathed to each of the independent republics.

The study of Central Asia has provoked much discussion around clans and their impact on political systems, and the degree to which clans differ from regions. The debate is over the impact of clans on mobilization of identities and the degree to which they have a debilitating effect on political change. If David Gullette (2007) is correct in redirecting us to the genealogical study of clans, then where does that leave us with the impact of clans on mobilization? Some authors see clans as a key stumbling block to democratization and key to unlocking why this region is authoritarian, as is debated in Chapter 4. This is not, of course, unique, since the post-Soviet space, as Thomas Carothers (2002) pointed out, remains stuck in the 'grey zone'. Also of interest is the fact that of the three that began liberalization paths in the 1990s, all have converged onto the path of authoritarianism. How satisfactory a lens is political culture in explaining the persistence of authoritarianism or are broader domestic and external explanatory frameworks more helpful?

With the exception of Askar Akaev who had 'broken with the republican party leadership by the end of the 1980s' (Huskey 2002: 75), all of Central Asia's first presidents were former Communist first party secretaries. Independent Tajikistan's first president, Rahmon Nabiev, had been the Tajik SSR's penultimate first secretary (1992–5) but once elected in November 1991 survived only until 1994, losing power during that country's tragic 1992–1997 civil war, to be replaced by Imomali Rahmonov in 1992 (Atkin 2002). While Rahmonov was able to remain in power into the second decade of the twenty-first century, Akaev, by contrast, was toppled by protests in 2005, as would be his successor in 2010, Kurmanbek Bakiev. Turkmenistan's Saparmurat Niyazov would most likely still be in power had he not died in 2006, replaced by Gurbanguly Berdymukhamedov. Kazakhstan's Nursultan Nazarbaev and Uzbekistan's Islam Karimov have remained so far these two independent countries' only presidents. These communists-turned-nationalists began to champion, successfully, new state identities, employing Soviet tools of state and nation-building outlined in Chapter 3. The challenges facing the leaders of the most multi-ethnic of the five: Kazakhstan, Kyrgyzstan and Tajikistan, were different to more mono-ethnic Turkmenistan and Uzbekistan that could rely on a greater congruence of ethnicity and state to sell the idea of a '-stani' to the population (even if both multi- and monoethnic polities have witnessed discrimination). Annette Bohr's (1998a) 'nationalizing by stealth' term became an apt formulation of how these countries' leaders hesitated to implement a rampant, exclusionary nationalism (thankfully). In part this was a legacy of Soviet psychic violence for some, or, for others, a genuine acceptance of the project that was Soviet rule and attempts to promote it.

A political system is shaped by the identities it embraces and protects and Chapter 5 analyses how varying types and levels of identities are constantly negotiated and renegotiated, by whom and to what purpose. In the absence of nationalist mobilization from below, the political container that was now an independent state could not automatically claim to be ruling in the name of a nation. The political elite, just as it had not learned compromise or competition in transition, did not have a sufficient national identity behind it. Identity and politics created a mixed set of challenges: how to create a state identity, how to further the titular national identity and how to deal with other sets of identities, be they supra- or sub-state.

One big question confronting scholars of the region is the nature of tradition and modernity and their transformation in the Soviet era. This forms the heart of identity and belief systems. Similarly for Islam: Islam, after the collapse of the Cold War and writings such as Samuel Huntington's *Clash of Civilizations*, has become a new priority for many writers of the region. Does the present portrayal of Islam obscure our understanding of Islam in the region and of security challenges? One exciting avenue of enquiry over the past 20 years has been to trace the links between pre-Soviet types of Islamic observance and post-Soviet expression. Did the Soviet era in this way freeze the development of Islam?

The politics of Soviet-era and independent Central Asia have been strongly shaped by the region's economics, and that is the focus of Chapter 6.

Much attention has been paid to the so-called new Great Game over pipeline access and the region's natural resources and I shall try also to show how competitive behaviour to gain access to Central Asia's resources has dominated great power interest. But I also look at writing that has attempted to understand the workings of a country exiting a Soviet planned economy and what sorts of factors have influenced different reform paths.

Chapter 7 places Central Asia in its international security context. Here Central Asia as a geopolitical configuration features as its strongest, both because of great power interests in the region and because emerging 'soft' security threats emphasize the broader region. The broader geopolitical region may be from where these threats emanate and with whose co-operation they need to be solved. What and who is threatening Central Asia and how relatively stable is the region? The region, like many others, has been subject to differing ideas of what constitutes 'security' and my final chapter explores the ramifications and implications of this. And, finally, in conclusion, I examine how the state and its transformation has provided a leitmotif for the book.

Before beginning, two important caveats. First, I apologize to all those authors I have not directly cited or have omitted in the text or bibliography. It is impossible to include every possible contributor whose work I have read in a work of this size. Second, the book cannot claim to address every question that could be asked about this region, for which another apology. In a book with the title 'Understanding' it is easy to give the impression that every aspect of the subject has been dealt with but no single work can ever do full justice to the vast and rich scholarly literature in all the fields that need to be considered. This is a book that touches on many aspects of its subject and does not claim to offer the last word on any of them. I hope it will inspire interest in a region that is deserving of further study, further questions and even further writing.

2 The region of Central Asia

What's in a name?

A central question with which to begin is to what extent is it justified to focus on the five ex-Soviet republics – Kazakhstan, Kyrgyzstan, Tajikistan, Turkmenistan and Uzbekistan, colloquially known as 'the five stans' – that form what we have come to know as Central Asia? In common with many other geographic regions, there is no neat answer to the question of what constitutes Central Asia and discussion of the topic is of long standing. The geographic expanse selected may depend on any number of reasons. It may be partly a function of the author's interests or specialization, their view on the region's leitmotifs that work to make this region 'discrete', or, again, what identities actors (external or internal) choose to give to Central Asia, either in how they imagine it (spatially or temporally) or how they try to perform it, even institutionally. Here each of these reasons is examined.

Terminological debates

'While not ideal, historians and political scientists are said to "know a region when they see one", and economists identify them through the existence of formal trading structures' (Fawn 2009: 12). In trying to understand the Central Asian region, the working language plays a role in how we see it. Take Russian and English language variations, for example, as shown in Table 2.1.

Despite its apparently clear-cut nature, the discussion will show that Table 2.1 is far from straightforward. Labels, for example, 'Russian' and 'English', obscure debates between individuals working in those languages (particularly in the community of explorers and geographers in the nineteenth century). But the table does suggest that the left-hand column is where this book lies, although I have not included north-eastern Iran, northern Afghanistan and southern Siberia in my delineation of the region.

Russian terminology is possibly the more straightforward. The Russian annexation of a greater part of the Central Asian territory, completed by 1884, led to the association of this region with Russian possessions and therefore, often to the use of Russian administrative terms for the region deriving from the Russian 'Governate General of Turkestan'. After the Bolshevik Revolution of 1917 and especially after the 1924–36 delimitation process Central Asia – in Russian 'Srednyaya Aziya', was used more narrowly to refer to the four Soviet

Table 2.1 Terminological debates

Terminology by language/date	Region		
	Western	*Eastern*	*Eastern and Western combined (if adopted)*
Current	*Generally* understood as area coterminous with five Soviet republics; sometimes including Western Turkestan and sometimes also northeastern Iran, northern Afghanistan and southern Siberia	*Generally* understood as area coterminous with Xinjiang, adjacent lands, Outer and Inner Mongolia and Tibet	*Generally* understood as coterminous with fusion of these two
Russian (1884–1917)	Western or 'Russian' Turkestan coterminous with the Russian annexed areas	Eastern or Chinese Turkestan	Turkestan
Russian in Soviet period (1917–1991)	'Srednyaya Aziya i Kazakhstan' (Middle Asia + Kazakhstan; Zentralasien +; Asie centrale+)	Tsentral'naya Aziya (Central Asia, Mittelasien; Haute Asie)	Sino-Soviet Border formalizing division
Russian (Post-Soviet)	Tsentral'naya Aziya referring to the five ex-Soviet '-stans' (as defined by the five themselves in 1993 and increasingly accepted by Russia)		
English Variations (twentieth century)	The twentieth century saw a proliferation of terms, including: 'High Asia', 'High Tartary', 'Chinese Tartary', 'Inmost Asia', 'Inner Asia', the 'Heart of Asia', 'Greater Central Asia' and 'Central Asia', with references also to Central Eurasia and Greater Middle East.		

Socialist Republics of the Uzbeks, Tajiks, Turkmen and Kirghizia, with the Kazakh SSR listed separately, hence, in the Soviet period, Central Asia and Kazakhstan (Bregel 1996). The term 'Tsentral'naya Aziya' 'was reserved for the lands further to the east that were, or had been, under Chinese rule, namely Mongolia (both the part formerly known as "Outer" Mongolia, and that known as Inner Mongolia), Xinjiang and Tibet (i.e. present-day Xinjiang/Tibet Autonomous Region, and adjacent areas of Chinese provinces with a significant Tibetan population)' (Akiner 1998: 4). The collapse of the Soviet Union brought further change to the term. The same term was adopted by the five newly independent states (with the inclusion of Kazakhstan) at a summit meeting of their presidents held in Tashkent in January 1993. Shirin Akiner (1998: 5) explains further that '[i]n Russia likewise, Tsentral'naya Aziya is increasingly used in this way (at least with reference to the post-Soviet period), thereby removing the old lexical distinction between the lands within the Russian sphere of influence and those within the Chinese sphere of influence'.

English terminology is rather more complex, particularly when we get into the post-Soviet period. In the pre-Soviet, and sometimes in the Soviet, the term 'Inner Asia' referred to both eastern and western parts. Writing in the Soviet period, Gavin Hambly comments that there were exceptions to this, with Central and Inner Asia treated as 'virtually synonymous' by some authors. He sees the region as comprising 'the five SSRs, the Mongolian People's Republic, and the three dependencies of China, known today as the Inner Mongolian Autonomous Region, the Sinkiang-Uighur Autonomous Region and the Tibet Autonomous Region, conflating Inner and Central Asia' (Hambly 1969: xi). That said, in the Soviet period, English and European usage basically referred to Western Central Asia as Central Asia, and with the Sino-Soviet border in place, generally excluded Western Xinjiang and therefore became coterminous with the five Soviet republics. It is also fair to say that English, French and German usage in the post-Soviet period, like the Russian post-Soviet usage, has frequently understood Central Asia or 'Tsentral'naya Aziya' to refer to the five ex-Soviet republics, leading many to view this as internationally the most commonly accepted use of the term. But this view is not universal and remains subject to both questioning and fluctuation.

While highlighting intraregional differences, some authors use Central Asia (Golden 2011) or Inner Asia (Sinor 1990) to mean both eastern and western parts. Bregel (1996: 1) explains further that '[I]n English, "Central Asia" would often mean the entire Inner Asian heartland, from the Ural River and the Caspian Sea in the west to Manchuria in the east, although just as often it would be used in a more restricted sense, being limited to the western part of the area'. For Svat Soucek (2000: xi–xii) Inner Asia 'designates the whole area in its historical and geographical sense; *Central Asia* [italics in original], as used in English, means the western portion of Inner Asia, roughly Western Turkestan and the western part of Eastern Turkestan, together with such adjacent areas as northeastern Iran and northern Afghanistan'. At its widest limits, the term may encompass a belt that stretches from the Hungarian plain in the west to the Ussuri and Amur rivers in the east, from the Arctic Circle in the north to the Indo-Gangetic plain in the south. More commonly, however, it is used to designate some part of the smaller (though nevertheless huge) area that is bounded by the Volga and Argun rivers, southern Siberia and the Himalayas (Akiner 1998: 4). Hambly (1969: xi) concludes: 'As a geographical expression the term "Central Asia" tends to elude precise definition'.

In the combined east–west usage, authors may distinguish between Islamic Central Asia (Bregel 1995), or western and eastern Central Asia (Golden 2011) between Islamic and Lamaist Central Asia. Still others continue to make a distinction between Central Asian as Western and Inner Asian as both Western and Eastern. The geographic limits 'western' and 'eastern', moreover, can change. Western can be limited to the five or it can be the five plus (Western) Xinjiang. The East can include Manchuria and Tibet, but sometimes does not.

The north–south extremes of the combined areas can differ, incorporating at times north-eastern Iran, additionally to northern Afghanistan, or, again, southern Siberia. Xinjiang is sometimes wholly placed in the West or split between its Muslim West and the remaining East. Turkey is sometimes included, sometimes not. Robert Canfield (1991: xi), for example, has referred to 'Greater Central Asia' as a region extending from 'Turkey to Sinkiang (Xinjiang) (or Chinese Turkestan) and, on a more southerly latitude, from the Euphrates to North India'. Cyril E. Black et al. (1991) refer to Iran, Afghanistan, Mongolia, Kazakhstan, Kyrgyzstan, Tajikistan, Turkmenistan, Uzbekistan, Tibet and Xinjiang while L. I. Miroshnikov (1992: 477–80) refers to Afghanistan, western China, northern India, north-eastern Iran, Mongolia, Pakistan and the former Soviet Central Asian republics.

Still another layer arises when Central Asia is related to its surrounding region because in the process of placing the region in its context the boundaries between it and the outside world are sometimes dropped. So, Central Asia and Central Eurasia may be used interchangeably by some (e.g. Hiro 2009), or including parts of each (Mackinder 1919). A more recent addition has been the Greater Middle East. Barry Buzan and Ole Wæver (2003: 423), employing their concept of 'regional security complex' (RSC), summarize the contemporary discussion as follows:

> Central Asia could be considered a candidate for a separate RSC (Peimani, 1998). In some studies of security regions, it is given its own chapter (sometimes together with the Caucasus, e.g., Schulz et al., 2001). Others have had difficulty deciding as part of which region to treat Central Asia. Is it (as the name seems to indicate) a part of Asia, or a part of the Middle East, maybe a 'northern tier' with Turkey, Pakistan, Iran, and Afghanistan (Ragigh-Aghsan, 2000)?

Buzan and Wæver (2003: 423) themselves classify it as 'a weak subcomplex whose internal dynamics are still forming and in which the involvement of Russia is strong'.

We may have to accept the conclusions of the first international meeting of experts on the study of civilizations of Central Asia, organized at UNESCO

Headquarters in April 1967, that the term 'Central Asia' 'may be understood in different ways' and that 'any attempt to define it would remain controversial' (Miroshnikov 1992: 479). If that is accepted, though, to what do we owe Central Asia's shifting qualities? Three principal ways of setting borders to the region will now be examined to underscore the region's malleability and the particular scope this therefore gives for the author's disciplinary specialization and interests to play an important role in what is left 'in' or 'out'.

Geography and its limits

In part, we can rely on disciplinary classification. Geography is perhaps the most obvious way to classify a region but this does not make it an easy exercise. 'Academic disciplines by necessity present a simplistic view of the world, and geography is no exception' (Lewis 1992: 3). The term 'Central Asia' began essentially as a reference to the centre and central regions because the term was 'used simply as a synonym of the terms "High Asia", "la Haute Tartarie" or "l'Asie intérieure"' (Miroshnikov 1992: 477). When used in this way no geographical boundaries of the area were mentioned; in other words, the emphasis here is on being landlocked and central.

The geographic core of Central Asia has often been located as Transoxania. The name 'Oxus' is the Latinized form of an Iranian word now called Amu Darya, and refers to the river of that name. The term 'Transoxania' (also rendered as 'Transoxiana') meaning 'across the Oxus' also corresponds to the medieval Arabic appellation *Mā warā al-Nahr* ('that which lies beyond the river'). The core Transoxania therefore lies between the Amu and Syr Darya rivers and also gives Uzbekistan its geographic status as Central Asia's centre, a landlocked country within a landlocked region. But this area's location as core is also qualified: 'Such a definition of Transoxiana, however, is rather artificial, and it may be better to emphasize only the undisputable fact that Transoxiana is that part of Central Asia which lies to the north of the middle course of the Amu Darya' (Soucek 2000: 14).

Natural boundaries also offer limits to Central Asia's geography. The region is enclosed by mountains on its east and south, by desert and arid steppe along most of the northern areas, and by the Caspian Sea on the west. The Dzhungarian gate in northeastern Kazakhstan (between the Tarbagatay Range and the Dzhungarskiy Alatau) provides a transitional area, as Peter Sinnott (1992: 79, 94–5) elaborates: 'This barren, narrow, constantly windy gorge, a graben formation, served as the portal for nomadic pastoral breeders and caravans as well as conquerors'. This topography has 'served to isolate much of Central Asia from the outside world'.

Between these northern and southernmost tips, zones in the region are at once distinct but merge seamlessly together. The tundra in the far north gives way to the forest zone (*taiga*) which stretches from the Baltic Sea to the Sea of Okhotsk, the Siberian forest zone marking where 'Central Asia ends' (Hambly 1969: 1). Forests become the steppe zone, and, in Akiner's (1998: 9) words, 'a broad expanse of grassland that stretches from the Hungarian and Ukrainian plains, across southern Siberia and the Kazakh steppe, to the Mongolian plateau and Manchuria. This is the natural habitat of the wild horse'. A stretch of semi-desert and then hot deserts follow further south. For Hambly (1969: 2), the 'eastern and western limits of Central Asia are less easily defined', the Great Wall of China and across the Manchurian forest approximately marking the east, but the western steppe-zone merges unbroken into 'the grasslands of the Ukraine, extending as far as Rumania and Hungary'.

The nineteenth century saw a push for geographic definitional precision, principally by German and Russian geographers and explorers. Alexander von Humboldt was the first to attempt a precise definition of the region, and in his major work *Asie Centrale*, published in Paris in 1843, he proposed to include in Central Asia a vast area lying between 5 degrees N. and 5 degrees S. of latitude 44.5 degrees N., which he considered to be the middle parallel of the entire Asian mainland. But not everyone agreed with Humboldt's approach. According to Miroshnikov (1992: 477), Nicolay Khanykoff, Russian orientalist and explorer of Central Asia, was the first to state that Central Asia required 'common physical features' not latitudinal definitions. The common physical feature was the absence of flow of water into the open sea, thus enlarging the geographic definition of Central Asia to include eastern Iran and Afghanistan.

Two decades later Ferdinand Richthofen, another German geographer, found this unsatisfactory, saying that the geological and topographical features in Khanykoff's region were too different to constitute one geographic whole. He pressed for the division of Asia into two types of natural region, 'central' and 'peripheral' (Miroshnikov 1992: 478). Ivan Mushketov, Miroshnikov (1992) recounts, while praising Richthofen's definition, nevertheless argued that the eastern and western parts of Inner Asia have so much in common in their geological origin and natural features that they should not be divided into Central (Central) and Inner (or Middle) Asia. He instead argued for a differentiation between Peripheral (or Outlying) and Inner (or Middle). By 'Inner' he meant the aggregate of 'all the land-locked regions of the Asian mainland, having no flow of water into the open sea and possessing the features of Khan-Khai'. He did suggest retaining the name 'Central Asia' for the eastern part of the area (i.e. for Richthofen's Central Asia). For greater 'Central Asia' he suggested two names: either 'Inner Asia' which was only used earlier sporadically, or 'Middle Asia', the term which, before Richthofen's definition, was widely used in nineteenth-century Russian literature as a synonym for Central Asia (Miroshnikov 1992: 478–9). Miroshnikov (1992: 479) concludes that the UNESCO studies takes as Central Asia therefore 'the whole interior of the Asian continent which largely coincides with greater Central Asia within geographical limits proposed by Humboldt and Mushketov'.

Historico-cultural definitions

If geography helps us to understand the northern and southern limits of Central Asia better than the western and eastern – partly because 'the Eurasian steppes and deserts have not been known by any comprehensive name' (Soucek 2000: 1) – cultural explanations for the east–west borders have sometimes stepped in where geographic ones have proven less satisfactory. Yuri Bregel (1995: viii) argues that, rather than as a geographic unit, Central Asia is best viewed, as 'a distinct cultural and historical entity'. Cultural cores and limits can take multiple approaches and two stand out in particular. One is the approach that stresses the Turko-Persian cultural world; the other is the one that stresses Islam. The former tends to unite the Western and Eastern parts, the latter tends to divide them according to which areas became Islamic and which did not. A third approach is also adopted – religious plurality as definitional.

A.H. Dani and V.M. Masson (1992: 27) argue that it is the type of peoples who settled in this region that determines its geographic expanse, since 'analogous natural conditions cannot but favour the birth of analogous modes of production as well as the appearance of similar cultures', the territory they examine thus including 'territories lying at present within the boundaries of Afghanistan, the western part of China, northern India, north-eastern Iran, Mongolia, Pakistan and the Central Asian republics of the USSR'. Relatedly, Shirin Akiner refers to how both eastern and western parts are united by ecology, a 'fragile environment'. Denis Sinor (1990: 2) argues for an interpretation of Central Asia based on historical and cultural criteria: his concern is with 'Central Eurasia or, to use a less cumbersome though less accurate term, Inner Asia'.

Bregel (1996: 3) summarizes the second approach, arguing that if we are looking at Central Asia as a distinct cultural and historical entity then it consists of:

> the western, Turko-Iranian, part of the Inner Asian heartland, whose indigenous population consisted of various Iranian peoples, most of whom have been by now Turkicized, and whose growing Turkic population has to various degrees assimilated its indigenous Iranian culture; in geographical terms, it spreads from the Caspian Sea and the Ural river basin in the west to the Altai mountains and the Turgan oasis in the east, and from the limits of the Inner Asian steppe belt in the north to the Hindukush and the Kopet-Dagh in the south. Beginning with the 8th century A.D., it was gradually incorporated into the Islamic world. Being a part of the Islamic world, it shares many cultural features with its Islamic neighbours in the south and the west, but it combines them in a unique blend with the features which it shares with the world of the Inner Asian nomads. It belongs, thus, to both these worlds, being a border area for each of them.

Bregel uses the term 'Islamic Central Asia'. Soucek (2000: xi–xii) similarly places Central Asia within a broader Inner Asia and likewise refers to it as Inner Asia's western part, 'roughly Western Turkestan and the western part of Eastern Turkestan, together with such adjacent areas as northeastern Iran and northern Afghanistan'. He argues that only with the arrival of Islam did the region become possible for the historian while previously the domain of the archaeologist. Similarly, Akiner (1998: 32, 19) writes that with the Arab conquest of Transoxania from about 10 AD and the securing of south-west Central Asia firmly within the Caliphate,

> the geographic boundaries between [Buddhism and Islam] gradually crystallized and the modern religious map of the region took shape.… As the local population converted to the new religion they acquired not simply a faith, but became part of the same intellectual space, participated in the same economic system, and importantly, came to share the same system of values as Muslims in the Middle East.

Political and geostrategic borders

Political borders, like their geographic and cultural counterparts, have changed in their reach and in the degree to which they have created clearly identifiable and fixed loci of power.

The only time in which Inner Asia (in the sense of both eastern and western areas) found political unity by default was in the Mongol period, where for the first time the whole region was united under one ruler, Genghiz Khan, creating 'the largest land empire ever to have existed' (Morgan 1990: 5). Already before his death (AD 1227) Genghiz Khan had divided his empire into vassal states, each headed by one of his sons. Both this unity and disunity meant that the Mongol period had a decisive impact on the development of Central Asian societies and their development into similar but distinct communities. The Mongol conquest also ended the political domination of the region's Persian population, although their cultural influence remained strong, especially in the territory of present-day Uzbekistan and Tajikistan. Turkic or Turko-Mongol princes now ruled.

A term that was once cultural may become political, and, in the process, cover a different geographic area. Turkestan, as Akiner (1998: 5) shows, is a classic example. A word of Persian origin meaning 'land of the Turks', it was used in the ninth and tenth centuries by Persian and Arab geographers to refer to the region north of the Syr Darya, outside the orbit of Islam. In the second half of the nineteenth century, 'Turkestan' acquired a political connotation when the term was incorporated into the official designation of the Tsarist colonial administration in the newly conquered Asian territories, hence the 'Governate General of Turkestan'. Less formally, this region was known as 'Western' or 'Russian Turkestan', in contrast to 'Eastern' or 'Chinese Turkestan' (i.e. Xinjiang and adjacent lands under Chinese rule). After the Bolshevik Revolution, 'Turkestan' was retained as the name of an Autonomous Soviet Socialist Republic before it was broken up into the five Soviet SSRs in the national delimitation process of 1924–36. In contemporary parlance, some groups continue to give it political meaning, especially those seeking independence for Xinjiang.

Prior to Russian annexation spatial power took two principal forms in the shape of nomadic and sedentary khanates. Peter Golden (2011: 15) writes how nomadic political organization did not amount to statehood, fluctuating between loose tribal federations and grand empires. In contrast, Scott Levi (2007: 29) refers to the sedentary Emirate of Bukhara and the khanates of Khokand and Khiva as 'Uzbek states'. Relative to contemporary states these khanates remained only loosely territorialized, however. Under Russian imperial annexation, whose process was completed by 1884, two of these three units retained a status of some independence, termed protectorates, while Khokand was absorbed into one of four territorial units administered by the Russians, the Governorate-General of Turkestan (Chapter 3).

According to Elizabeth Bacon (1980) and Levi (2007), we cannot deny the huge socio-economic and cultural transformation brought on by imperial Russia's encounter with Central Asia. Andreas Kappeler (2001) shows that at the political level Russian rule in Central Asia remained largely pragmatic. There was 'no master plan' for the *inorodtsy* (aliens) from whom, in classical colonial style, Russian rulers extracted resources while hoping that political non-interference would keep them quiet. Partly to this end, Tsarist policy turned a blind eye to local practices and beliefs and retained Islamic Shari'ah and customary law, *Adat*. (Golden 2011: 126, 128). By contrast, the Soviet project, while also retaining pragmatism and realpolitik, was nevertheless shaped by the ideological and deliberately transformative project, communism, and this set at least three new meanings for political borders of the region. First, Central Asia, as a region, disappeared from within the Soviet whole which created external borders that sealed a divide between the capitalist and socialist worlds (and within that between Communist Russia and China) and were tightly controlled and highly impenetrable. This also created further impediments to the region's interaction with the wider Muslim world, and cemented the political divide administratively enacted under Tsarist rule, between Western and Eastern Xinjiang. Second, in terms of borders within the western Central Asian region, Soviet authorities, for a brief period, maintained the broader regional area of Turkestan (which combined more or less the four former administrative areas of Tsarist rule), opting instead to divide the area in the national delimitation process of 1924–36. Third, delimitation created five of the 15 Soviet Socialist Republics (SSRs), each of them bearing the titular name of five Central Asian ethno-linguistic groups identified by Soviet authorities and ethnographers. For the first time in their history, therefore, Central Asian political borders were given ethno-linguistic content (with all the contradictions that this involved, to which we return in Chapter 3).

When Soviet power imploded in 1991, these five separate Soviet republics were to become, almost seamlessly, the five independent states, providing both continuity (same political borders) and change (different political meaning). As mostly unaltered since their Soviet beginnings, the borders still carry the rationale of Soviet 'dual assimilation' (Hirsch 2005) at both Soviet and ethno-linguistic levels. Independent leaders have adapted Soviet templates to stress how their now sovereign political vessels contain both wider civic identities (read Soviet) and also particular titular ones (read ethno-linguistic) (Chapter 5). Sometimes borders express where lands naturally come to an end, such as the Dzhungarian gate, or where mountains or rivers, particularly in the region's southern borders, coincide. Most graphically they signify domestic and external sovereignty in an imported Westphalian system of statehood (Chapter 4).

These varied meanings placed on borders create multiple contradictions in an early independence era. Leaders have not contested these borders (Chapters 5 and 7), but rather the borders both among and external to the five republics remain fluid. Admittedly, some borders are less porous than the one with Russia, for example with Afghanistan. Fluidity is in part a function of their infancy as sovereign entities, the borders still being often ineffectively guarded (Chapter 5). It is also a function of topography. While geographically easier to pass than those in the south, the sheer length of the Kazakhstan-Russian border – at 6,846 km (Golunov 2001), the longest single-segment land border in the world – makes comprehensive border controls very difficult. Mountainous borders, or rivers as a border, for example in the Tajik-Afghan case, create their own sets of policing challenges and fluidity, or the drive to retain fluidity, and is a result of imperfect drawing, with co-ethnic or economic communities trying to keep their ties as they find themselves suddenly straddled across borders.

Two years into independence, in 1993, regional leaders decided to meet and call their collective affiliation 'Central Asia'. Little research has been done on why and how this particular appellation was chosen but one factor in this assembling was the snub the leaders felt to the region in having not been invited by European states to the meeting of the first institutional replacement of the defunct Soviet edifice, the Commonwealth of Independent States. Despite these noble beginnings the record to date has indicated few successes at meaningful regional co-operation, let alone integration. The affiliation amounted neither to the dismantling of their borders to build one big borderless region on the lines, say, of a new Turkestan, or to construct a regional institution that, while co-functioning alongside five independent states, would integrate the five. No equivalent project to the functionalism of the 1970s surrounding the EU currently exists, for example. Authors explain this absence of regional institutionalization in different ways, ranging from the emphasis on cementing rather than pooling sovereignty, the primacy of regime security, or the absence of a meaningful regional identity (Chapters 4–7). Roy Allison (2008) has aptly coined these states' interaction as 'virtual regionalism' (Chapter 7).

In the early twentieth century strategic and geopolitical considerations also began to enter the debate about where Central Asia begins and ends (Yapp 1994: 1–10). Their most popular manifestation was in the geopolitical contest of the nineteenth century which saw England and Russia competing for territorial influence and its eventual resolution in the carving out of the famous Afghan finger of land. The notion of a 'Great Game' was coined and has stuck ever since. Halford Mackinder's speech of 1904 set in motion the idea that Central Asia as a region distinguished itself above all in geopolitical terms. As a landmass that was in between of Europe and Asia, it was pivotal, in an era of rail travel, in providing links between distant parts of the globe. Giving 'exact borders' to this land that is in between was 'not necessary to describe a strategic concept'

(Mackinder 1919). Geographer Saul B. Cohen (1999: xxii) in *Geography and Politics in a World Divided* proposed a new framework dividing the globe into geostrategic regions corresponding to the spheres of influence of the major world powers, and geopolitical regions that include independent regions like South Asia, and what he called 'shatterbelts, large, strategically located regions occupied by a number of conflicting states and caught between the opposing interests of the adjoining great powers'. Central Asia can be categorized as both.

Leitmotifs

Central Asia as 'heartland' has become one of several leitmotifs associated with the region. This is briefly explored here, along with three others: a geography of extremes with a unique ecology; a space where nomadic and sedentary lives symbiotically and dramatically interacted; and a highly penetrated region that housed multiple empires and peoples. These leitmotifs, common to whether one takes the 'small' or the 'big' version of Central Asia, encourage further ideas about what, if anything, is regionally distinctive.

A geography of extremes with a unique ecological habitat

Whatever the geographic boundaries, and whether or not one agrees with a latitudinal measurement of where Central Asia begins and ends, few dispute its distinctive geography. 'It is characterized by isolation and extreme aridity over the greater part of the area' (Hambly 1969: 1) and, due to the fact that it is 'wholly unpenetrated by waterways from the ocean' (Mackinder 1919: 183–4), the rivers have been practically useless for purposes of human communication with the outside world. The drainage of the region's two largest rivers, the Amu Darya and the Syr Darya, requires major technologies to tap for irrigation purposes. Particularly indomitable is the Amu Darya, known also as the 'mad river' because sharp inclines on its course can lead to dramatic and sudden rises in water levels, though oasis cities have sprung up in the loess foothill valleys of Soviet Central Asia. The Ferghana valley, while at the centre dry and salty, has scattered among its mountains 'flourishing oases among the rolling hills or *adyrs*' (Masson 1992: 33–4; 33). Small changes in global temperatures can significantly alter the resulting water off-flow, changing the amount of grazing land and shifting the frontier between desert and agricultural land (Gunder Frank 1992).

The region boasts among the hottest deserts and highest mountains in the world. Described by archaeologist Sir Aurel Stein as 'probably the most formidable of all the dune-covered wastes of this globe' (cited by Soucek 2000: 2), the Lop Nor, Taklamakan in western Xinjiang is one of several inhospitable vast deserts. Others include the Betpak Dala ('Plain of Misfortune'), Kyzyl Kum ('Red Sand') and the Kara Kum ('Black Sand') in the west and the Gobi of southern Mongolia and eastern Xinjiang. By contrast, the vast steppe covering the contemporary area of Kazakhstan, southern Russia and southern Ukraine, known to medieval Muslim authors as Dasht-I Kipchak ('The Steppe of the Kipchak

[Turks]'), has become nameless and thus, some argue, its borders even harder to pinpoint. Both terrains are home to various indigenous species, such as the Snow Leopard, the gazelle, the Bactrian camel and the Przhevalsky horse.

Known to the Chinese as the Heavenly Mountains, the Tien Shan is one of the grandest ranges of Asia, with Khan Tengri reaching a height of 23,600 feet, and the 'Roof of the World' that embraces the Kunlun, Karakoram and Himalayas are the highest mountain complexes in the world (Hambly 1969: 3). While a barrier to southward expansion of the nomadic steppe empires, their passes have allowed for the travel of trade and religion (Soucek 2000: 2). Life cycles and mountains were deeply connected for the nomad, a site of rituals, burials and communication with *tengri*, the nomads' celestial deity. The region therefore possesses an ecology of vast expanses with relative population scarcity, inhospitable terrain and water scarcity.

A space where nomadic and sedentary lives dramatically interacted

Central Asia witnessed 'possibly [the] most stark interaction of the economies of pastoral husbandry and settled agriculture experienced in world civilizations'. The nomadic and the sedentary worlds, whose coexistence emerged at the outset of the first millennium BC 'to some extent were complementary to each other but in certain respects were mutually antagonistic' (Hambly 1969: 10). Towns in areas like Semireche developed on the banks of oases and river banks and nomadic tribes of the steppe favoured a pastoral economy, bartering food, clothing, shelter, fuel and transport for grain and metalware. René Grousset (2005: ix) describes the inherent tension to this nevertheless mutually profitable interaction as analogous to 'the feelings of a capitalist society and a proletariat enclosed within a modern city.... In these circumstances, the periodic thrusts of the nomads into the cultivated areas were a law of nature'.

Nomads replaced their direct predecessors, Bronze Age stockbreeders, transforming the steppe into an area of intense development. As 'a sophisticated economic specialization for exploiting the resources of the steppe' (Barfield 1989: 20), pastoral nomads were not a transitional phase from hunting and gathering to agriculture. 'Even the Bible ascribes temporal precedence' to agriculture, Frank (1992: 3–4) writes. Further '... we should hasten to get rid of the popular image of Central Asia as the home of "barbarian nomads." Central Asia was also home to many highly civilized and urbanized peoples. Yet even when many people were nomadic pastoralists, they were no more "barbarian" or "savage" than many of their sedentary "civilized" neighbours'. The steppe's 'horse-breeding, highly mobile Eurasian nomad' (Soucek 2000: 1) 'developed military powers capable to change the course of history of urban civilizations' (Azarolli 1985: 66). Grousset (2005: xi) explains again:

> The mounted archer of the steppe reigned over Eurasia for thirteen centuries because he was the spontaneous creation of the soil itself: the offspring of hunger and want, the nomads' only means of survival during years of

famine .... The cannonades with which Ivan the Terrible scattered the last heirs of the Golden Horde, and with which the K'ang-his emperor of China frightened the Kalmucks, marked the end of a period of world history. For the first time, and for ever, military technique had changed camps and civilization became stronger than barbarism.

Bukhara and Samarkand were the most important urban centres of this early Muslim period which saw significant achievements in areas of commerce, manufacture and culture. The region produced a disproportionate number of Muslim scholars, artists and craftsmen of exceptional calibre (e.g. al-Bukhari, al-Tirmizi, al-Khwarezmi, al-Farabi, al-Biruni, Ibn Sina) and occupied a key place in 'transcontinental commerce between the Far East, the Middle East and the Mediterranean world' (Hambly 1969: 6). Before the 'cannonades' of Ivan the Terrible and Tsarist rule, China and Iran particularly were key cultural and commercial contacts for nomads. These two contiguous powers interacted in quite different ways with the region. While Iran, 'unified by the dynamic ideology of Shii Islam, to a considerable degree blocked direct communications of merchants, pilgrims, and scholars between the eastern and western parts of the Muslim world', China, when not practising open diplomacy, operated a closed frontier system (Hambly 1969: 14). The result was often tense or absent relations with Iran as opposed to a relatively stable and mutually fruitful relation-ship between tribal and Chinese farming communities. When balance was lost, however, particularly when Central Asian societies were growing too slowly, they were 'seen to become easy prey to active and energetic neighbours' (Dani and Masson 1992: 475), including China.

In the ensuing pages, we will encounter references to nomadic and sedentary lifestyles in our understandings of contemporary change (Chapter 4). For some, the onslaught of modernity has rendered the distinction between nomadic and sedentary ways of life of lesser import (Chapter 3). For others, these references have been used as content for new state ideologies. The sedentary nature of their pasts is celebrated by the Uzbeks and Tajiks as long-established nationhood, well before the arrival of Soviet power. A nomadic legacy and its concomitant horde/clan structure, is seen by some as an impediment to democratization (Chapters 4 and 5).

Unity in diversity? A region of overlapping empires and peoples

The 'active and energetic' Russia in the nineteenth century was the last in a long line of imperial rulers of this territory, and its encroachment marked the begin-ning of substantial Russian migration to the region (Demko 1969). This modern wave of ethnic migration is in keeping with a region that has seen the mixing of peoples since as far back as the third to late first millennium BC with the proto-Indo-Europeans encountering the Mongoloids (including proto-Mongols, proto-Turks, proto-Tibetans and proto-Tungus). The first recorded peoples were of Iranian origin, the central area of Transoxiana they inhabited, later known as

Sogdia, and many place names end in the Iranian word meaning 'town' – 'kent', – 'kand', – 'klat'. Up until the eighteenth century the 'general trend has been for Turkish peoples and languages to supersede or overwhelm their predecessors. Even the thirteenth-century Mongol conquests did little to modify this trend, the Turkish tribal aristocracies thereafter claiming descent from Chingiz Khan or his paladins with as much pride as did the true Mongols' (Hambly 1969: 9). Central Asia as 'a crossroads for major ethnic migrations and a meeting place of the ancient world's great civilizations – Persian, Greek, Indian, Chinese and Islamic' (Hunter 1996: 3) is a third leitmotif.

This meeting place has resulted from the region's cradling of successive empires to include the Achaemenid Empire (556–330 BC) through the Graeco-Bactrian (ca 308–128 BC) to the Sasanids of the third century (see Table 1.2). As already noted, the region has also produced its own empires, of which the Chingizid in the thirteenth century is the most famous. But this was not the first indigenous nomadic steppe empire, the Hsiung-nu's rise in the eastern steppe in the third century BC (the first recorded even if the origins of these peoples remain unknown) and the Turk Empire in the third century already attesting to how it was 'the frontier zones occupied by peoples of mixed cultures' that provided 'the source of conquest dynasties and not the open steppe' (Barfield 1989: 12). The arrival of the Arabs in the eighth century brought to the western region a shift from Sogdian language to Farsi and a new creedal religion, Islam, leading Soucek (2000: 56) to conclude that '[S]ignificantly, the two giant neighbors to the south-east and northwest – China, and, a millennium later, Russia – would remain unable to change the effects of the two catalytic factors – Islamization and Turkicization – despite their recurrent or eventual domination of the area'.

Despite the homogenizing forces of Turkicization and Islamization, the ethnic, linguistic and religious picture remains a brilliant mosaic. The modern-day Tajiks are direct descendants of the region's Iranian heritage and the other four titular groups are Turkic. Muriel Atkin (1994a: 91) states that the 'Tajiks of the former Soviet Union and the dominant nationality in Iran, the Persians, as well as the various Persian speakers in Afghanistan, are similar – though not identical – in language and other aspects of culture' and further that, although the term 'Tajik' has a venerable tradition of use, not only in Central Asia, to differentiate Persian speakers from Turkic peoples, the use of that name to designate a nationality in a political sense is a twentieth-century creation of the Soviet regime.

Diversity is shown to be the product of change, in an environment that negotiates, renegotiates and metamorphoses identities. Some disappear in the process of this renegotiation. As a central feature of ethnicity, language must have changed several times and the population of the Central Asian area was using mainly Indo-European languages towards the end of the second and at the beginning of the first millennium BC: Islam in the western part did not enter a vacuum, but it entered a space where the creedal religions of Zoroastrianism, Christianity, Manichaeism and Judaism had long existed (Akiner 1998: 33), along with local beliefs such as shamanism and animism, indigenous to both Mongol and Turkic tribes.

Table 2.2 Empires and peoples

Date	Empire (name/origins)	Type/Rulers	Notes
First inhabitants	Persian peoples		
3–1 millennium BCE	Proto-Indo-Europeans encountering the Mongoloids (including proto-Mongols, proto-Turks, proto-Tibetans and proto-Tungus)		
556–330 BCE	Achaemenid Empire of Iran	Sedentary; mainly covering southern area	
308–128 BCE	Graeco-Bactria	Sedentary; Alexander the Great, West	
209–155 BCE	Hsuing-nu	Eastern; Leader (shan-yü) of Hsuing-nu in 209 is Motun	Mixing of proto-Indo-Europeans and Mongoloids (inc. proto-Mongols, proto-Turks, proto-Tibetans and proto-Tungus); Iranian peoples with Turkic superimposed.
202 BCE – 220 AD	Han Dynasty	China	
Between first century BC and first century AD to 270s	Kushan Empire	Central/southern	
226–651	Sasanid Empire	Central/southern	
375	Huns across the Volga	Attila dies 453	
450–567	Hephthalite state	Afghanistan and neighbouring areas	Destroyed by Türks and Persians

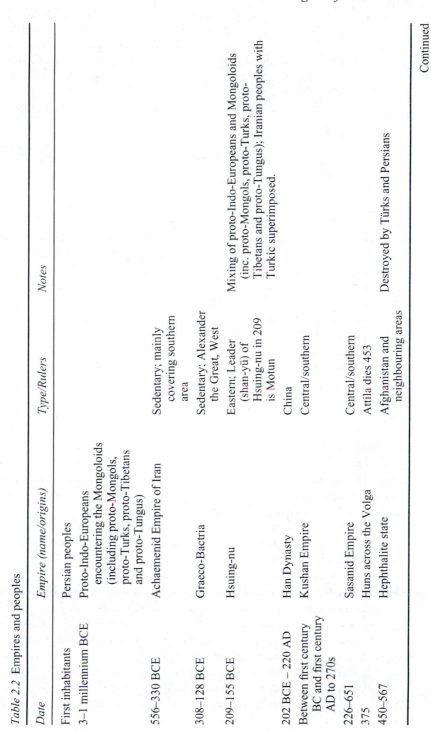

Continued

Table 2.2 Cont'd

Date	Empire (name/origins)	Type/Rulers	Notes
552–630	First Türk Qaghanate	Eastern	White Huns, Turks from Mongolia
682–742	Second Türk Qaghanate	Eastern	
744–840	Reign of the Uighur Qaghanate		
Eighth to twelfth centuries	Arab conquest	Western	Abbasids, Uighur Qaghanate, Qarluqs, Samanid Dynasty; in 651 Arabs complete conquest of Persia and begin advance into CA; major conversion of Turkic tribes to Islam (960).
992–1212	Karakhanid dynasty	Western and eastern Turkistan	First Turkic Muslim dynasty; Uighurs and Manichesim; allowed for indigenous Muslim identity to grow.
1218–1220	Mongols conquer Central Asia	Ghengiz Khan (died 1227) (united eastern and western)	Before his death vassals (*uluses*) to sons, Jochi, Chaghadai, Ögödei and Tolui
1368	End of Mongol rule in China		
1370–1405	Timur	Timur (Tamerlane), died at Otrar. Followed by reign of Timurids (ending 1507).	Timur claiming Genghisid descent but in reality not a Genghisid, he never used the title qaghan. Turkic-speaking and Muslim; Islamic monarch claim; capital is Samarkand; one of the most famous Timurids was Ulugh Beg (1394-1449), not only a monarch but a mathematician and astronomer. His capital-Samarkand.

1451	Abu'l-Khayr Khan	Emerges as leader of Uzbeks	Mongol
1502	Collapse of Golden Horde		Early to mid-sixteenth century Kazakhs divide into Great Horde, Middle Horde, Small Horde, plus Inner Horde.
Seventeenth to early eighteenth centuries	Jungar Empire	Dominates eastern parts	With the Jungar defeat, Xinjiang comes under Chinese rule
1917	Bolsheviks assume control of Central Asia		
1924–1936	Soviet Delimitation		
1991	Collapse of Soviet Union		

Sources: Adapted and compiled from Golden (2011: 142–6); also consulted: Sinor (1990, especially Chapters 1, 5, 11); Soucek (2000, especially Chapters 2, 3, 7, 8, 9, 19); Morgan (1990).

Today these leitmotifs feed into discussions of where Central Asia fits in the Islamic world, the search for cultural authenticity (competition over who is the true 'aboriginal group'), ethnic self-descriptions, cultural cohesion of the region (see below in the discussion of regional identities) and battles over scripts as identity markers. Contrast two views of where this mosaic leaves us in terms of regional cohesion: on the one hand, Gregory Gleason (1997: xv) writing about western Central Asia maintains that:

> Geography, history, language, and culture had closely linked the societies of Central Asia. Present-day Kazakstan, Kyrgyzstan, Tajikistan, Turkmenistan, and Uzbekistan shared common languages, historical traditions, and values in a way that bound them together as inheritors of common cultural traditions. None of these states had ever existed as an independent country. They were linked by their common traditions much more closely than were, for instance, the countries of Western Europe, Latin America, Africa, or even colonial America.

On the other hand, Denis Sinor (1990: 14), in answer to the question of whether any objective criteria specific to Inner Asia (eastern and western) taken as a whole exist, says: 'the links which usually hold together or create a cultural entity – such as script, race, religion, language – played only a very moderate role as factors of cohesion'.

Heartland and Pivot

As part of these imperial encounters, the Great Game between the empires of Russia and England in the nineteenth century has inspired even the sleepiest of imaginations. Citing often 'Now I shall go far and far into the North, playing the Great Game...' (Rudyard Kipling, *Kim* 1901), writers on the Great Game proceed to emphasize our fourth and final leitmotif, Central Asia as heartland. As noted above, the Heartland thesis stems from a body of writing by Mackinder written in 1904, 1919 and 1942. The material from 1904 remains to this day one of the most widely publicised works by a geographer, as Nick Megoran (2005) points out. In 1904 Mackinder presented a paper entitled, 'The Geographical Pivot of History', reprinted in *Introduction to Democratic Ideals and Reality*, pp. 175–193. Mackinder (1942: 188, 186) asks: 'Is not the pivot region of the world's politics that vast area of Euro-Asia which is inaccessible to ships, but in antiquity lay open to the horse-riding nomads, and is today about to be covered with a network of railways?' Mackinder referred not so much to Central Asia as to the 'continuous land-mass of Euro-Asia', or, as he states, 'half of all the land on the globe' (excluding the deserts of Sahara and Arabia), concluding that: who rules East Europe commands the Heartland; who rules the Heartland commands the World-Island; who rules the World-Island commands the World (Mackinder 1942: 50).

While pivot and heartland are the most common terms, core/periphery or stagnant/creative are to a degree variations on this theme. Gunder Frank's (1992)

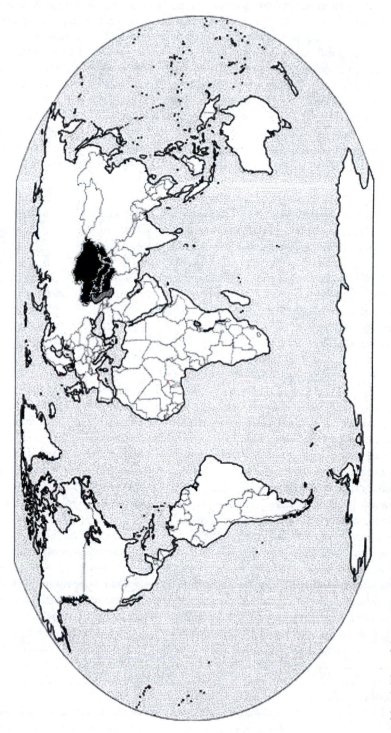

Map 1 Map of the world, with Central Asia highlighted.

preoccupation is also with geopolitics, less as a passageway than as a discussion of whether regionally Central Asia can in accumulation terms (wealth, ideas, resources) be classed as a centre rather than a periphery. Others view Central Asia as important because it is in a unique position to play a role for great power interests elsewhere, even if those interests are not its direct concern. The concept is applied to the competition over influence by Great Powers and given the modified title of new Great Game in which the prize is no longer territorial possession but access to Central Asia's markets and resources and to 'a form of neo-imperialist hegemony' (Edwards 2003: 89).

In its original formulation, some critics accused Mackinder of exaggerating rail power and thus the potential of the Heartland, superseded as it soon was by the advent of air power. Still others contended that geopolitical determinism was suspect, particularly discredited by the development of German Geopolitik during the interwar years. Others have been tempted to use the heartland thesis as a political culture argument for authoritarian rule, in that only autocratic rule would be able to hold sway over a landmass this size.

Its contemporary application as a new Great Game has also attracted a number of criticisms. As an analytical tool it downplays the role of the Central Asian states themselves, portraying them as simple reactors to great power behaviour (Chapter 4). On the other hand it assumes that the powers involved have clearly defined strategies for the region which further foreign policy analysis has often shown not to be the case (Chapter 7). Others call the game 'not-so-great' (Sokov 2005) because of its destabilizing influences and given the low percentage of oil resources relative to other parts of the Middle East (Lieven 1999). However, its incorrect (deliberate or not) interpretation can carry 'ethical concerns' (Megoran 2004: 347). This relates to how the 'tendency is to cite some feature from the distant or recent past, say, understandings of the meanings of racial categories, and then project these forward or backward in time as if they were structural features of thought rather than ones with distinctive historical trajectories' (Agnew 1999: 126). Edwards (2003: 97) concludes that: 'The linking of the New Great Game with geopolitics does neither justice as their contemporary use has often been intellectually lax and capriciously all-embracing, driven by the obscure romanticism of a bygone era'.

Despite any serious shortcomings, the Great Game narrative continues to feed both the discourse and the behaviour of contemporary external and domestic actors. For example, many of independent Uzbekistan's leaders and intellectuals have used the heartland theory both to portray their own country as the main player in Central Asia and to draw the international community's attention to broader transnational problems, which, because they are situated in the heartland, concern a broader region (Chapters 5 and 7).

Conclusions

Questioning the essence of Central Asia, S.A.M. Adshead (1993: 27) asks whether it is: 'core or periphery, active or passive, living heart or dead centre?

Central Asia, it has been said, suffers from every geographical liability, but enjoys one asset: its central position between the homelands of Europe, Iran, India and China. This centrality has allowed it to be alternately a point of diffusion and a point of convergence'. Thomas Barfield (1989: 12) similarly has argued that Central Asia cannot be considered separately from the surrounding states and any analytical category that attempts to understand it must incorporate the broader region: 'The Mongolian steppe, north China, and Manchuria must be analysed as part of a single historical system' and Inner Asia's trajectory is closely linked to that of China's. Gunder Frank (1992: 1), writing that from '[his] non-specialist perspective the region appears as a sort of black hole in the middle of the world', any 'analytical framework must embrace the entire Afro-Eurasian world system, the hub of which was Central Asia'. 'Central Asia is of fundamental importance for understanding Eurasian History.... It is the missing link in World History' (Beckwith 1993). The primary paradox driving Central Asia's existence is that it is both central and isolated.

Central Asia refuses to be neatly compartmentalized. It has both elusive borders and an elusive core, the former being responsible to some extent for the latter. Boundaries are created in reference to both 'out' and 'in' and in both cases neither is readily identifiable. This is in part because the region is so often subsumed as part of a greater whole. As part of a continuous landmass it is very hard for the region to be discrete. Sinor (1977) describes Central Asia as a volcano that periodically erupts, the outflowing lava reducing the 'centre' of 'inner' Asia. Consequently 'Central Asian peoples have been mostly losers in two ways. They have lost out to others on their home ground, and their Central Asian homelands ceased to be so central to world history' (Gunder Frank 1992: 2). Gunder Frank argues that even if military superiority was the case for Central Asia it never rose to become a core region because it was never the core of capital accumulation. If economically peripheral, culturally, however, the region 'can no longer be regarded as a marginal area for it lies within the hub of great civilizations as much as it is itself the home of ancient civilization' (Lal 1992: 437).

Central Asia as a meta-geographical construct can be highly contingent, serving a particular purpose (e.g. aid policy or political mobilization) at a particular moment – and with often quite different implications. If the above has presented a picture of negotiable borders and possibilities, what does the independence era tell us about how actors interpret and enact these repertoires? Domestically, Dru Gladney (1990) writes that the people of Central Asia do not call themselves Central Asian. Gül Özcan (2010: 6) writes that 'Central Asia, a term originating in Russian, does not carry any particular cultural or historical meaning for the people in the region apart from reminding them of a sense of being in-between'. Security demands and their resolution have tended to make outside players want to consider Central Asia as more than just the five states. Roy Allison and Lena Jonson (2001: 23), while focusing on the five countries, also explain how 'the term "wider Central Asia" will be used to indicate the areas of Russia, China and Afghanistan, which border the core Central Asian states and share sizeable ethnic minorities with them'. Analysing hard and soft security threats, Swanström (2010: 37) argues for a 'Greater Central Asia [that] is here defined as including the former Soviet republics of Kazakhstan, Kyrgyzstan, Tajikistan, Turkmenistan and Uzbekistan, as well as Afghanistan and the Western Chinese Xinjiang-Uygur Autonomous Province'.

Outside players handle the region differently: Beijing is often seen to be promoting its national security aims through the promotion of multilateral security or 'Washington sees the region, so long in limbo, as an extension of the Middle East, fraught with the same perils and problems' (Hopkirk 1993: vii). Russian foreign policy makers for some time after Soviet collapse differentiated between the world that used to belong to them and the wider world by their use of the term 'near abroad' as a shorthand way of saying those parts that used to belong to Russia, and, in those who were predicting Russia's neo-imperialist tendencies, parts that would once again belong to the motherland. In Chapter 7, we shall see that 9/11 accentuated how Russia could no longer assume that the West would keep out of what it perceived (and the West had been happy to concur, busy as it was with the former Yugoslavia) was its own back yard.

These two understandings, domestic and external, can be harmonious, such as in the immediate aftermath of September 11, but those particular moments have proven the exception rather than the rule (Chapter 7). Condoleezza Rice's coining of the 'Greater Middle East' served a US foreign policy purpose of linking Central Asia with the Middle East partly to justify the use of airbases from Central Asia for its policies in Afghanistan and Iraq. This coupling of Afghanistan with Central Asian security concerns has been driven from the outside; if the understanding is that after withdrawal Afghanistan becomes a local problem needing local solutions, but without local commitment by actors, who often lack resources or who are too consumed by their own security concerns, it is easy to see how the problem arises.

The modern historical and contemporary processes of transformation seem to be most repeatedly used as reference points for organizing analysis around the five ex-Soviet republics. In contemporary terms, the Soviet prefix to this region continues to have relevance. Not all authors qualify Central Asia with 'post-Soviet' but many write with that understanding, that is, that Central Asia refers to 'the former Soviet South' (Herzig 1995) which in the Soviet era was known as 'Middle Asia and Kazakhstan'. The practice of defining a region according to where it belonged politically in the immediately preceding period is not unusual. An obvious parallel is the prefix post-colonial, where states in Africa and the Middle East continued to be defined as post-colonial for some time after colonial powers had withdrawn. As described in Chapter 3, the comparison between post-Soviet and post-colonial has become a major area of debate in our attempts to understand this part of the world. The populations themselves and those observing and working in the region have therefore unsurprisingly sought to understand processes of change through the lens of post-socialism. Politically, therefore, the region can fit quite neatly into broader understandings of Central Eurasia, as much of Central Eurasia has gone through communism. Thus, politically, the region has commonalities with China and Mongolia to the East, as well as North to Russia and West to the Caucasus.

Promoting the need to replace the 'myth of continents' with a 'world regional framework' which emphasizes 'the spatial contours of assemblages of ideas, practices, and social institutions that give human communities their distinction and coherence', Martin Lewis and Karen Wigen (1997: 187–8) argue that Central Asia should be instated as just one such world region: 'While Southeast Asia as a category may be questionable, it is nonetheless ubiquitous in world regionalization schemes. Central or Inner Asia (the area once called Tartary), on the other hand, is a historically clear-cut region that is nonetheless almost invisible in contemporary global cartography'. At the same time, however, they (1997: 181) argue that:

> Central Asia's deep internal rifts render it a less satisfactory category for contemporary analysis. Still, the delineation of a Central Asian world region has two signal advantages: it highlights the cultural separation of such areas as Tibet and Mongolia from the Chinese realm to which they are habitually attached and it underscores the as-yet uncertain position of the five former Soviet republics in the area.

The survival of Central Asia as a discrete region has been and continues to be questioned. History tells us that the region has not always succeeded in surviving for long stretches of time independently of outside powers, even if it has sometimes managed to act as buffer or intentional go-between. The big difference today is that the region is composed of sovereign states in a modern era where autonomy and non-interference are largely respected. This new international framework, a framework of states that has taken over from empires, is the single biggest factor in favour of the survival of the five entities as independent states.

3 Empires, Soviet rule and sovereignty

In 1991 five sovereign Central Asian republics emerged from the collapse of the Soviet Union. The story of how the former Soviet republics originated and were transformed into sovereign entities is the subject of this chapter. It is easy to forget the short time-span between the creation of a republic and its gaining independence, and we must keep in mind that upon independence an average of barely 60 years had gone by since these countries' creation as republics.

The transformation of this region into Soviet Central Asia has sparked five main debates about change and continuity. First, scholars focus on how and why imperial powers, particularly imperial Russia in the eighteenth and nineteenth centuries, came to play a dominant role in the region and with what cultural and political effects. Second, more recent scholarship in particular has focused on the links between Soviet rule and national identity and the simultaneous creation by leaders of political spaces called republics where borders were territorialized and ascribed an ethnic name corresponding to the titular majority (Kazakh, Kyrgyz, Tajik, Turkmen and Uzbek). Third, scholars have come to ask whether Soviet rule was or became another form of imperial rule and therefore whether the study of Central Asia could benefit from incorporating the findings of post-colonial studies. Fourth, the degree of transformation under Soviet rule is assessed: if prior to 1917 this region had seen neither industry nor mechanized transport, what, by 1991, had survived of tradition and what had changed and modernized? Finally, authors have assessed the legacies of Soviet rule, the paths to independence, and the difficulties of embracing Westphalian sovereignty.

The Russian Empire and the establishment of Soviet power

The previous chapter illustrated how the changes to and confusion of cultures and rulers has complicated even a regional definition of Central Asia. It underscored how prior to the Russian empire, most types of empire had occupied a place in Central Asia – from steppe to dynastic and classical empire. Up to the sixth century AD the region was dominated by Iranian empires and peoples, to be either displaced or submerged by Turks from the east thereafter (Levi 2007). Shirin Akiner elaborates (1998: 32):

> The boundary between the Turkic and Iranian ethnic and linguistic spheres in Central Asia came to be, in approximate terms, the Kopet Dag and Hindu Kush mountain ranges and the Amu Darya river, with the Turkic peoples located mainly to the north of this line and the Iranian peoples to the south. The chief exceptions to this division are, amongst the Iranians, the Tajiks of Tajikistan and of the Bukhara-Samarkand area of Uzbekistan; amongst the Turks, some Turkmen tribes and a few nomadic groups that are located in northern Iran.

The effective isolation of Central Asia from Iranian influence for over three hundred years thus in this account facilitated Russian expansion.

This Russian expansion southward went through four main stages. The first stage, 1580–1644, involved the conquest of Siberia bringing the southern borders of Russia close to the area of contemporary Kazakhstan. During the second stage, 1680–1760, Kazakh tribes sought protection from Russia in the face of onslaughts by the Dzhungarian Oirat tribes from the east, with the result that by the early nineteenth century most of the Kazakh tribes had been fully incorporated into the Russian empire. Growing trade connections between these areas pushed imperial Russia to secure safe passage of people and goods. Between 1785 and 1830 Russian powers conquered the territory between the Black and Caspian Seas and further annexations followed also in the Amur region (1850–65). The last areas to be conquered were Transoxania and Transcaspia (approximately today's Uzbekistan and Turkmenistan, respectively). On 15 June 1865 Russian troops under the command of General M.G. Cherniaev entered Transoxania's third largest city. This was the first major urban site in the sedentary region annexed by Russian power. In the fourth and final stage, between 1864 and 1884 the three major city-states, Bukhara, Khiva and Khokand were unable to resist Russia's further subjugation of Transoxania. Russian formal annexation of this area was completed with the capture of Merv, the main outpost of Turkmen resistance, in 1884 (Akiner 1998).

In this final subjugation, the Russians annexed large chunks of territory from each of them but left the three rulers on their thrones to rule their rump states as Russian protectorates (Khokand was later wholly annexed). By 1889, when the Turkmen tribes of the Qizil Qum desert had been completely subjugated, Russia had emerged as the paramount colonial power in the region. The lands annexed from the local states or tribes were consolidated in the province of Turkestan, ruled by a governor-general answerable directly to the tsar. The two protectorates of Bukhara and Khiva were enclosed within Russian customs boundaries and denied the ability to conduct foreign relations on their own. In 1895 the Anglo-Russian Boundary Commission fixed the northern boundary of Afghanistan, creating the so-called geography of the 'Afghan finger' and marking Russia's southernmost frontier for the next some hundred years.

Russia's drive southward and its subsequent annexation of the region carried substantial military, politico-economic and socio-cultural implications. Militarily, a line of defensive posts had been established in the territory of contemporary Kazakhstan and many of these were to become important towns in the coming period. The establishment of these military forts was in a great many ways enabled by the absence by that time of other great powers in the region. Soucek (2000: 151) particularly refers to how Iran, 'unified by the dynamic ideology of Shia Islam, to a considerable degree blocked direct communications of merchants, pilgrims, and scholars between the eastern and western parts of the Muslim world'. Even if trade relations between Central Asia and the Indian subcontinent continued and even if by the late nineteenth and early twentieth centuries Central Asians had access to publications from the Ottoman Empire, Egypt, Iran, and India, Russia's presence was far more tangible than that of Iran's.

Russian imperial rule was pragmatic, not ideological. A colonial administration for the region (the Governate-General of Turkestan) was created in 1867. It encompassed most of western Turkestan (i.e. the land between the Caspian Sea and the Tien Shan), except for the khanates of Bukhara and Khiva, which retained a nominally independent status as protectorates, along with Transcaspia, which was ruled from the Caucasus. 'As the administrators of many other European colonial empires had discovered, protectorates were much cheaper than direct rule' (Khalid 2007: 34–5). Russian administration for the first time territorialized power in the Kazakh steppe and even in the protectorates, khanates and emirate by enshrining autonomy, possibly making rulers and people more aware of boundaries and their implications. At any rate the colonial administration introduced internal provincial and district boundaries and, even if internally largely left to their own devices, the two protectorates of Bukhara and Khiva were enclosed within Russian customs boundaries and denied the ability to conduct foreign relations on their own.

The triple military, political and economic onslaught into the Kazakh steppe lands revolutionized the traditional way of life of the Kazakh nomad. 'Many Tsarist officials had difficulty in understanding the flexible nature of Kazakh political organization' (Bacon 1966: 97). Complications arose as nomads registered in one volost often migrated to another. Some of the Kazakh tribal chieftains were co-opted into the Russian imperial administrative system. Elections introduced an unfamiliar and now competitive method of selecting a leader. Traditionally, 'families enjoyed rights of usufruct within the territory of their tribal group, but no one owned land' (Bacon 1966: 99–100). Politically, new forms of Russian power were used, weakening paternalistic leadership. Taxation of the yurt rather than livestock weighed most heavily on the poor nomad family (Demko 1969; Akiner 1995; Olcott 1995; Svanberg 1999).

While the settled areas did not see any comparable revolution, the Russian administration in exchange for its provision of manufactured goods, set out to develop the cotton monoculture of the region. In both nomadic and sedentary areas, Russian economic colonialism also brought with it an increased dependence on trade goods, transforming material culture. Some goods became part of Kazakh culture: green tea and tea bowls from China, for example, and the Russian samovar for heating tea water. Cultural practice transformed among the elites of the steppe through increased exposure to Russian culture.

The nature and timing of Russian involvement in the region created, in terms of Russian influence, a two-tier Central Asia. Kazakhs had already long been under Russian control by the time the Russians created the Governate-General of Turkestan, while Russian peasants had long settled on Kazakh pasturelands, until 1910 when a clause in the statute of government barred Russian peasants from settling on lands other than those newly brought under irrigation. Bacon (1966: 93–5) observes that 'Russian influence on oasis social culture was for the most part limited and superficial'. Despite revolts and resistance on the Kazakh steppe, Russian influence in among the Kazakhs and Kyrgyz had thus already become stronger and the narrative of anti-Russian (and later anti-Soviet) resistance fresher in the Transoxania and Transcaspia regions.

Some 30 years later the establishment of Soviet power met resistance, violence and eventually some accommodation. Immediately prior to the Bolshevik assumption of power in 1917, the call-to-arms of 1916, in which every young male was expected behind the lines to support the war effort, had provoked significant revolt, persecution and attacks. Coming as it did just a few months prior to the Bolshevik triumph, 1916 was to prove important for the support that some Central Asians were to give to the communist cause. This proved particularly the case for the Kyrgyz; while many Russian lives were lost in skirmishes, many Kyrgyz were either killed or forced to flee, either to the hills or China. One of the major sources of resistance or accommodation was found in how leaders in these regions navigated a precarious balance between heeding orders from above and listening to demands from below.

This balance was particularly precarious in Turkestan where conservative leaders had to listen to demands for modernization from Muslims which became associated with the Jadids, who were 'the first generation of modern Central Asian intellectuals' (Khalid 1998: 1) and for whom the nation (millat) became the 'the locus of Jadid reform' (Khalid 1998: 184). In 1917 the Provisional Government created a Turkestan Committee based upon the old governor-generalship, but in both Turkestan and the steppe towns dual authority structures emerged. Only by the middle of 1917 had the Bolsheviks begun to become prominent allowing for the duplication of central institutions of power at the local level. A key challenge was for different communities, especially communities lobbying for Muslim and national rights, to be included into the Bolshevik project and discussions of representation (e.g. of Islam, women) dominated the first All Union Muslim Congress held in Moscow in May 1917.

During 1917 the Alash Orda nationalist movement on the back of demands by the Kazak intelligentsia (Kendirbaeva 1999) formed on the Kazakh steppe and the first All-Kazak conference was held in Orenburg in July 1917, Orenburg being at that time still part of the Kazakh steppe area. This movement would endow Kazakhs with a collective memory of, albeit short-lived, autonomy since '[b]ecause of Cossack indifference and Bolshevik weakness, the Alash Orda government was left more or less on its own to govern the Kazakh community' (Olcott 1995: 143). Steven Sabol (2003: 133) writes that the Alash Orda government 'did achieve a degree of independence during the civil war that was unique and is now regarded by many Kazakh scholars as the first modern independent Kazakh state'. As with the All-Union Muslim Congress, their agenda was dominated by discussions of rights and representation, but included discussions about land use. Kazakh nomads had seen their rights to land severely reduced by the settlement of Russian peasants (Demko 1969). A few months later in December 1917 the Fourth Congress of Central Asia Muslims was held in Khokand in December. Chaired by Mustafa Chokaev its membership and proceedings tended to be dominated by Uzbeks. A dual power situation was briefly created but, in February 1918, forces of the Tashkent soviet seized Khokand and massacred many of its inhabitants.

From the summer of 1918 Whites and Reds contested for victory in the steppes, whilst Kazakh nationalists sought to preserve some form of independence. Increasingly, however, White rejection of their claims for authority pushed leading figures in Alash Orda into the arms of the Bolsheviks. In November 1919 the Military Revolutionary Council issued an amnesty for Alash members, and the following month saw the start of formal negotiations. With the vast majority of Kazakhstan in Bolshevik hands by March 1920, the formation of the Kirgiz (Kazakh) ASSR within the Russian Federation was announced in April 1920. By this time most of the Alash leaders had joined forces with the Marxist forces (Anderson 1997: 20–7).

Tsarist imperialism in Central Asia would matter for its Soviet successor for at least three reasons. First, it transformed the region culturally and demographically. When the Soviets arrived they were coming into a region that had already become acquainted with Russians and Russian rule. While Russian rule was largely pragmatic, the Soviet state, in contrast, penetrated and transformed society to a degree unprecedented for the region. Second, Russian imperial power had already territorialized rule and, according to Khalid (2007: 35) 'Central Asia had seen many empires in its long history, but the Russian conquest brought new forms of political control and new forms of knowledge to justify it. It brought Central Asia into the modern world via colonialism. This fate was shared by much of the world outside Europe and North America in the nineteenth century'. Third, the undisputed practice of colonialism in the Russian period was a key facilitator behind the emergence of Soviet communism and Soviet power in the region: it championed the rights of oppressed peoples, promoted national rights and declared itself, in Terry Martin's (2001: 19) words, as 'the world's first post-imperial state'. The importance of precedent was far-reaching and ironic: Soviet authorities and plans for national 'liberation' and 'modernization' were 'at the heart of a process to mitigate the consequences of "imperialism" and "colonialism"' (Teichmann 2007: 499), in short to de-colonize.

Border delimitation in Soviet Central Asia (1924–1936)

Between 1924 and 1936 a process known as the Soviet 'National-Territorial Delimitation' (*natsionalno-gosudarstvennoe razmezhevanie*) was brought to its completion. In the course of this process the Soviet Union was divided into 15 republics along national lines. The largest assigned ethnic group gave its name to the republic it inhabited. Five of these 15 were Central Asian republics and are, in the order of their formation: the Turkmen and Uzbek Soviet Socialist Republics (SSRs) in 1924, the Tajik SSR in 1929 and the Kazakh and Kyrgyz SSRs in 1936. Why would the 'internationally-minded Bolsheviks' (Haugen 2003), whose ideological platform was predicated on the withering away of the nation-state in the march to a socialist future, decide to carve up its territory along ethnic lines and ascribe them ethnic names? Why build into the system these basic contradictions that Adrienne Lynn Edgar (2004) rightly observes change over time but never disappear? Why did the Tajiks lose their ancient cities of Bukhara and Samarkand to the Uzbek SSR? Why did Kazakhstan end up so vast?

It is worth expanding a little more on just how radical this project was. The Soviet Union was the largest multi-ethnic polity to systematically base its political units on ethnicity (Suny 1993). For the first time in Central Asia's history, nationality and borders were declared congruent. The ethnic component of the Bolshevik project, furthermore, did not 'stop' at the drawing and naming of borders: it used ethnicity as the cornerstone of socio-political transformation. In addition to national territories, the Soviet regime fostered the idea of national cultures which were promoted among the various national groups. No doubt, this was a national culture that was designed by Soviet authorities so as to be compatible with the overall Soviet communist ideology, but also conceptually it was a national culture based on territory and ethnicity. The development of national literary languages for the various groups was a key element in the institutionalization of nationality. The selection, codification, elaboration and implementation that is necessary for any language standardization all had to be put in place (Landau and Kellner-Heinkele 2001) so that the 'national languages' could be officially established, no easy task given the supremacy of Russian as a *lingua franca* throughout the region, not to mention the multiple script and orthographic changes that came later. By the close of the 1920s 'education for the vast majority of the children in the Soviet Union was being conducted in his or her national language' (Smith 1997: 307). Finally, the Soviet state made nationality a main category in its classification of the population. The famous fifth point in Soviet passports represented (supposedly) genealogical information about the holders. In short, the Soviet state made nationality a decisive criterion in the distribution of goods and resources such as jobs, education and positions in bureaucracy (Martin 2001).

The content of the Soviet nationalities policy was finally delineated in resolutions passed at the Twelfth Party Congress in April 1923 and at a special Central Committee conference on nationalities policy in June 1923 (Martin 2001: 9). These resolutions promoted national languages and national elites, soon known as *korenizatsiia* (indigenization). Stalin famously defined Soviet national cultures as being 'national in form, socialist in content'. Federation for the Soviet Union also had clear limits, indeed, 'it did not involve federation, if this term means anything more than the mere formation of administrative territories along national lines' (Martin 2001: 13). To follow the nationalities principle, in descending size units were administratively organized into full Union republics, Autonomous republics, Autonomous Oblast and then smaller administrative units, such as regions and districts. In 1924 the Bukhara Emirate and Khivan Khanate (briefly termed the People's Republics of Bukhara and Khiva) and the Turkestan republic became the newly formed Uzbek SSR (incorporating the Tajik ASSR) and the newly formed Turkmen SSR. In 1924 the Kara-Kyrgyz Autonomous Oblast (AO) (present-day Kyrgyz Republic) and the Kyrgyz ASSR (present-day Kazakhstan) were incorporated into the Russian RFSR. In 1929 a separate Tajik SSR was created. After a renaming of Kyrgyz ASSR to Kazakh ASSR in 1925, alongside an upgrading of the Kara-Kyrgyz AO to ASSR status, finally in 1936 each was granted its own Union Republic, the Kyrgyz and Kazakh SSRs.

Debates that have emerged surrounding delimitation are more than debates about border drawing. They drive at how the Soviet state legitimated itself and the degree to which identities in this period were developed or stunted. We can identify the following four major reasons that have been proposed for the drawing of borders or national delimitation: the strategy of *realpolitik* (economic and political) and 'divide-and-rule', which was a view that dominated in the Soviet period and served also as a tactical concession to win round dissenters and oppressed colonial peoples from abroad by framing the new state as an anti-colonial regime; 'an active, prophylactic strategy of promoting non-Russian nation-building to prevent the growth of nationalism' (Martin 2001: 8); a belief in the necessity of creating nations to hurry up their eventual demise and the march to socialism and therefore the birth of a 'chronic ethnophilia' (Slezkine 1994), with authors such as Arne Haugen (2003) also suggesting that the territorial borders do reflect territorialized national identities; linked to the last, the outcome of participation from local elites. Border delimitation was regarded as a strategy aimed at securing political power and control by the centre over the non-Russian peripheries. Borders were meant first to divide and thus destroy what were perceived as genuine nationalist movements or the perceived supra-national identities of pan-Turkism and all-Muslim movements (Carrère d'Encausse 1992) even if in reality there was no strong pan-Turkish movement. The Soviets would outdo their ideological competitors. Rule would also be facilitated by the administrative and organizational help that borders bring to a large multi-ethnic empire, and economic divisions would ensure that no single republic could secede with any chance of survival. Walker Connor (1984) emphasized how the international dimension forced such divide-and-rule policies, a point made previously also by Bennigsen and Lemercier-Quelquejay (1967: 134):

> There is little doubt that the wish to forestall the fashioning of a pan-Turkestan national consciousness … was central to the 1924 decision. One need only to recall that the Bolshevik leaders had to combat at the same period the ideas of Sultan Galiev and his followers on the union of all Turks of Russia into a single republic, Turan.

Stephen Blank (1994: 128) much later would also argue that the national delimitation of Central Asia was a part of a great divide and rule plan, the essence of which was to accomplish the 'fragmentation of Muslim unity'. Edward Allworth (1990) also agrees that delimitation was part of a divide-and-rule strategy and that a segregation strategy was essentially anti-Uzbek because the Uzbeks, by virtue of their numbers and geographic spread, posed the greatest threat to central power. In further defence of a divide-and-rule argument, scholars pointed to how divisions did not usefully express nationality and nationhood. According to Bennigsen and Lemercier-Quelquejay (1961: 27), if nationality had been a real organizational principle, then a Kazakh-Kyrgyz entity, an Uzbek-Tajik entity and finally a Turkmen entity would have made more sense (in other words how the project started out). Steven Sabol (1995: 235) offers a number of reasons for the dynamics behind delimitation, including that the 'concrete goal was to separate the main tribal units of Ferghana Valley'. Roy (2000) sees in the tortuous border drawing of the Ferghana Valley partly economic imperatives, ensuring that no single republic would be able to become truly independent.

Sometimes following on from this, but analytically separate, was that borders drawn along national lines were intended as a transitional solution. Even if temporary, some would see already this creation as a genuine commitment to equality. But many saw it as tactically ensuring the loyalty of peoples living at the borders of the Soviet state. It provided a showcase to peoples who were still living under colonial powers. Particularly it would appeal to kinsmen across borders. It was also a tactical response to the weakness of and resistance to Soviet power (notably by the Basmachi movement) in the early years, and Lenin's perception of how nationalism might be tapped for the support of Soviet power. And tactically it suggested the Soviet Union adhered to the norms of sovereignty and statehood then increasingly prevalent in the international system, particularly promoted by Woodrow Wilson.

By contrast the next two reasons – delimitation as the wider nationalities principle as a 'prophylactic' and expression of 'chronic ethnophilia' – argue precisely the opposite, namely that nationhood had become a real organizational principle for the Soviets. The nation was perceived as axiomatic to the success of the Soviet project, particularly in the early years when faced with the weakness of Soviet power and resistance by the Basmachi movement.

At first the deliberate fostering of nationhood might seem anathema to the Soviet ideal of a stateless socialist world. But Terry Martin (2001) gives us three reasons why the Soviets saw the nation as integral to Bolshevik doctrine: class-creation, modernization and staving off Great Russian chauvinism. By granting nationhood, the Bolsheviks stole from the nationalists their biggest card and ensured that the above-class alliance that was nationalism would become a socialist one. Society would thus again splinter into classes, allowing the Bolsheviks to recruit further proletarian and peasant support for the construction of socialism. Second, since a phase of national consciousness was viewed as inevitable, the Soviets thought to hurry it along by deliberately fostering such awareness. It was part of a more comprehensive plan for societal transformation. And third, citing Lenin, 'Scratch any Communist and you find a Great Russian chauvinist.... He sits in many of us and we must fight him' (Martin 2001: 1): to stave off Russian nationalism, or at least to counter it, non-Russian nationalisms were to be promoted.

As a measure of how seriously the task was taken authors point to the army of Moscow-based officials and ethnographers that Soviet power put to work to document, in detail, ethnic groups. Why, if the purpose had simply been to 'divide-and-rule'? The panoply of measures and the extent of this project is well documented by Francine Hirsch (2005) and captured in Yuri Slezkine's (1994) term of 'chronic ethnophilia'. The commitment to the task was shown by how its sheer enormity was not off-putting, one writer commenting on how ethnographers sent to Central Asia 'would come across clans and tribes that had not yet worked out their national consciousness' (Vakhabov 1961: 388). Bartol'd had written: 'When you ask a Turkistani what is his identity, he will answer that he is, first of all, a "Muslim," then an inhabitant of such or such city or village …, or if he is a nomad, member of such or such tribe'. Ronald Suny (1999: 168–9) also writes how '[N]ames like "Uzbeks", "Kazakhs", and "Tajiks" had referred to social or military categories or patterns of settlement (sedentary, nomadic, or oases)'. Haugen (2003: 29, 7) argues that this consciousness was built on 'existing patterns of identity' and the new republics expressed 'a considerable degree of continuity' and 'to a great degree corresponded to historical divisions and formations in Central Asia' and therefore 'the delimitation should be seen as an attempt to unite rather than to break up the region'. Edgar (2004: 5–7), writing on the creation of Soviet Turkmenistan, argues that 'the crucial contribution of local elites in shaping Soviet nations has not received enough attention', that 'a sense of "Turkmen-ness" based on genealogy long predated the Soviet era' and that this 'segmented genealogical structure that potentially united the Turkmen groups was equally prone to divide them'.

With access to new archival evidence, Haugen (2003: 29) also argues that 'discussions in connection with the delimitation also reflected that identities were changing' and that 'local forces were able to influence the project to a much greater degree than has usually been acknowledged'. One part of this transformation concerned the role that local actors came to play in defining the demarcation process. Here the specifics of each republic become very relevant. Martin's (2001) research on early delimitation shows how the forces at work in drawing borders in Kazakhstan were quite different to elsewhere in Central Asia. The difference arose primarily from large Slav settlement of the steppe lands in the Russian era and the staunch defence by Kazakhs of their land and territory and resistance to further such encroachment. The multinational, European-settled regions of Kazakhstan and to a lesser degree Kyrgyz territory placed land ownership at the centre of debates over delimitation. The recognition of earlier Kazakh calls for autonomy (Sabol 2003) was also important.

By contrast, the Tajiks lost their most prized territory to the Uzbeks, and this, coupled with their own republic's relatively later formation, is explained partly by an inactive and inexperienced local elite that was unable to promote the Tajik cause – even if, almost as soon as the Tajik ASSR was created, Tajik leaders became vocal about how Uzbekistan's leaders discriminated against Tajiks.

From 1924 to 1929 the Tajik Soviet Socialist Autonomous Republic existed within the Uzbek SSR; only in 1929 did the Tajiks get their own SSR. Dov Lynch (2001: 52) writes that delimitation left Tajikistan:

> with unfavourable structural circumstances for the emergence of a unified political community. Tajikistan had four main administrative regions in Leninabad (Khujant), Kurgan-Tyube, Kulob (these last two were merged in early 1993 to create Khatlon) and Gorno-Badakhshan, as well as several important "areas of republican subordination" in such central districts as Gharm and Hissor. The new Tajik Republic was left without the two "city symbols" of Tajik culture and history. Bukhara and Samarkand were attributed to Uzbekistan. The loss of these cities, with the concomitant loss of their intellectual elite, left Tajikistan bereft of natural historical and cultural centres. … the new Tajik Republic contained only 300,000 of the total Tajik population of 1.1. million, based mainly in Uzbekistan. The small republic was dominated by mountains, with 93 percent of its territory above 1500 meters. These geographical circumstances led to the preservation of strong local identities, based around 'identity-regions' consisting of the six main regions and districts.

The result of 1929, then, was far from perfect, 'even [Russian] "orientalists" could not help noticing that the Tajiks of the cities of the plains, like Samarkand and Bukhara, were not only living "all mixed up" with the Uzbeks but were indistinguishable from them in appearance' (Bergne 2007: 127). Even if they 'did not always win' (Bergne 2007: 54), the Uzbeks, by contrast, had been vocal and well organized from the beginning. Their militancy, Olivier Roy (2000: 73) notes, in turn spawned action by other ethnic groups, concluding that: 'Stalin's great victory was that he made the intellectuals in Central Asia defend their own languages and "nations" against their neighbors, and not against Moscow, who instead was called upon for mediation and the settlement of conflicts'.

Similarly Donald Carlisle (1994: 104) emphasizes 'the play of local politics and the place of native populations whose cooperation with the Center was essential for the success of the project'. These tensions existed precisely because, as Carlisle proceeds to argue, they were essentially political and they produced patriotisms that were also regional or geopolitical, not merely 'national'. While for Carlisle the Jadids of Bukhara themselves militated for national delimitation, Allworth argues that Moscow exploited Bukhara. The incorporation of '[s]ignificant numbers of Central Asians' into the Communist Party and other organs of power 'influenced the outcome of the delimitation process' (Haugen 2003: 8).

The reality of motivations behind border drawing probably lay somewhere in between, combining various reasons, not even necessarily in a linear way, and often dependent on region or republic. Whatever the reason, the outcome is undisputed: it became the largest multinational polity in history. And Mark Von Hagen (2004) is probably right when he says the collapse might not have happened had the Soviet Union been less federalized. The outcome, intended or unintended, was a sense of growing national belonging, which began to take on a life of its own. In Martin's (2001: 22) terms, 'the paradox is less that Soviet communism actively promoted nationalism than how in practice nationalism came to have permanent tensions with the Soviet construct that would not disappear'. In Central Asia emerged the added paradox that, unusual among Soviet republics, their titular nations for the first time had (albeit nominal) borders ascribed to them. Thus, the Soviet and the national were created and about to be experienced simultaneously.

Empire and 'becoming'

These tensions became part of the bigger paradox that was to play itself out in the emerging realities of Soviet Central Asia, and finally in its collapse. The collapse of the Soviet Union encouraged a renewed discussion about what constitutes empire, whether the Soviet Union can be neatly classed as empire, and whether we can 'apply Postcolonial Theory to Central Eurasia?' (Adams 2008). This has also involved ideas about how best to conceive empire: as intention (anti-imperial or imperial), experience ('alien or close') or outcome ('becoming').

At the core of these debates is whether, on the one hand, the commitment to cultural and national equalization, and, on the other, the sheer intensity of Soviet transformation, still allows for classification of the Soviet Union as an empire. One answer sees the Soviet Union not as an empire but as an 'activist, interventionist, mobilizational state' (Khalid 2006: 232), rather like its Kemalist predecessor in Turkey. Khalid (2006: 233) further argues that '[c]olonial conquest transformed colonized societies, but colonial empires seldom used state power to transform societies, cultures, or individuals in the way attempted by the Soviet state'. A second sees it as 'an empire with a caveat' (Kassymbekova 2011: 21), while a third prefers to keep it as, straight, empire.

Martin (2001: 19), by contrast, does not replace empire with state. He does, however, also underline the project's radically transformative nature and its commitment to rights:

> The Affirmative Action Empire was not a traditional empire. I am not aligning myself with those who now argue that the Soviet Union, as a result of its shared characteristics with other empires, can be classified in objective social science terms as an 'empire.' The term *Affirmative Action Empire* represents an attempt to capture the paradoxical nature of the multiethnic Soviet state: an extraordinarily invasive, centralized, and violent state formally structured as a federation of sovereign nations; the successor state to the collapsed Russian empire that successfully reconquered most of its former national borderlands but then set out to systematically build and strengthen its non-Russian nations, even where they barely existed.

In 1967, Alec Nove and J.A. Neweth (1967: 122) puzzled over a state that seemed to privilege its eastern periphery while simultaneously holding it in subjugation, concluding that 'if we do not call the present relationship colonialism, we ought to invent a new name to describe something which represents subordination and yet is genuinely different from the imperialism of the past'.

A second position is close to the latter but more categorical: yes, the Soviet Union was different but it was still an empire. These differences made the Soviet Union unique without, however, questioning that rule by Moscow was imperial and its effect on Central Asia a partly colonizing one. Scholars here show how, specifically in the cultural domain, nationalities policies had worked to produce outcomes not seen anywhere else among empires (or multinational states for that matter). Francine Hirsch (2005) emphasizes the policy of dual assimilation in which Soviet authorities promote both a Soviet-wide identity and a nation-wide one. Douglas Northrop (2004) on the unveiling campaign (as part of the broader *hujum* or assault on traditional ways) and Paula Michaels (2000) on medicine illustrate how the state was highly interventionist but simultaneously similar in effects to those produced by the cultural technologies of the classical empires such as Britain and France.

Northrop (2004: 21-2) says:

> Some elements of the Bolshevik approach to Central Asia, therefore, are not colonial per se. Yet it would be wrong to conclude from the surface similarities in representations of Slavic and Central Asian peasants that the USSR was no more than a modernizing state or that its policies did not differentiate meaningfully between regions. ... One of my main premises, then, is that the USSR, like its tsarist predecessor, was a colonial empire. Power in the Soviet Union was expressed across lines of hierarchy and difference that created at least theoretically distinct centers (metropoles) and peripheries (colonies).

Thus while this may have been an empire of nations or even an affirmative action empire, the USSR still ensured that ethnic Russians remained the titular nationality with the most economic, political and cultural rights; that the Russian language was the trans-republican lingua franca; and, that Central Asia particularly was made the 'dumping ground' for 'unwanted peoples'. These writers further emphasize how the periphery itself participated in the construction of the Soviet Union and how the 1927 unveiling campaign, for example, 'had had to adjust to its new empire and rethink what it meant by a "Soviet" Policy in the colonial non-Russian periphery. What would a Soviet society look like in Muslim areas such as southern Central Asia? ... In the local encounter between Soviet power and Central Asia, both sides emerged transformed' (Northrop 2004: 344).

The third position that regards the Soviet Union unequivocally as empire is adopted also (Barkey and Von Hagen 1997; Dawisha and Parrot 1997). The economic relationship between Soviet centre and Central Asian periphery comes probably closest to the classic imperial mould and yet, paradoxically, few have given this particular scrutiny. Martin (2001: 14) explains how compared 'to the commitment to cultural and national equalization, through Affirmative Action in education and hiring, the Soviet commitment to economic equalization was never institutionalized'. Similarly, Khalid (2006: 232, Footnote 3) comments on:

> the curiosity that there has been little interest in the economic relationship between Central Asia and the Soviet state, which is where the colonial argument is the easiest to make. Soviet economic planning turned the whole region into a gigantic cotton plantation in order for the USSR to achieve 'cotton independence' ... Scholars who invoke postcolonial studies in the study of Central Asia have been much more interested in the cultural work of Soviet power, a much sexier topic than the history of cotton.

Deniz Kandiyoti's (2007) edited collection on cotton does, however, make for compelling reading and underscores how Central Asia's economies had been subject to the wildest of projects with the sole aim of enriching the centre and with scant regard of these schemes' human and environmental costs. This claim can be made in spite of peculiarities, such as the still disputed subsidy transfer issue, referring to how, given the huge investments industrializing Central Asia, who received more, the core or the periphery (*kto kovo?*). To continue with the story of 'white gold', Kandiyoti (2007: 1–2) writes that 'the extent of surplus transfer to the centre from Central Asia also became a matter of debate since these transfers were offset by substantial subsidies to the Soviet periphery from the All-Union Budget'. Empires, in short, can modernize and still remain empires.

The economies of Central Asia under Soviet rule became first and foremost providers of raw materials to the core. Cotton, wheat and oil were key examples. Under Stalin 'the twin goals of collectivization and "cotton independence" were pursued' (Kandiyoti 2007: 1). While before the October Revolution cotton production in Central Asia was reasonably balanced between fruit and cotton, under Soviet rule it would become 'the major provider of raw cotton for the Russian and Ukrainian textile factories' (Spoor 2007a: 56).

Otto Pohl (2007: 12) argues that 'not since the defeat of the Confederate States of America had any other region in the world been so dependent on cotton' and 'the acreage devoted to cotton was expanded continually until it reached a peak in the 1980s'. By the 1980s the diversion of the Amu Darya and Syr Darya river basin water to irrigate cotton production had led to a 40 per cent desiccation of the Aral Sea. Already by the 1970s a nomenklatura around cotton had developed which was falsifying output and yield data and encouraging forced labour and corrupt practices. All this became publicized after the death of Communist Party leader Sharif Rashidov in 1983. Post-Brezhnev Moscow in its anti-corruption campaign purged thousands of cadres in Uzbekistan in what became known as the 'cotton affair' (Gleason 1997).

The Virgin Lands programme of the 1960s transformed the Kazakh steppe into the Soviet Union's breadbasket. This followed forced sedentarization of nomadic peoples and the collectivization of agriculture in the region as a whole (Economakis 1991). In the Kazakh case, '[e]stimates of deaths and destruction vary' some, Bhavna Dave (2007: 56) points out, naming the period 1929–33 'a tragedy bordering on genocide'. According to Zhuldyzbek B. Abylkhozhin, Manash Kozybaev and Makash Tatimov (1989), 2.3 million Kazakhs perished. Industrially, Soviet power deliberately ensured that Central Asia was unable to process and refine oil on its territory; furthermore, the economic relationship of Central Asian economies to Moscow conformed to the 'spokes of the wheel' analogy made by Alexander Motyl (2001) where each republic (spoke) was directly connected only to Moscow (hub). All pipelines transporting oil and gas travelled through Russia.

To use income gained from cash crops to fuel the ever growing and hugely expensive military-industrial complex, production goals were raised to unthinkable levels and with scant regard for ecological balance. The command-administrative system, with its inbuilt five-year plan, became an incentive to over-fulfil as regional elites vied for influence and status (Sakwa 1989). The resultant degree of intervention and penetration in the economy was thus decidedly greater than anything practised to date by imperial powers elsewhere in the world. In this view, then, the Soviet Union differed from its Tsarist predecessor in degree and speed of intervention but the fundamental premise of economic exploiter/exploited remained.

This brings us full circle to the discussion of how much a post-colonial lens might be applied to discussions of post-Soviet Central Asia. Do claims matter more than, as time passes, the assessed experience of living under empire? Edward Said (2003) argues that all empires frame their aims as benign civilizing missions. So perhaps an emphasis on claims can take us only so far. We cannot speak of one period of Soviet rule, one region of Soviet rule, or even of uniform policies and effects across Soviet time and space, so we need to detail those differences and isolate Central Asia for our purposes. Perhaps, then, Soviet Central Asia experienced a mix of socio-political modernization, economic imperialism and cultural semi-colonization.

Politically it had the most clear case of modernization even if it remained subject to central control. While economically it was, on the one hand, industrialized and subsidized, on the other, it was exploited in a classical colonial sense. Cultural colonization is a particularly difficult area to categorize because the experience is not only ambivalent but also internalized. *Mankurtism* – the phrase coined by internationally renowned Kyrgyz writer Chingiz Aitmatov (1983) to refer to attempts to erase the pre-Soviet past in these societies – was juxtaposed to examples of cultural empowerment. Both Russians and non-Russians were subject to large-scale persecution, extermination and incarceration, both Russians and non-Russians were given citizenship. But at the same time the core itself claimed that its relations with the periphery were to be similar to those practised by its imperial Russian predecessor; moreover, Russian language was prioritized and Russians were given top jobs. And because of Stalin's reliance on Russian nationalism, Russians were generally not deported on ethnic grounds to Siberia and Central Asia. In short, as a mobilizing empire, we can expect change in the way empire is experienced over time and its longer-term effects on popular behaviour.

Mark Beissinger (2004: 17) argues that the Soviet Union:

> should be understood instead as one of the first of a new form of empire whose crucial contributions were its denial of its imperial quality and its use of the very cornerstones of the modern nation-state system – the norms of state sovereignty and national self-determination – as instruments of non-consensual control over culturally distinct populations, thereby blurring the line between state and empire.

At the same time, he (2004: 33) continues, the Soviet Union only began to be framed as an imperial one by the periphery in the 1980s and even then '[o]n the eve of the collapse of the USSR, few observers treated the USSR internally as an empire'.

Whether we accept or reject the imperial label, it is hard to contest the radical nature of Soviet rule and its profound effect on both the outer and inner realm of human existence in this region. Unlike other parts of the Soviet Union which were already sedentarized and somewhat industrialized, Soviet industrialization in Central Asia occurred in the unique context of either pastoral economies or largely, if not exclusively, settled agrarian economies organized around water. The Soviets introduced industrialization in two decades, bringing the chapter to its penultimate section, the place of tradition in the modernizing Soviet experiment.

Tradition, modernization and transformation

Faced with these visible transformations, it may seem curious to ask how much *did* change, and with what effect(s). The tensions between traditionalism and modernization are variously interpreted and these interpretations fall roughly into three types. One type looks at tradition and Soviet modernization as incompatible competitors and tradition as therefore resisting modernization attempts. The second, by contrast, sees Soviet modernization as transforming traditional structures, even if not always in the form expected or intended. The third views the relationship between Soviet modernization and traditionalism as symbiotic, each experience transforming the other.

Sergei P. Poliakov (1992: 4) uses:

> 'traditionalism' and 'traditional society' to mean the complete rejection of anything new introduced from the outside into the familiar, 'traditional' way of life. Traditionalism does not simply battle novelty; it actively demands constant correction of the life-style according to an ancient, primordial, or 'classical' model.

In this view, everyday practices were a form of resistance to Soviet rule and defended as an ideal vision of Central Asian tradition. M. Nazif Shahrani (1984: 36) writes that transformation 'failed for at least two reasons: First, because of the power of the informal structure of sufi orders in Soviet Central Asia; Second, because social identities are multiplex'. By the end of the Soviet period, approximately two-thirds of the Soviet Union's Muslims resided in Central Asia (Ro'i 2000). The survival and practice of Islam in this framework constituted a triumph of traditionalism, and the survival of Soviet Muslims 'will be an important chemical agent in the future brew' (Bennigsen and Wimbush 1985: 4) causing eventual Soviet collapse. This view assumed that '[a]dherence to Islam automatically was supposed to have a political meaning in the Soviet context' (Khalid 2003: 574). Michael Rywkin (1988: 90) explains further that:

> In the decade remaining in this century, the political, economic, and cultural weight of Central Asia – propelled by an unprecedented demographic boom – will inexorably grow. The sheer numerical strength and the continuing unassimalability of the Soviet Muslim masses, in the context of political liberalization, economic decline, and resurgent nationalism throughout the USSR as a whole, including among Russians, will present the Soviet state with its greatest challenge as the world's last great multinational empire prepares to enter the twenty-first century.

As we shall see, the Muslim peoples of Central Asia were the last to declare independence from the Soviet Union.

The Soviet approach to understanding and defining religious life is similar to its approach to understanding and defining identity. Nationalities policy positively encouraged the search by national republics for their 'cultural authenticity' and nation-building with a strong cultural content was not seen as anathema to Soviet power. In its attempts to build nations, it championed tradition but not just any tradition. The Soviets had a deep disdain for anything they deemed archaic, notably clans and folk/popular Islam, the latter becoming known as 'parallel Islam', and viewed it as directly opposing the state. In his study of musical styles and cultural identities in Tajikistan Federico Spinetti (2005: 186) writes how 'traditional musics were transformed into national monuments in order to comply with Soviet internationalism'. But if a particular tradition could be slotted into its essentialized view of identity then it could be permitted. To ensure Islam toed the official line, the Soviets set up the Spiritual Boards or Directorates of the Muslims, the largest of which was of Central Asia and Kazakhstan (SADUM) in Tashkent (the other three based in Ufa, Makhachkala and Baku).

But historians of the Soviet period were already questioning this monolithic view of Islam. While acknowledging that:

> Islam undoubtedly constitutes some sort of bond of union among the Soviet Muslim nationalities, and also between them and non-Soviet Muslims.

But this does not necessarily mean that there is such a thing as Muslim nationalism or Turkic nationalism or Turkestani nationalism.

(Wheeler 1968: 74)

Or in Atkin's (1989: 27) words 'Sufism means too many different things to
different adherents, and too much of it has nothing to do with politics'.
Furthermore, writing before Soviet collapse Mark Saroyan (1993: 38) questioned
the validity of the very notion of a 'paired opposite' of 'modern' and 'traditional'.
Continuing by describing 'the paired opposites that inform Western writing on
Islam in the Soviet Union' he lists:

state (pro-state)	society (anti-state)
Soviet	Muslim
modern	traditional
artifice	authenticity
nationality	pan-Turkism/pan-Islam
"official Islam"	"parallel Islam"
illegitimacy	legitimate social authority
false ideology	true religion

Saroyan (1993: 29) traces the first use of the term 'parallel Islam' in 1980 by
'the dean of Soviet Islamic studies, Lusitsian Klimovich', later adopted by
'Bennigsen and Lemercier-Quelquejay and later Bennigsen and Wimbush'
(Saroyan 1993: 29). He suggests that through an analysis of discourse and power
such misleading dichotomies can be debunked. We will pick up on this again
in Chapter 5.

Disputes today remain about what constitutes 'tradition' and who matters in
considering what constitutes 'tradition'. Russ Kleinbach and Lilly Salimjanova
(2007) argue that non-consensual bride kidnapping is not a Kyrgyz *adat* (traditional customary law) tradition. Cynthia Werner (2009: 327) notes 'a strong
divide between the public notion that bride abduction is a traditional practice and
the scholarly opinion that non-consensual abduction was rare in the past'.

The second approach emphasizes how Soviet rule used tradition for its modern
aim of nation-building, but not always with the results or the form expected.
From 1927 onwards, the regime conducted a full-scale campaign against Islam.
Religious properties were confiscated, madrasas and mosques were closed, their
buildings requisitioned for more "socially useful" purposes (schools, clubs, ware-
houses), or, in many cases, destroyed. *Ulama* (clergy) were persecuted (Keller
2001). At the same time it sought to invest in nation-building. Edgar's (2004)
earlier noted depiction of local Turkmen showed elites eager to help in building
a new republic and a vernacular language. But how they defined themselves, such
as genealogy, they wanted to maintain and '[a]s a result, many Turkmen were
unpersuaded that Soviet-style modernity was essential to the formation of a strong
and cohesive Turkmen nation' (Edgar 2004: 263). Despite the 'huge changes'
brought by the twentieth century, 'Turkmen villagers continued to follow many

of the customs that began under nomadic conditions of life, particularly those that had to do with marriage and the family' (Edgar 2007: 43).

With a similar objective, tribes were to be broken up and mixed around to serve bigger national allegiances. For Roy (2007) sedentarization and collectivization led paradoxically to tribes becoming stronger through their territorialization and this in turn consolidated nationhood. Roy (2007: 137–8) also points to the relatively high number of forced population resettlements in the Tajik SSR as a principal reason for the insecure regional identities found there on Soviet collapse. Waves of 'territorialization' occurred in the 1930s, during the drive to collectivization, and in the 1950s, in pursuit of cotton production. Large numbers of Gharmis and Kulobis were resettled in the areas around Qurghonteppa. This experience solidified regional differences as maintained in kolkhozes (collective farms). In the words of Roy (1997: 139), in these areas, the kolkhoz represented an 'expression of a solidarity group [...] or the object of a power struggle between rival groups'. In Pauline Jones Luong's (2002) study of the Kazakh, Kyrgyz and Uzbek SSRs, by contrast, tribal identities were subsumed into strong regional identities. Central Asian languages were developed as part of this essentialized view of identity and, through universal literacy and script changes, were modernized. Either way, the indigenous becomes Sovietized.

In the third perspective the lines between Soviet projects and traditional concepts were much more blurred, and the Soviet may become indigenized. Both fed into each other. Soviet policy in Central Asia came to focus especially on gender relations as a substitute for class, in the hope that this approach would bring about wholesale revolutionary change. To continue on unveiling, Northrop (2004: 346) states that:

> '[t]radition' came to mean veiling and seclusion – and *all* Uzbek women not just those in wealthy urban families. A panoply of associated 'traditional' practices (bride-price and polygyny, circumcision ceremonies, religious funerals, pilgrimages, and a host of others) were reimagined as universal; together they became stabilized, and in the end they were nationalized as emblems of the Uzbek people. These practices thus became expressive of an un-Soviet, even anti-Soviet identity – a richly ironic outcome, since the Uzbek national identity was itself largely a Soviet creation. The party's own actions, therefore, played an important albeit inadvertent role in spreading the practice of veiling, especially in rural areas, by equating it with Uzbek religio-cultural and now national traditions, and thereby giving it new depth and political meaning.

Devin DeWeese (2002: 306) writes that 'religious boards thus stand among the structures of Soviet life that became "indigenized" and assimilated into Islamic religious life, and not only as a means of control' and 'it is one of the strange ironies of Soviet history that the Communist party and the Soviet academic establishment were essentially allied with the official Islamic clergy (not to mention fundamentalists abroad) in adopting a "rigorist" interpretation of what constituted "real" Islam', a point also made by Saroyan (2003).

Continuing on the everyday effects of the unveiling, Northrop (2007: 95) writes that:

> [t]he campaign against the veil was complicated, contested, and contradictory; over the next fifteen years it transformed all sides. Soviet reformers and their Muslim opponents alike came to define their cultural practices and social values through the everyday customs of millions of individual women …. this common ground of debate ultimately helped define a specific, local and deeply gendered vocabulary for both Central Asian Bolshevism and Uzbek national identity.

Marianne Kamp (2007: 113) also writes on the contradictory effects of Soviet modernization: 'Gulshad's wedding feast is illuminated with electric lights, another rare wonder of modernization for rural people. At the same time, Soviet modernization also meant massive government control and intervention in everyday life'. Discussions about change and continuity matter for the independence period. In discursive terms, 'tradition' and 'modern', and their associated narratives of 'golden ages', 'revival', or again, 'cultural authenticity' are placed in a broader continuum. Second, the debates acknowledge how the everyday experience of Soviet rule mattered both for confirming existing notions of self and for embracing or at least adapting to the challenges of modernization. This layer of modern bureaucratic and industrial structures is real to the region: Central Asia is more than simply a configuration of tribes and clans. Finally, it enables us to better grasp what would soon become the legacies of the Soviet world and therefore the sum of what varied interpretations and experiences of 'the Soviet' means for the early independence period.

Paths to sovereignty and independence: enduring Soviet legacies

Just as Soviet Central Asia provides us with interesting challenges to our preconceptions of empire, so it, finally, does for sovereignty. As Martha Brill Olcott (1992) writes, Central Asian states were 'catapulted to independence'. Prior to independence, incumbent leaders and those of social movements that had sprung up under Gorbachev's policies of perestroika and glasnost, were reacting to the implosion of the centre. The All-Union referendum of 17 March 1991, which was to be the last Soviet-wide referendum, had included the question: 'Do you agree that [name of republic] will enter the renewed union (Federation) as a (*ravnopravnaia*) republic enjoying equal rights [with others]?', was essentially about whether republics wanted to stay in the Union, albeit on promised new 'equal' terms. All five Central Asian populations voted into 90 percentages for retention of the Union. Countries began to declare independence only once it was clear that the centre had imploded, and cultural leaders, such as Olzhas Suleimenov (1995), were quick to express their reservations:

> We were in opposition but we were constructive. I myself view the collapse of the Soviet Union as a tragedy for Kazakhstan ... Gorbachev wanted to draft a more equal Union Treaty. But then Yeltsin wanted to remove Gorbachev. In order to achieve that, he exploded the whole Union. We say that it is not worth burning the whole fur coat to kill one flea. But that is exactly what Yeltsin did.

If we accept the notion of independent sovereignty as popular sovereignty, one that needs to be willed and owned by the people, then we run into problems when we apply it to Central Asia. Michael Walzer (1977) following John Stuart Mill, points out that, by definition, self-determination must be willed by the people. Others have argued that leaders of movements militating for change still stopped short of demanding outright independence already viewing sovereignty as a significant achievement and were fearful what independence would bring. Uzbek activist Muhammad Solih explains that '[they] realized that independence does not equal democracy' (Suyarkulova 2011).

The fact that the Soviet Union incorporated notions of sovereignty and self-determination already under empire significantly altered the ways that sovereignty was uttered in the perestroika and glasnost periods and in the sovereign eras, The Soviet Union, as noted, had ruled by 'fuzzying the boundary between state and empire' (Beissinger 2004: 25). The union republics became statelets in embryo, with complete institutions of government, national symbols, traditions of cultural production in their own literary vernaculars, a legitimate standing in Soviet law and even the (theoretical) right to secession written into the federal constitution. Thus, through federalism, the union republics were in effect furnished with the institutions, organizations, and access to resources to forward their national interests and to mobilize their constituents behind securing a greater measure of national self-determination. On top of that we have the specificity of Central Asia in which these notions were new to the peoples concerned and were understood in the context of the order in which they had been introduced, namely sovereignty within imperial borders which theoretically, in traditional Western language, is a contradiction in terms. In Central Asian terms, however, and to a degree like several other SSRs, it was quite natural to militate in favour of 'more sovereignty'.

Prior to Bolshevik victory, Lenin saw that championing the national cause and incorporating national sensibilities would ensure political victory: 'In forwarding the right of nations to self-determination, which he saw as linked exclusively with the right to political secession, Lenin was adopting a political strategy for resolving Russia's national question' (Smith 1996: 4–5). After 1917, Lenin radically changed his position. In the 1918 Constitution the Party opted for the state to have a federal form, and in 1919 was proposing 'a federated union of states, organized in a soviet manner ... as one of the transitional forms on the road to complete unity' (Peters 1964: 146). The Union Treaty of 1922 was a compromise reached as a result of the Civil War and Stalin's notion of 'proletarian self-determination'. The 'larger non-Russian nationality groupings were offered equality of union republic status within a Soviet federation which would honour their right to secession and would grant their major nationalities considerable cultural and administrative autonomy. In return for these guarantees, the nationalities would give up their present form of state sovereignty and become part of a socialist federation of states' (Smith 1998: 5–6). After Khrushchev's attempts to hasten the merging of nationalities into a new 'Soviet man', under Brezhnev official policy throughout the 1970s and 1980s continued to accept tacitly the existence of a multiethnic society of culturally distinct yet integrated nationalities. Brezhnev made it clear he wanted to retain, in the 1977 Constitution, the (albeit nominal) right of union republics to territorial secession (as included in the 1924 and 1936 constitutions).

By the Gorbachev era the Soviet Union had become a hybrid, a part imperial, part federal structure. While Central Asian leaders were required to keep control and meet production targets, 'these elites were treating their territories as feudal fiefs and that by the Brezhnev era even the loyalty of local Russians could not be taken for granted, as such people could be coopted, bribed or intimidated into supporting traditional modes of rule' (Anderson 1997: 36). Also, under Gorbachev, 'part of the explanation for the enhanced legitimacy of local politicians is that they have distanced themselves from the central leadership' (Fierman 1991: 55). Despite perestroika and glasnost, Gorbachev refused to treat the nationalities question seriously; until the mid-December 1986 events that ironically came from the region which was to resist the end of the Soviet Union, then capital of the Kazakh SSR, Alma-Ata. Riots had been triggered by the replacement of a Kazakh First Party Secretary with a Russian, which broke with the previously universal practice of appointing a native to such a post. By the summer of 1989 Gorbachev declared that 'inter-ethnic conflict threatens to determine, not only the fate of perestroika, but also the integrity of the Soviet state'. On 11 March 1990, the Lithuanian parliament became the first republic to declare its independence from the CPSU. Four months later, in July 1990, the Lithuanian parliament became the first republic to declare its independence from Moscow. Although the other 14 union republics did not go so far, the Lithuanian decision paved the way for sovereignty declarations by them throughout 1990.

Authors have differed in the kinds of Soviet legacies they analyse and on how specifically they matter. The absence of large-scale independence movements exerted a profound effect on the psychology of these young sovereign states. As a basic starting point, the absence of alternatives and civil society meant that incumbent leaders were barely challenged and, monopolizing economic and political resources, were able very swiftly to don a sovereign coat. The leaders who assumed power were in the main those who had ruled their countries already prior to Soviet collapse. In the absence of self-determination movements, what

Table 3.1 Major ethnic groups in Central Asia

Year	Kazakhstan	Kyrgyzstan	Tajikistan	Turkmenistan	Uzbekistan
1989	Kazakh 40%, Russian 38%, German 6%, other 16%	Kyrgyz 52%, Russian 21%, Uzbek 13%, Other 14%	Tajik 62%, Russian 8%, Uzbek 24%, other 6%	Turkmen 72%, Russian 9%, Uzbek 9%, other 10%	Uzbek 71%, Russian 8%, Tajik 5%, other 16%
1993	Kazakh 41.9%, Russian 37%, Ukrainian 5.2%, German 4.7%, Uzbek 2.1%, Tatar 2%, other 7.1%	Kyrgyz 52.4%, Russian 21.5%, Uzbek 12.9%, Ukrainian 2.5%, German 2.4%, other 8.3%	Tajik 64.9%, Uzbek 25%, Russian 3.5%, other 6.6%	Turkmen 73.3%, Russian 9.8%, Uzbek 9%, Kazakhs 2% other 5.9%	Uzbek 71.4%, Russian 8.3%, Tajik 4.7%, Kazakhs 4.1%, Tatars 2.4% (includes 70% of Crimean Tatars deported during World War II), Karakalpaks 2.1%, other 7%
Most recent data	Kazakh 63.1%, Russian 23.7%, Uzbek 2.8%, Ukrainian 2.1%, Uighur 1.4%, Tatar 1.3%, German 1.1%, other 4.5% (2009 census)	Kyrgyz 64.9%, Uzbek 13.8%, Russian 12.5%, Dungan 1.1%, Ukrainian 1%, Uighur 1% other 5.7% (1999 census)	Tajik 79.9%, Uzbek 15.3%, Russian 1.1%, Kyrgyz 1.1%, other 2.6% (2000 census)	Turkmen 85%, Uzbek 5%, Russian 4%, other 6% (2003)	Uzbek 80%, Russian 5.5%, Tajik 5%, Kazakh 3%, Karakalpak 2.5%, Tatar 1.5%, other 2.5% (1996 est.)

Sources: (2011) *The World Factbook*, Washington, DC: Central Intelligence Agency. (1993) *The World Factbook*, Washington, DC: Central Intelligence Agency; retrieved through Project Gutenberg. (1989) 'Tablitsa 9c: Distribution of population by nationality and language'; from 1989 Soviet Census, retrieved from the Working Archive, Goskostata Rossii, available at; http://www.demoscope.ru/.

really changed in the nature of domestic sovereignty, other than at the declaratory level? Are such states which emerge by default hollow and weak, easily malleable by outside forces and prone to imminent collapse? In the coming chapters statehood will be reviewed from four angles: politics, identity, economics and security.

4   Authoritarian alternatives

Saparmurat Niyazov ruled Turkmenistan for 16 years after the Soviet Union fell apart, imprisoning, torturing and exiling political opponents, while appointing himself President for Life. Few dictators have been more megalomaniacal. Niyazov outlawed ballet and opera, replaced the word 'bread' with his mother's name, swapped January with his own name and built golden statues of himself, one of which rotated to continue to face the sun. He also closed libraries, shut down internet cafes and included himself in the national anthem. He produced his own national ideology, the *Ruhnama*. Meanwhile, he allegedly siphoned off into his personal bank account some $3 billion from the country's hydrocarbon revenues. He died of a heart attack in 2006.

While no other president in Central Asia comes close to this degree of abomination, all have presided largely over authoritarian systems. This chapter will discuss the reasons behind this authoritarianism and the consequences of it through four sets of questions. The first concerns the countries' domestic and external sovereignties and how the peculiarities of sovereignty have led to particular state-building challenges, domestic and foreign. A second debate addresses the apparent entrenchment of authoritarianism and presidential rule in Central Asia. Why has this region 'failed to democratize'? A subset of questions concerns why we have seen the five opt for different types and speeds of authoritarianism, some more personalistic, some later than others, and one – the Kyrgyz republic – opting in 2010 to establish a parliamentary democracy. Third, how is authoritarian power maintained? Here I shall look at how formal and informal institutions and networks interact, and the role of international actors, in maintaining or overthrowing regimes. Finally, what has Central Asia shown about that critical tipping point when change becomes violent? What I intend to propose is that there is nothing inevitable about authoritarianism or its consequences in Central Asia.

Sovereignty and the meaning of independence

External sovereignty: establishing new foreign policies

As we saw at the close of Chapter 3, there was also nothing inevitable about the transition from the Soviet Union to 15 independent national republics.

Russia's 'involuntary disengagement' from Central Asia was the midwife to this region's independence. Russia's clear message that it no longer sought to subsidize their regimes caused leaders to scramble for domestic and external formulae that would help launch them into these unchartered waters of independence.

In acquiring a monopoly of political violence over their state boundaries, Central Asian leaders busied themselves with cementing four types of this newly acquired sovereignty. The first was Westphalian sovereignty or political organization that excludes external actors from authority structures in a defined territory; and the second, domestic sovereignty, or how political authority is organized domestically so that they are able to exercise control over a defined territory. The others, international legal sovereignty and interdependence sovereignty, are of lesser concern here (Krasner 1999).

To assist with the exclusion of external actors from authority structures and to secure international legal sovereignty, the five faced the challenges of building up armies and police forces to protect their borders. By the close of the 1990s, while Kazakhstan, Turkmenistan and Uzbekistan were guarding their own borders, the Kyrgyz Republic had signed bilateral agreements with Russia on the joint co-operation for protection of their borders. The Tajik case, on account of the civil war, was decidedly different. Throughout the 1990s, Russia continued to help Tajikistan maintain the over 1,400 km border with Afghanistan as it had done now for some 100 years; when Russia withdrew this aid in 2005, the US, the Organization for Security and Cooperation in Europe (OSCE) and the EU stepped in to assist with tightening border security.

In Tajikistan's case also, the Russian military was deployed the longest and continues to have a sizeable presence there. Upon independence, the Russian military presence included 25,000 Russian peacekeepers and 25,000 Russian border guards, though this cannot be taken as accurate since, as Catherine Poujol (1997) writes, their precise numbers were difficult to determine. Sergey Gretsky (1995: 26) writes that the 201st Motorized Rifle Division was renamed the Fourth Base in 2004 and downsized to 5,000. It continued to exert important influence, however. The Central Asian countries had inherited very different militaries and police forces, all of which had been effectively run by ethnic Russians, with Central Asians very rarely gaining a leadership role. Uzbekistan's army was by far the strongest (Marat 2009). Poujol (1997: 100) concludes: 'As for the creation of a Tajik national army, it is scarcely on the agenda. The [Tajik] republic was not as lucky as Uzbekistan, which had in Tashkent the headquarters of the Turkestan Military District (abolished on 30 June 1992), as well as three of the former USSR's military academies'.

Simultaneously, the Central Asian states set about designing and implementing independent foreign policies, and all five opted – in keeping with generalized presidential rule – to give the president a veto over foreign policy decision-making. Following an amendment to Stalin's constitution, in 1944 each of the Central Asian republics gained their own ministries of foreign affairs but these were, like the right to secession, nominal only. Formerly the strict preserve of Moscow, the foreign-policy elite establishment thus had to be created more or

Table 4.1 The military in Central Asia (2010)

Country	Army	Navy	Air Force	MoD	2010 Budget (USD)	2010 US Foreign Military Aid (USD)	Deployments
Kazakhstan	30,000	3,000	12,000	4,000	1.12 bln	3.0 mln	OSCE (Armenia and Azerbaijan): 1
Kyrgyzstan	8,500	0	2,400	n/a	96 mln	3.5 mln	OSCE (Bosnia-Herzegovina): 1; UN (Liberia): 3; UN (Sudan): 7
Tajikistan	7,300	0	1,500	n/a	84 mln	1.5 mln	OSCE (Bosnia-Herzegovina): 1
Turkmenistan	18,500	500	3,000	n/a	261 mln	2 mln	n/a
Uzbekistan	50,000	0	17,000	n/a	1.42 bln	n/a	OSCE (Serbia): 2

Source: Compiled from (2011) *The Military Balance*, London: International Institute for Strategic Studies.

less from scratch. An independent foreign policy required the training of diplomats and the cultivation of new partners. The political content of these foreign policies is closely linked to the economics and security of these states, which we shall discuss in Chapters 6 and 7. In all five, presidential advisors and assistants and National Security Committees assist in the foreign policy output.

The five have, however, diverged in their foreign policy direction. Kazakhstan's foreign policy has officially been described as a 'multivector foreign policy' (Cummings 2004); Kyrgyzstan's under Akaev was associated with the concept of Kyrgyzstan as a Silk Road (Huskey 2004); Tajikistan's since 2002 as an 'open door policy' (Jonson 2006); Turkmenistan's since 2005 UN approval as 'positive neutrality' (Cummings and Ochs 2002; Denison 2006; Anceschi 2008); and Uzbekistan's as self-reliance with Karimov, 'the least willing to assent to the creation of supra-state coordinating organs and the delegation of certain powers to them' (Bohr 1998b: 43). Niyazov declared Turkmenistan's desire to play the role of Central Asian Geneva or Vienna. Akaev noted how 'Central Asia plays a special role in establishing relationships with the East and West, being a sort of link between them'. Nazarbaev's 1994 proposal for a Eurasian Union is very much in the spirit of multivectorism. In foreign policy, 'forecasts that cultural or other factors would eventually dominate the CARs' foreign policies did not materialize. Neither Turkey, nor Iran nor Pakistan became exclusive partners of the CARs' (Abazov 1999: 22).

What explains the pragmatism on the one hand and these divergences on the other? Foreign policy analysis variously points to bureaucratic politics, national identity (including culture and geographic location), personality and leadership, and institutional arrangements. However, most analyses of Central Asian foreign policy behaviour have emphasized either domestic factors (broadly understood) or the international system (explored in Chapter 7). Few studies have as yet provided in-depth understandings of how elites make foreign policies and what sort of factors and processes go into that decision-making. In domestic factor terms, particularly, societal identity (ethnic mix and the identification of national identity and nationalism) and geographic location are stressed. Thus Cummings (2004) and Hanks (2009) look at how Kazakhstan's close relationship with Russia is set to continue to make Russia primus inter pares among foreign policy state relations. Jonson (2006) also argues that Russia will retain its primacy for Tajikistan but for different societal and geographic reasons. Huskey (2004) sees Russia also as remaining key for the Kyrgyz Republic and Abazov's (1999) analysis of these three states stressed the continued relevance of Russia for foreign policy making. Turkmenistan and Uzbekistan's isolationist and self-reliant policies, even if ideologically framed, are also driven by pragmatic considerations.

Domestic sovereignty: establishing meaning in political independence

As detailed in Chapter 3, the distinguishing feature of Central Asia's path to sovereignty was the absence of national independence movements. Sovereignty needed also to acquire domestic meaning. In some other parts of the Soviet Union republican movements went to the streets to fight for independence (Beissinger 2002). In many post-colonial settings the creation of independent states came from national liberation movements and sometimes a period of mandates (Burgis 2011). By contrast, Central Asia experienced a process of non-rupture, in which the old Soviet container almost seamlessly metamorphosed into one of a new national state. In part, this absence of independence movements was directly linked to the absence of dissident movements in Central Asia (Cummings and Hinnebusch 2011).

The catapulting to independence (Olcott 1992) initiated a process of bureaucratic sovereignty (Lewis 2011) that almost without exception saw the old nomenklatura remaining in power after Soviet collapse. The Kyrgyz Republic's election of Askar Akaev, a laser physicist who had been based at the Academy of Sciences in Moscow, to the post of new leader in 1990 was the only case of a non-former Communist Party First Secretary managing to stay in power. By contrast, Tajikistan's Rahmon Nabiev, who was a former Communist Party chief (albeit penultimate), was forced to resign in 1991, his appointment insufficient to harness the liberalization processes. With the exception of Turkmenistan, the other four had all seen attempts by grassroots movements to seize the opportunities provided by perestroika and glasnost of the mid-1980s but only in Tajikistan did the incumbent leadership fail to keep itself in power in the early independence years.

Specific circumstances conspired to make Nabiev resign (Atkin 2002). First, political parties emerged that sought to forge a new Tajik 'idea' challenging the interests of the dominant regional groups. Second, the disintegration of the Soviet economic system placed a premium on the weakness of Tajik institutions. Third, as noted by Stéphane Dudoignon (1997a: 63–4), these groups were also responding to burgeoning Uzbek nationalism in the *Birlik* Popular Movement, always seen as a potential hegemonic threat to Tajik identity. The broad common ground among the opposition groups was the intention to pursue genuine Tajik national sovereignty. To reduce tensions, Nabiev agreed to the legalization of the Islamic Renaissance Party (IRP), supporters of which made up a large percentage of the demonstrators in Dushanbe, to restore the ban on the Communist Party, and to step down as Acting President during the election campaign. In the election, which had been rescheduled to the end of November, he won two-thirds of the vote. The relatively poor showing of filmmaker Dawlat Khudonazarov, the candidate of the united opposition, seemed to discourage the opponents of Communist rule. Soon after his election Nabiev lifted the ban on the Communist Party which quickly re-established itself as the country's dominant political organization. But eventually he agreed to resign even if he appeared on television the same night to say his decision had been voluntary (Brown 1997: 89–92).

All Central Asian leaders had reportedly embraced the prospect of independence with some trepidation but, now it was in their possession, were not about to renounce it. Societies, by contrast, were slower to adapt, widening the gap between what they on the one hand, and elites on the other, thought about independence. Even nationalists in Central Asia had opted to stop short of full-blown independence, seeking instead increased cultural rights within the existing Union. For the ordinary citizen the working of political institutions – such as the presidential advisory groups or parliament, or the choices elites made between them – did not have immediate repercussions until much later. Furthermore, these citizens' individual experiences of everyday sovereignty affected young and old, urban and rural, workers and farmers quite differently. For example, several years into independence communities in northern Kazakhstan continued to use the Russian rouble in place of the newly introduced Kazakh national currency, the *tenge*. In part this was a function of geography and particularly borders. Border communities experienced sovereignty most immediately and tangibly. Communities sprawled across borders were unable to make sense of newfound restrictions posed by national checkpoints to their travel and trade when before they had lived outside their parent republic with no problem, since the Soviet Union included all these parts. Into independence, border communities have continued to defy customs and disregard state presence, while elites upheld and sought, as noted often with international assistance, to strengthen the borders. In three cases – Kyrgyzstan, Kazakhstan and Tajikistan – elites agreed to a change in border demarcation but in all cases this was a Chinese demand in exchange for assistance, economic and otherwise. These land swaps were shrouded in secrecy and still little information is available on the full extent of territory handed to China, particularly in the Kyrgyz and Kazakh cases. The agreements provoked much popular discontent, in the Kyrgyz case contributing to overall dissatisfaction with Akaev. But, with the exception of some unilateral border demarcation by the Uzbek regime, the Central Asian regimes have agreed to keep the borders intact and worked to make them impassible rather than fluid.

Authoritarian alternatives

As elites busied themselves with crafting new foreign policies and anchoring their borders, the arduous task of embarking on a journey away from one-party, communist rule had also begun. The Soviet political system briefly described in Chapter 3 bequeathed to all five the dominance of the Communist party, the absence of civil society and the fusion of state and party.

The degree to which newly independent rulers are faced with choices about the political institutions they craft remains the subject of debate. Simplified, promoters of historical institutionalism see a country's culture and past as determining the sorts of choices it has open to it in the future. This path-dependency explanation places emphasis therefore on structure. On the other hand, those who see agency as key, primarily in the elites running the country, explain decisions often in rational choice, profit-maximizing terms. Some see the possibility of the two co-existing, with elites working within, but not prisoners of, the templates given to them by culture, geography and history.

In her analysis of one institutional choice in Central Asia, the electoral system, Pauline Jones Luong (2002: 275–6) charts this middle ground by explaining how 'Central Asian elites were motivated to adopt democratic reforms as long as they believed that it would enhance their ability to capture distributive gains during the transition'. The absence of mass mobilization and popular protest ensured that elites did not perceive their relative power to have significantly changed once the Soviet Union had collapsed, and, in turn, encouraged 'the persistence of the political identities that they adopted under the previous regime. This enabled them to maintain the primary mechanism for distributing political and economic resources and the system for settling political disagreements – that is, regionalism'. The different forms the electoral system took depended on the relative power perceptions of central and regional leaders, which were partly a function of the degree to which the regions had been, and were continuing to be, decentralized. Thus, in the Kyrgyz Republic's case, regional players perceived themselves as having the upper hand, in Uzbekistan, the centre and in Kazakhstan, both, and a compromise resulted. Kazakhstan decentralized 'by default' (Cummings 2000; Jones Luong 2004).

All five leaderships preside over authoritarian presidential political systems. Authoritarian political systems concentrate power in a small, usually closed, political elite, who may be elected or unelected by the population and who possess disproportionate power over any other institution or group. All Central Asian regimes have paid lip service to elections and have had their leaders go through the process of so-called 'free and fair' elections. Because the process has been far from 'free and fair' governments are perceived as generally unaccountable to the masses. They exercise power with a high degree of arbitrariness, with civil society only occasionally proving cumbersome (Kyrgyzstan and Tajikistan, and to a lesser degree Kazakhstan).

The independence years have seen authoritarianism in all five become more rather than less entrenched, and in this authoritarianism the institution of the president has dominated all other formal institutions (governmental, parliamentary and regional). The choice by elites of presidential-style authoritarianism is in part a legacy of strong leadership in the Soviet period and the preference for an individual to symbolize and represent the polity. The president has a formal veto over all foreign policy decisions. He has the power to appoint the Prime Minister, the Head of the Constitutional Court and often some members of parliament and heads of quangos, such as the Assembly of Peoples' Deputies, a forum that exists in both the Kyrgyz Republic and Kazakhstan to promote interethnic dialogue.

At the same time, and even if converging, the five systems continue to display important differences in degrees of power-sharing and ruthlessness. These shades of authoritarianism, functions of institutions, personalities, foreign actors and civil societies, have been described in a variety of ways, with 'semi-authoritarianism', 'competitive authoritarianism', 'liberalized autocracy', 'delegative democracy', 'managed democracy', 'defective democracy' and 'electoral authoritarianism' all attempting to capture the Central Asian experience. Although in the last years of Akaev and under Kurmanbek Bakiev (2005–2010) civil society suffered heavily from increased repression, the Kyrgyz Republic remains the most liberal of all the five and continues to have the most vibrant contestational politics. It boasted the only independent printing press of the region and its freedom levels to the mid-late 1990s were regionally unsurpassed. At the time of writing, new presidential elections were imminent and there was talk with varying degree of conviction about the viability of parliamentary democracy. Some point to Akaev's personality as a factor in his country's early liberalization, others to his decision to embrace a liberal ideology as a way of anchoring his rule and attracting foreign assistance. In any case the joint economic and political liberalization that followed the Kyrgyz leadership's agreement to implement International Monetary Fund (IMF) and World Bank recommendations, led both to a more active civil society than anywhere else in Central Asia, but at the same time a de-institutionalized polity that failed to harness this newly active society. Deep fragmentation has come to characterize Kyrgyz politics as a result. The Tajiks were also early political liberalizers but the descent into civil war prevented liberal institutions taking off at the same time as they did in the Kyrgyz Republic. Also, the regime after the peace agreement has been increasingly rather than less authoritarian (see below).

The other less authoritarian system has been Kazakhstan's but, with hindsight, the 1992–1994 period of some political liberalization seemed more of a tactical compromise in the setting up of a tightly run presidential system. That said, early economic liberalization enabled the formation of several elite economic groupings and, while still pro-presidential, has entailed intra-elite competition and political compromises. Multiethnic fragmentation and de facto decentralization have also made compromise and greater sharing a necessary feature (Cummings 2009). The personality of President Nursultan Nazarbaev (in power since 1990) is often viewed as having been a decisive factor in the authoritarian nature of the regime, its dual civic and national character and in the art of compromise and nepotism.

In contrast to the parliaments of Kazakhstan (in its early years) and the Kyrgyz Republic, those of Turkmenistan or Uzbekistan have not managed to become a forum of debate. In both cases, furthermore, civil society has often been brutally repressed. Political refugees are common for both countries, dialogue is stifled and non-governmental organization (NGO) activity has been shut down. Here debate is often instead about the degree to which the personalities of the president have dominated the system. Uzbekistan's ruling elite is similarly thought to comprise several big groupings (Ilkhamov 2007), and despite external appearances of a monolithic structure, its rule involves sustained bargaining and compromise. Turkmenistan's first president, Saparmurat Niyazov, had been in power already for some five years when the Soviet Union collapsed and by the time of his death in 2006 he had become the longest-serving leader of the post-communist space. The smooth transfer of power to his successor Berdymukhamedov suggested a greater institutionalization of power than had been supposed;

Table 4.2 Freedom House indicators for Central Asia since independence

Civil liberties (1 = most free; 7 = least free)

Country	1991	1992	1993	1994	1995	1996	1997	1998	1999	2000	2001	2002	2003	2004	2005	2006	2007	2008	2009	2010
Kazakhstan	4	5	4	5	5	5	5	5	5	5	5	5	5	5	5	5	5	5	5	5
Kyrgyzstan	4	2	3	3	4	4	4	5	5	5	5	5	5	5	4	4	4	4	5	5
Tajikistan	5	6	7	7	7	7	6	6	6	6	6	5	5	5	5	5	5	5	5	5
Turkmenistan	5	6	7	7	7	7	7	7	7	7	7	7	7	7	7	7	7	7	7	7
Uzbekistan	5	6	7	7	7	6	6	6	6	6	6	6	6	6	7	7	7	7	7	7

Political rights (1 = most free; 7 = least free)

Country	1991	1992	1993	1994	1995	1996	1997	1998	1999	2000	2001	2002	2003	2004	2005	2006	2007	2008	2009	2010
Kazakhstan	5	5	6	6	6	6	6	6	6	6	6	6	6	6	6	6	6	6	6	6
Kyrgyzstan	5	4	5	4	4	4	4	5	5	6	6	6	6	6	5	5	5	5	6	5
Tajikistan	5	6	7	7	7	7	6	6	6	6	6	6	6	6	6	6	6	6	6	6
Turkmenistan	6	7	7	7	7	7	7	7	7	7	7	7	7	7	7	7	7	7	7	7
Uzbekistan	6	6	7	7	7	7	7	7	7	7	7	7	7	7	7	7	7	7	7	7

Source: (2011) 'Country ratings and status, FIW 1973–2011' *Freedom House*, available at http://www.freedomhouse.org/template.cfm?page=439 (last accessed on 06-Dec-2011).

Table 4.3 Transparency International's *Corruption Perceptions Index* (1999–2010)

Country	1999	2000	2001	2002	2003	2004	2005	2006	2007	2008	2009	2010
Kazakhstan	2.3	3	2.7	2.3	2.4	2.2	n/a	2.6	2.1	2.2	2.7	2.9
Kyrgyzstan	2.2	n/a	n/a	n/a	2.1	2.2	n/a	2.2	2.1	1.8	1.9	2
Tajikistan	n/a	n/a	n/a	n/a	1.8	2	2.1	2.2	2.1	n/a	2	2.1
Turkmenistan	n/a	n/a	n/a	n/a	n/a	2	1.8	2.2	2	1.8	1.8	1.6
Uzbekistan	1.8	2.4	2.7	2.9	2.4	2.3	2.2	2.1	1.7	1.8	1.7	1.6

(10 = least corrupt; 1 = most corrupt).
Source: Compiled from annual releases of Transparency International's *Corruption Perceptions Index* from 1999 through 2010. Available at: http://www.transparency.org/policy-research/surveys-indices/cpl (last accessed on 06-Dec-2011)

previously the personality and cult of the president had given at least the impression of a highly personalistic rule, one that would end with Niyazov's death.

While Niyazov cut a figure of aberration in spite of his rule's tragic consequences, Uzbekistan's Islam Karimov is known for his brutality. Both have built extensive cults but Niyazov's became known for its extreme nature and also its eccentricities. Although several buildings and a university are now named after him, Nazarbaev has stressed that he is against such cults, making a public point of refusing a presidency for life. Karimov, by contrast, has often stated his willingness to order the use of violence, by boiling or cutting off heads, particularly of those he dubs extremists. To the question 'Is this one region or many?' that we asked in Chapter 2, the political joins a cultural, regional-wide perspective: can Kyrgyzstan's attempts to build a parliamentary democracy be placed in the same category as Turkmenistan's excessive cult of personality? The above suggests not and that differences in degree matter, both in terms of the 'why' and the 'so what' of these systems.

Various reasons are advanced as to why Central Asia is authoritarian. Thomas Carothers (2002) points out how this is by no means unique to Central Asia, with much of the post-Soviet space a decade after Soviet collapse stuck in the 'grey zone' of (semi-) authoritarianism. Central Asia seems to distinguish itself, however, in the personalized nature of the authoritarianism, and in the region's growing similarities in that personalization of rule, even if important differences of degree between the five remain. This has led some to ask whether there is something specific about Central Asian political culture that lends itself to personalized authoritarianism. In this interpretation societies are viewed as patriarchal and hierarchical: 'while culture may not determine outcomes, it is hard to avoid the conclusion that it serves to shape and constrain the choices made by élites' (Anderson 1997: 47). 'Central Asian traditions of patriarchy, popular submissiveness, deference to authority and to elders and weak democratic institutions would seem to impel Central Asian societies towards an authoritarian future' (Gleason 1997: 38). As in the Soviet period, others see Central Asian tradition as having been, and continuing to be, immutable, 'the complete rejection of anything new introduced from the outside into the familiar, "traditional" way of life' (Poliakov 1992: 4).

Several problems arise with explanations of authoritarianism that use political culture, however. Even if the concept has travelled far, political culture is still too often conceived as a static set of properties handed down from one generation to the next. We must also consider which political culture we are referring to. Debate, meritocracy and matriarchal roles are as much a part of Central Asian societies as are respect for elders and strong leadership. Muriel Atkin (2010) stresses that good governance was a concern of traditional rulers. Political culture arguments all too often end up furthering unhelpful stereotypes, adopted by Central Asian presidents themselves. In his autobiography, *The Kazakhstan Way*, Nazarbaev (2008: 14) refers to how 'it was already clear then that the people attempting to transfer Western liberal ideas directly to Kazakhstan would run up against cultural difficulties in the broadest sense, including political culture as well'. The bigger danger with political culture arguments is that post-Soviet Central Asian leaders, already steeped in the essentialist ethnography of the Soviet era, use those very arguments to repress and stifle contestation and change.

Another contested view is that authoritarianism better serves these societies' goals at this particular juncture of their development. Paul Kubicek (1998), for example, outlines arguments of morality and effectiveness that can be used to explain why authoritarianism may be a 'cure' rather than 'curse' for Central Asia, including the avoidance of the nationalism trap that often comes with democratization (Snyder 2000) and the propensity of authoritarian leaders to reform (even if Kazakhstan's Nazarbaev is the only post-Soviet president to have had a former advisor tried for corruption in the US, he has simultaneously sought to strengthen state economic and security institutions). Furthermore, writing before Osh 2010 but just after the Tajik civil war, Kubicek (1998: 41) asks: 'Is a democratic experiment "worth" the possible cost of another Tajikistan? In fact, one might even go so far as to say that one can be sanguine about the situation in Central Asia because these states have managed to avoid or overcome the sometimes intractable dilemmas posed by democratization'. This early independence period has seen a correlation between absent liberalization and social stability but whether this amounts to causation and how long stability on the basis of repression can be maintained is another question. The argument that authoritarianism is the outcome of deliberate preference by elites to serve their needs rather than a system by default is a point developed also by Neil J. Melvin (2004: 138) who also notes that by the late 1990s 'there was evidence of a convergence of authoritarian forms, indicating that authoritarian rule in the region was being transformed and sustained by new factors; the engagement of key sections of the elite with international capital and political interests, geopolitics and the struggle with terrorism and radical Islam'.

Another way of asking why these systems are authoritarian is, of course, to posit why they are not democratizing and more often than not this is the way the question has been posed. Again, this has provoked discussion. In these debates, working definitions of democracy and democratization are sometimes inexplicit, which of course obstructs our ability to judge whether democracies have been consolidated and whether backsliding is likely. The most widely held view of what constitutes a consolidating democracy is the holding of free and fair elections and the peaceful change, twice, of a government. This minimalist, Schumpeterian view of democracy has been the benchmark for a large number of international institutions, foremost the election monitoring arm of the OSCE, the Office for Democratic Institutions and Human Rights (ODIHR).

Two main approaches have been used to explain why Central Asia has not democratized. The modernist/structural approach, epitomized by Seymour Martin Lipset (1960), suggests that without a certain level of economic development or class configuration, the middle class will not develop to sustain a liberalization path. The transitional approach, spearheaded by Dankwart Rustow (1970) who emphasizes the importance of political will, places primacy on leadership, and the ability of a new elite to forge unity and negotiate with oppositional elites. Rustow speaks about the need for rupture, bureaucratic sovereignty rendering this absent in Central Asia. He also speaks about the need for national consolidation which echoes some of the concerns of scholars of Central Asia who argue that the competitor identities such as clans create enduring obstacles to the possibility of democratization (Collins 2002). John Ishiyama (2002) argues that authoritarian presidentialism is largely a function of 'neo-patrimonialism', which has been partially inherited from the Soviet era.

Perhaps it is just too early to judge whether Central Asia is on the democratization path but analysts nearly a decade earlier wondered whether the democratization lens was the best one through which to view this region. Valerie Bunce (1995) argued that Latin America and Eastern Europe are unhelpfully bunched together having, as they do, quite different starting points. Many have chosen instead to discard the discussion of democratization altogether in favour of a comparative politics approach, in which basic questions about political institutions and development are asked, or in favour of a political anthropological approach, which locates 'the political' in micro-realities and provides a more nuanced picture of how cultural context can transform the political and vice versa.

Central to discussions about erroneous assumptions, paradigms and interpretations of current political transformation are questions of legitimacy. Discussions about how to maintain power and how to nurture legitimacy are analytically separate. Legitimacy in the absence of popular mobilization movements is difficult but Central Asian leaders were strikingly adept at turning communist legitimation slogans into national ones (Dave 2007). Chapter 5 shows how the attempts by leaders to craft top-down state identities drew on essentialist notions of the titular nationality (Bohr 1998a). When this was practised in multiethnic states, a careful accompanying rhetoric of internationalism was introduced (Schatz 2000).

John Heathershaw (2009), in a study of Tajikistan, argues that the international community's logic is based on a flawed understanding of legitimacy, namely that legitimacy can only be of the democratic kind. Still employing classic works on legitimacy, such as David Beetham's (1991), he shows how legitimacy should not be regarded in substantive or procedural terms. Instead it is an inter-subjective process that is highly contingent and may not involve democratic representation. Replying to Heathershaw's conceptualization, Atkin (2010: 221) asks:

> Does simply getting by as best one can under a regime render that regime legitimate in any meaningful sense of the word? In past centuries, long before liberal democracy was a possibility in Tajikistan or elsewhere, the Tajiks' ancestors had concepts of good government. A crucial component was the ruler's interest in the concerns of the governed and his efforts to meet their needs. That is a standard of legitimacy that does not require the culture-bound naivety the author decries, but it is also one which, by the author's own account, Tajikistan does not meet.

In sum, ordinary Tajiks show 'endurance, not acceptance of the regime'. Heathershaw (2010a: 227) replies that: 'such endurance can be considered in terms of legitimacy'.

Ultimately, the Heathershaw–Atkin interchange captures what authors view as appropriate goals of government and who – outside and inside to the state – should decide on those goals. In a post-conflict situation such as Tajikistan's, the goals of government are understandably very much about preventing another descent into violence. Stability becomes the mantra. The government can begin to justify and measure its actions in terms of the degree to which it has avoided another civil war. Necessary reforms become therefore: 'not so much how a democracy can be established, but how reforms can be made palatable to the ruling regime so that it will want to introduce them'. Furthermore, rapid democ-ratization, 'promoted by outsiders (opposition groups as well as international mediators) who are not intimately familiar with culture and society in the region and with the internal workings of the Tajik government', raises a different sort of worry: 'once free and fair elections are held at some time in the future, and all Tajik parties win some seats in a liberal, multi-party assembly or parliament, will these groups be willing and able to cooperate with each other?' (Brenninkmeijer 1997: 208). In his book, *From Voting to Violence*, Jack Snyder (2000) articulated such hazards of early liberalization for countries in flux more generally. The question has also been posed by numerous commentators about whether a parlia-mentary democracy best suits Kyrgyzstan after the 2010 violence.

For the moment leaders in all five countries have viewed authoritarianism as the best way to maintain their power. The regime of authoritarianism infuses perceived predictability into the system by avoiding competitive elections, and ensures that the system remains closed to competitors. But the system is not static, it is dynamic and in need of constant maintenance, all of which is hard work. We turn next to some of the ways in which leaders have actively sought to sustain their rule.

Maintaining power and ensuring compliance: (in)formal politics, clientelism and pervasive corruption

To keep themselves in power the leaders have attempted to: a) shape both the informal and formal opportunity structures by de-ethnicizing the political space and strictly limiting opportunities outside executive power; b) de-territorialize and centralize; and c) adopt a cadre policy of simultaneously seeking out allies and protecting technocrats as part of a broader patron–client network (Cummings 2005).

The degree to which a particular regime is successful at maintaining power depends on the relationship between its state and society, and legitimacy of rule is a key element of that relationship. The case of Kazakhstan is interesting here. Kazakhstan's state capacity – in administrative, financial, technical and ideational terms – is stronger than that of any of its Central Asian neighbours (Cummings and Norgaard 2004). The ability of Kazakhstan's leaders to harness change is thus more powerful. It has been better placed to co-opt oppositional leaders. Its revamped constitution of 1995 increased presidential powers and references to the Constitution are made to justify presidential action. Deliberate contradictions in the Kazakhstani Constitutions allowed President Nazarbaev to escape accusations of non-constitutionalism, while at the same time couching his actions in legal terms. The institutionalization process outside of the executive has been strictly controlled, in particular with regard to the judiciary and legislative spheres; party political formation; and the deliberate obstruction of the development of an indigenous bourgeoisie. The ruling elite has also de-ideologized the political space by opting for a largely technocratic style of rule and strategic management goals.

In the multinational states of Kazakhstan and the Kyrgyz Republic, the titular nations were occupying state positions disproportionate to their demographic weight in the early independence years. In both countries Presidents Nazarbaev and Akaev used the language of internationalism. In this context a de-ethnicization of the political space became easier. This discourse of de-ethnicization has helped the elite to remain in power because it has disempowered alternative ideologies in the political space and slowed the formation of non-Kazakh movements because they already felt protected by the state. By contrast, Turkmenistan and Uzbekistan have used ideology over management strategies to run the state, partly because in a mono-national setting, their leaders could more easily appeal to a national ideology. But in all cases the leaderships have been able to steer the debate away from ethnicity to issues of loyalty and opposition. In Kazakhstan's oppositional leader Petr Svoik's terms: 'Most akims [regional heads] are loyal to the government which illustrates the ideology of nationalism is secondary to the ideology of power' (cited by Edmunds 1998: 467).

The study of Central Asian political institutions may have sometimes paradoxically underemphasized the formal, with consequences for analysis. In any discussion of how power is sustained and change enacted, it is important to consider how much the formal institutions matter and, perhaps more importantly, how much they are perceived to matter. The import of formal institutions to Central Asia is partly a Soviet legacy. They regulate behaviour between political actors in that they provide templates for action and limits to the resources that any one institution can possess. Electoral systems have thus excluded the rights of potential competitor candidates to campaign, such as the barring of Akezhan Kazhegeldin in the 1998 presidential elections. In Tajikistan's 1997 peace agreement formal rules obliged a newly formed government to institutionalize consociationalism. In Uzbekistan, political parties that the formal political power institutions had outlawed sometimes reportedly transformed into NGOs. Formal institutions also regulate and legitimate irregular behaviour (Isaacs 2011). For better or for worse, the Soviet period bequeathed to the five states a sense of modern institutionalism. We should not imagine Central Asia simply as a vast terrain of unregulated, ungoverned groupings who only use contacts or bribes to get matters resolved.

Furthermore, a neat conflation of clan and network is misleading. Sometimes networks are based on kinship (real or fictive), sometimes not. Often networks are social or economic; they may express common educational, regional or work backgrounds or a simple economic transaction (such as the purchase of a position or the granting of mutual economic favours). They may provide 'a certain security in the face of the state and allowed access to scarce goods' (Pétric 2002: 14).

It is likely that power actually resides somewhere between the formal and the informal. Few can deny the importance of patronage networks for sustaining social, political and economic life and for mobilization. Gretchen Helmke and Steven Levitsky (2004) consider four categories of informal politics, defined by two dimensions. The first dimension concerns the convergence or divergence of institutional outcomes (complementarity or competitiveness); the second measures institutional effectiveness. This classification shows the variety of informal politics, which in the Helme and Levitsky study includes corruption and gentlemen's agreements, culturally rooted norms and informal arrangements between institutional players. The discussion in Chapter 3 of the degree to which traditional institutions have survived into the post-Soviet era is in part asking whether they provide a competitor to today's formal institutions, and whether the term 'informal' necessarily always means 'customary'. For example, Kyrgyz local *aksakal* courts are investigated to see if they provide real functioning alternatives to the modern formal local council or court (Beyer 2007). The Uzbek social institution of the *mahalla* is seen as a substitute service provider to the state. At the same time, the workings of formal institutions exert a real impact on people's lives and if they do not work, people lose faith in their leaders and the overall justness of the system. This is certainly true when leaders are seen to abuse public office for private gain which is the case in all five. Central Asian regimes rank among the most corrupt in the world.

To ensure control and the suppression of alternative constituencies, authoritarian systems tend to be unitary systems. Only Kyrgyzstan followed the international community's advice to decentralize and, under Akaev, its system gave formal powers to regional heads. In Kazakhstan's case, the President resisted pressures for decentralization even if financially de facto decentralization occurred in the 1990s. Some of these rights and responsibilities of leaders are enshrined in the constitution, others are not. In most cases the constitutions are crafted carefully enough to allow for freedom of interpretation. President Nazarbaev (2008: 87) declared that 'Our Constitution is not a mirror image of reality, but a representation of how society and the state ought to be'.

Just as the regimes have sought to de-emphasize ethnic identities, so they have sought to downplay regional identities or interests. The centralization of politics has been achieved in a number of ways: by harnessing territorial representations through executive national institutions; by ensuring control over the economic reform process; and by attempting to centralize the recruitment process. In Kazakhstan, centralization enabled the elite to oust regional competitors and to monopolize regional economic resources. It has been achieved by emaciating regional powers, weakening the regions through a process of regional consolidation, moving the capital to the periphery, creating top-down parties and ensuring centre-regional crossovers in the recruitment process.

US Assistant Secretary of State Elizabeth Jones recounted how in early 2002 she urged Kazakhstan's Foreign Minister Kasymzhomart Tokaev to ensure that 'elections to members of the parliament should be absolutely free and fair, and not back to the old days, when the president said to me, in one conversation, "Yes, we have lots of political parties here. I started them all"'. Presidents have sought to control their personnel and recruitment networks by creating top-down transmission-belt parties, such as Kazakhstan's Union of People's Unity (SNEK), formed in 1993 in the run-up to the 1994 parliamentary elections, or, again, the Liberal Party, headed by the president's then Press Secretary Asylbek Bisenbiev in the run-up to the January 1999 elections. All Central Asian leaderships have built variations of top-down presidential parties. By creating a series of top-down centrist parties, the elite itself has attempted to monopolize the political space.

Turkmenistan's political development has managed to keep itself the most tightly sealed from wider currents of change, and this already in the Gorbachev era. But elsewhere, presidential parties have not always dominated the Central Asian scene. These were not political parties in the Western sense of the term since they lacked broad-based social constituencies but to varying degrees they propagated alternative ideologies. In the Tajik case, the political groups that emerged centred on Tajik nationalism. These movements responded partly to the already formed Birlik Popular Movement formed in the Uzbek SSR and whose initial aim had been to form a united Central Asian opposition movement on the lines of the Baltic Popular Fronts. One such Tajik group was the Islamic Renaissance Party (IRP), the only registered opposition Islamic party in the post-Soviet space, and the only Islamic party to gain seats in government after the 1997 Peace Agreement.

Opposition parties have, however, fared poorly in Central Asia. Saodat Olimova (2000) notes how already in 2000, not long after the peace agreement, the IRP gained only 8 per cent of the national vote. The unity achieved between the three movements in 1991 in the Tajik Republic could not be maintained as it soon emerged that:

> the Democratic Party and Rastākhez, both products of the intelligentsia of the Soviet period, on the one hand, and the Islamic Rebirth Party, created by a clandestine network of Islamic intellectuals, on the other, essentially fought over the same constituency, in the Dushanbe suburbs and the most impoverished parts of the Tajik countryside, which were divided into networks of regional and local solidarity dominated by the hierarchies of traditional chiefs.
>
> (Dudoignon 1997a: 69)

The Tajik case showed how unity in political breakthrough had helped challenge the ruling elite. İdil Tunçer-Kilavuz (2011: 286) argues that 'the unification among opposition groups in Tajikistan but not in Uzbekistan, and the key role played by a mediator in uniting the opposition in Tajikistan, were important differences between the two countries and it seems clear that the networks which Turajonzoda created, and his decision to activate them, influenced the outcome in Tajikistan'. Opposition parties elsewhere have also been fragmented. For example, Kazakhstan's social grouping *Lad,* failed to unite broader Slavic movements and was devoid of charismatic personalities. Eugene Huskey and Gulnara Iskakova (2010) note that division between opposition parties in the Kyrgyz Republic has been a considerable barrier to their development. Even here where the opposition is the most developed its leaders have often moved in and out of government, causing confusion for the voters.

If the Kyrgyz regime has been able to co-opt opposition leaders as elsewhere, it has not managed to sustain this co-option through presidential party networks or other patronage means in the way that other Central Asian leaders have managed. Neither Akaev nor Bakiev succeeded in forming lasting transmission belt parties. A compelling reason for this must be the greater fragmentation of elites in the early independence years. The elusiveness of ruling elite unity was decisive for the 2005 and 2010 events which saw the toppling of Akaev and Bakiev. The International Crisis Group (2005: 8) cited an interlocutor on Akaev's fall 'Everybody in his circle knew that this could not all continue ... but even their sense of self-preservation had gone. They didn't even agree to negotiations. They just thought: they're all a bunch of cattle, and we are the elected gods'. A group of opposition leaders claimed power, with former Prime Minister Bakiev becoming interim head of government and then president – but only for five years. The experience in the 1990s of a relatively open political environment and shift towards narrow family interests also played a central role in the events leading to Bakiev's ousting. In late 2006, he had moved to face off the challenge of the opposition against him, seizing more power from the parliament for the presidential administration. However, he did so in a political environment that since 2002 had become familiar with the power of protest and open conflict between elite factions. His efforts to co-opt and control the conflicting factions were limited and ultimately unsuccessful. Thus, even if many remain sceptical about the existence in Central Asia of any meaningful party system, the role of oppositional parties and their effects remains important to understanding the successes of mobilization and democratization.

Timeline 1 The Tulip 'Revolution' (March 2005)

27 February 2005: Parliamentary elections are held in Kyrgyzstan; international observers claim the elections do not meet international standards (Saidazimova 2005).

13 March 2005: Run-off elections held.

21 March 2005: A police station in Jalalabad is stormed by thousands of rioters in protest of alleged election fraud (*BBC News* 2005); an administration building in Osh is overtaken by rioters as well (*The Guardian* 2005).

24 March 2005: Demonstrators gather in Bishkek (*The Guardian* 2005); rioters break into the Presidential Palace; leading opposition figure Feliks Kulov escapes jail; and President Askar Akaev flees the country (*EurasiaNet* 2006).

28 March 2005: The new unicameral legislature elected on 27 February and 13 March is confirmed as legitimate by the Central Election Committee; opposition leader Kurmanbek Bakiev is named interim prime minister (*EurasiaNet* 2006).

04 April 2005: President Askar Akaev submits his resignation (*EurasiaNet* 2006).

11 April 2005: Akaev's registration is accepted by the parliament; presidential elections are set for 10 July; and Feliks Kulov is acquitted by the Supreme Court (*EurasiaNet* 2006).

13 May 2005: Kulov decides not to run for president; two other candidates withdraw and Bakiev becomes the clear favourite (*EurasiaNet* 2006).

01 June 2005: Rioters break into the Supreme Court building to protest the court's rejection of appeals to the 27 February and 13 March elections; they

---

call for the resignation of all judges appointed under Akayev, along with the head of the Supreme Court (*EurasiaNet* 2006).

10 June 2005: MP Jyrgalbek Surabaldiev is murdered in Bishkek; three days later rioters in Osh storm a hotel in protest, claiming MP Bayaman Erkinbaev is responsible (*EurasiaNet* 2006).

27 June 2005: Supporters of presidential candidate Urmatbek Baryktabasov, disqualified during the election because of his Kazakh citizenship, storm the presidential building in Bishkek; acting President Bakiyev blames Akaev supporters; former Parliamentary Speaker Mukar Cholponbaev is believed to be connected and is arrested (*EurasiaNet* 2006).

10 July 2005: President elections are held (*EurasiaNet* 2006).

11 July 2005: Acting President Bakiev is declared the winner with 89 per cent of the votes; he calls for negotiations regarding the US presence at the Manas Air Base (*EurasiaNet* 2006).

13 July 2005: Russian officials announce they will double their military presence at their base in Kant (*EurasiaNet* 2006).

27 July 2005: Protestors block the road to the Kumtor gold mine, demanding further compensation for an accident in 1998 in which a truck carrying cyanide fell into a local river (*EurasiaNet* 2006).

14 August 2005: Bakiev is inaugurated and immediately nominates Kulov as acting prime minister (*EurasiaNet* 2006).

01 September 2005: Kulov's nomination is approved by the parliament (*EurasiaNet* 2006).

21 September 2005: MP Erkinbaev is killed in Bishkek, a suspected retribution killing for the death of MP Surabaldiyev in June (*EurasiaNet* 2006).

20 October 2005: MP Tynychbek Akmatbaev is killed in a prison riot while visiting the prison's hospital; his brother, Ryspek, organizes protests the next day calling for the resignation of Prime Minister Kulov, who he believes is responsible (*EurasiaNet* 2006).

8 January 2006: Raatbek Sanatbaev, a former Olympian, is killed during his campaign to become the next chair of the Kyrgyz Olympic

Committee, a post originally held by MP Erkinbayev; the National Security Service tries to hide the incident from the public, but MPs eventually find out (*EurasiaNet* 2006).

25 January 2006: Rsypek Akmatbaev is acquitted of charges that he killed a police officer; he vows to run for his deceased brother's seat in parliament (*EurasiaNet* 2006).

30 March 2006: The Central Election Commission rules that Akmatbaev is ineligible to run for office on grounds that he does not meet residency requirements; protests ensue the next day (*EurasiaNet* 2006).

3 April 2006: The Supreme Court rules that Akmatbaev is eligible to run for office; a counter protest is later held, critical of the alleged corruption that allowed Akmatbayev, suspected of ties to organized crime, to run for office (*EurasiaNet* 2006).

9 April 2006: Akmatbaev wins 79 per cent of the vote but is withheld from his position on account of murder charges brought against him (*EurasiaNet* 2006).

19 April 2006: Bakiev claims that he will annul the 2001 bilateral agreement allowing US-led forces to use the Manas Air Base unless the US pays USD 200 million per year (*EurasiaNet* 2006).

29 April 2006: Thousands of demonstrators meet in Bishkek's central square to protest the government's failure to reform (*EurasiaNet* 2006).

2 May 2006: Several cabinet ministers submit their resignations after receiving poor grades from parliament; Bakiev rejects all resignations (*EurasiaNet* 2006).

10 May 2006: Akmatbaev is shot dead in Bishkek; Bakiev, in response to the late April demonstrations, shuffles the cabinet; protest leaders deem the moves insufficient (*EurasiaNet* 2006).

12 May 2006: Alleged members of the Islamic Movement of Uzbekistan invade southern Kyrgyzstan from the Tajik-Kyrgyz border; at least five Kyrgyz citizens are killed (*EurasiaNet* 2006).

14 June 2006: The US agrees with the Kyrgyz government to pay USD 20 million per year for the Manas Air Base along with USD 150 million in aid (*EurasiaNet* 2006).

7 August 2006: Ethnic violence continues following the suspected IMU raid in southern Kyrgyzstan; ethnic Uzbek Mullah Muhammadrafiq Kamalov is killed by Uzbek and Kyrgyz security forces pursuing suspected IMU members; protests ensue in southern Kyrgyzstan in opposition to the government's treatment of ethnic Uzbeks (*EurasiaNet* 2006).

2 November 2006: Protests begin to grow calling for a constitutional reform; by 9 November, Bakiev signs, unwillingly, a new constitution that cedes much of the executive branch's power to the legislature.

Timeline 2 The April events, Kyrgyzstan (April 2010)

Early 2010: Rising electricity tariffs in Kyrgyzstan cause significant unrest among the population; local protests are reported across the country (RFE/RL 2010c; Wood 2010).

9 March 2010: News reports emerge connecting an American businessman accused of fraud by an Italian court to Kyrgyz President Bakiev's family; Kyrgyz websites posting the report immediately suffer from technical problems and over the course of the next few months, the Kyrgyz government shuts down several news outlets, particularly those supported by opposition groups (Trilling 2010a, 2010b).

3 April 2010: United Nations Secretary-General Ban Ki-moon, in response to demonstrations outside the UN building in Kyrgyzstan, denounces the government's stifling of free speech (Trilling 2010a).

6 April 2010: Protestors storm a government administration building in the Kyrgyz town of Talas; reports are mixed as police clash with protestors; residents in Bishkek report an internet outage and opposition leaders announce demonstrations for 7 April in Bishkek (*EurasiaNet* 2010).

7 April 2010: Demonstrations in Bishkek are estimated to be as large as 10,000 people; clashes between law enforcement and protestors result in more than 80 deaths and several hundred injuries; protestors storm government buildings, taking control of the government; Rosa Otunbayeva is named as interim leader (Levy 2010a; 2010b; Lillis 2010a).

8 April 2010: Otunbayeva calls for Bakiev's resignation, notes that an interim government will remain in place for six months when a referendum will be held on a new constitution, and cancels the rise in electricity tariffs; Bakiyev, located in southern Kyrgyzstan, responds soon after that that he has no intention of resigning (Levy 2010b; Trilling 2010b).

15 April 2010: Bakiev submits his formal resignation and flees Kyrgyzstan to Kazakhstan (Golovnina 2010; Lillis 2010b).

Mid June 2010: Ethnic violence erupts between ethnic Kyrgyz and Uzbeks in the city of Osh; the final death toll is placed at close to 470 people with approximately 400,000 displaced because of the violence (including in nearby Jala-Abad) (Najibullah 2011) (see alternate chronology, 'Osh 2010 Timeline').

27 June 2010: A national referendum results in a new constitution for the country which reduces the executive and strengthens the parliament; parliamentary elections will be held every five years, with the first elections in October 2010, and a president will be elected every six years, though the position will be largely ceremonial (Harding and Gabbatt 2010).

3 July 2010: Otunbayeva is sworn in as president until the end of 2011 (Dzyubenko 2010).

10 Oct 2010: Parliamentary elections are held but no party manages to win an outright majority (*BBC News* 2010).

15 December 2010: After months of negotiations, a ruling coalition within the parliament is formed between Respublika, the Social-Democratic Party of Kyrgyzstan and the Ata-Jurt Party (Marat 2010).

The Kyrgyz republic is a curious hybrid in which mobilization occurs both within and without the system, captured by Scott Radnitz's (2010: 197) use of the term 'subversive clientelism'. In this interpretation, 'Akaev thus followed in the footsteps of other leaders whose policies inadvertently empowered critical actors in society who would later come to oppose or topple them'. For Radnitz (2006: 132–3), March 2005 'was something decidedly more limited, namely a transfer of power'. Similarly, Fairbanks (2007: 55) says: 'the "Tulip Revolution" only replaced one former communist apparatchik with a less sophisticated one, and the northern elite with a more parochial southern elite'. We turn now to a broader examination of the Tulip Revolution and the Andijan events that were soon to follow.

The Tulip Revolution and Andijan in 2005

Rubin and Snyder (1998: 150) rightly point out that 'where the state provides a legal framework for an autonomous civil society, control over administration is not the only means of collective action, as the development of political mobilization during Gorbachev's glasnost showed, but the dominant apparat clans of Central Asia did not permit any such civil society to develop'. The partial exception here has been the Kyrgyz Republic but, in the Kyrgyz case, to continue the discussion of subversive clientelism, the question becomes the degree to which civil society affected elite mobilization.

It is questioned whether civil society, or its potential, exists at all (Anderson 1997). Here the definition encompasses not just political parties but broader social movements and civic action groups. The reasons given for the weakness of civil society are many (Ruffin and Waugh 1999). Part of the debate is whether the concept itself is too Eurocentric, and concern is expressed about the concept's possible overstretching. The debate is somewhat resolved by making a distinction between communal civil society and Western civil society, where communal civil society can be based on pre-existing social (kinship or fictive) networks while Western-style groups occupy a space between society and the state and operate outside pre-existing bonds, having created new networks.

The Tulip Revolution of March 2005 and the tragic events of Andijan in May 2005 encapsulated these theoretical discussions. Claiming that the elections of 27 February and their second round of 13 March had been rigged, on 15 March opposition leaders created a Coordinating Council of Kyrgyz National Unity, selecting Jusupbek Jeenbekov as its chairman. As this parallel system of authority consolidated itself on 20 March violent clashes erupted in southern Kyrgyzstan as officials attempted to reassert their authority by forcibly dispersing protestors from government offices in the southern major cities of Osh and Jalalabad. By 24 March a significant number of opposition supporters had arrived in the capital (Cummings 2008: 225). Writing at the close of 2004, Eugene Huskey had predicted that:

> [i]t appears unlikely that the current semi-authoritarian equilibrium, which has been in place for several years, can be maintained. Set against the presidential 'family' desperate to maintain its power and perquisites is a growing opposition that is drawn not just from the ranks of the permanently disillusioned, but from leading government officials. This contest between two irreconcilable forces sets up the possibility, although not the likelihood, of a 'yellow revolution in Kyrgyzstan'.

Analysts were quick to further examine the role of foreign actors in the Tulip Revolution and Russia's reaction to those events (Ortmann 2008) and whether civil society had played a role in Akaev's rapid abdication of power.

On 13 May 2005 government troops opened fire on demonstrators in Uzbekistan's eastern town of Andijan. Five years on, the official death toll was

Timeline 3 Andijan Uzbekistan (May 2005) (unless otherwise noted, from RFE/RL 2005)

Early to mid May 2005: Demonstrations begin in Andijan in protest of 23 businessmen on trial for alleged involvement in an Islamic group banned by the government; as the demonstrations grow, the government uses force to push back; rioters overtake a local government building but fail to take over the National Security Service headquarters in Andijan; hundreds of Uzbeks flee to Kyrygzstan; estimates of the death toll range from 70 to several hundred; President Islam Karimov accuses radical Islamic groups of the violence and denies having ordered troops to fire on demonstrators; foreign media is blacked out.

18 May 2005: Foreign diplomats receive a restricted tour of Andijan; China supports the government's handling of the situation while the EU calls for an independent inquiry.

19 May 2005: Karimov rejects calls for an independent international inquiry.

21 May 2005: The US calls for an independent international inquiry.

25 May 2005: Karimov continues to reject calls for an independent international inquiry.

2 June 2005: The Russian government claims that IMU, Taliban and Chechen terrorists were involved in the Andijan events.

6 June 2005: Visas for US Peace Corps members in Uzbekistan are not renewed, forcing the US to suspend its Uzbek Peace Corps mission.

13 June 2005: EU foreign ministers threaten sanctions if Karimov does not agree to an independent inquiry.

15 June 2005: The US military confirms that operations out of the Uzbek-based Karshi-Khanabad Air Base have been narrowed under Uzbek order; days later the Uzbek government denies a link between the restricted operations and the US position on Andijan.

11 July 2005: The government prosecutor in Andijan announces an official death toll of 187, 94 of which, he claims, were terrorists, 20 law-enforcement officials, 11 soldiers, 57 ordinary citizens, and five unidentified.

29 July 2005: The US is formally evicted from the Karshi-Khanabad Air Base (Wright and Tyson 2005).

July – September 2005: Foreign media organizations continue to be subject to harassment by the Uzbek government.

October – December 2005: Over 150 people are convicted of terrorism charges in often closed trials related to the Andijan events, and sentenced to jail terms as long as 22 years.

still put at 189 but eyewitness accounts and human rights activists put the numbers closer to 1,000. The authorities accused local protesters, who were reacting to a trial of 23 local businessmen accused of membership of what they termed were Islamic radical groups such as Akramia, Hizb-ut-Tahrir and al-Qaeda. The situation suddenly escalated over the night of 12–13 May when a group of the 23 men's supporters raided a local military base and seized weapons. Then they stormed the prison and freed the defendants along with all the other inmates, sparking a quite separate debate about how information is gathered and the role of scholars in such events (Megoran 2008). Fiona Hill (2005: 112) concluded 'from [her] interviews conducted with survivors who fled the Kyrgyz Republic that government forces fired indiscriminately, killing men, women, and children, and that troops pursued those who fled the square'. In response to demands for an independent investigation, the authorities closed and expelled foreign NGOs involved in media and civil society development. Furthermore, relations between Uzbekistan and the US, already worsening, deteriorated sharply.

Akiner (2005: 10) argued that Andijan 'was not driven by religious or socio-economic demands' but it seems hard to ignore the effect of political and economic trends in Uzbekistan and the broader region. Coming as it did just after the Tulip Revolution in the Kyrgyz Republic, Tashkent authorities were particularly vigilant that no domino effect or toppling of the regime was to happen in their country. Kandiyoiti argues that it epitomized 'a fundamental breach of the social contract between state and citizen in Uzbekistan' (Kandiyoti 2005). It exposed the dilemmas of a country that continued to have an important cotton production sector, run according to command principles, where input prices were high but sales prices were well below global prices. 'In rural Andijan's increasingly tight economic environment, being able to sell at Karasu (Korasuv) bazaar and cross the border to Osh in Kyrgyzstan to trade more profitably became important "safety-valves"' (Kandiyoti 2005). On 11 July 2002 bazaar traders were badly hit when the government imposed a punitive tax on imports and strict regulations on trade. These regulations were also a reaction to the IMF demands to bring about the convertibility of the Uzbek sum by eradicating differences between official and black-market foreign exchange rates (Chapter 6). The government pushed ahead with convertibility at an artificially high rate by effectively closing its borders to private trade and introducing high tariffs for goods to restrict demand for foreign currency. A further significant development followed. As the government grew increasingly suspicious of the activities of donor-assisted NGOs, their modest infusions of cash into the economy began to be choked. Stringent political and fiscal controls, ostensibly to combat money-laundering by local NGOs, made the work of foreign donors increasingly difficult.

International organizations, the EU among them, have spent considerable amounts of money trying to encourage the development of civil society. Authors soon commented on the paradox that democracy-building was leading to non-democratic outcomes (Jones Luong and Weinthal 1999). Successful international grant recipients often became elites divorced from the wider community, their projects often failing to provide the sustainability that was essential to their being effective. Some NGOs receiving money are in fact government-sponsored or – linked. Disillusionment with the development of civil society was largely a result of disillusionment with these democratization efforts, both domestically and abroad.

September 11 and its aftermath provided added incentives, it seemed, for the international community to focus less on building civil society than on strengthening states. Strengthened states might be better equipped to combat terrorism. Both the Tulip and Andijan events exposed doubts over the viability of a Western agenda for democracy promotion twinned with Operation Enduring Freedom (OEF) (Jones Luong and Weinthal 2002). Security concerns seemed increasingly to trump those of a human rights agenda. Few reacted to Akaev's crackdown in Aksy in 2002 and little pressure was exerted on Karimov after OEF was launched at the close of 2001.

External promotions: democratization and authoritarianism compete

The misfit between external goals and domestic contexts is partly voiced in writing that analyses how international democracy promotion efforts or development conditionality might best be achieved. In 2007 the EU finalized its 'Strategy for a New Partnership' with Central Asia in which the promotion of democracy and the rule of law figured strongly. Anna Matveeva (2009b: 5) comments thus on the EU: 'The EU needs to keep its expectations of what can be achieved in Tajikistan proportional to the context and be mindful that its political system may not be conducive to any substantial reform, as its resilience lies in projection of power and predictability'.

Interviewed, former ambassador-at-large for the former Soviet Union, Stephen Sestanovich (2002) explained that 'social and cultural awareness are not all you need to have an impact' but similarly that 'elites have to believe that the rule of law and market economies and political pluralism serve their interests, or they won't embrace them'. US policy became increasingly associated with Bush policy (Schatz and Levine 2008: 26) and 'attributing the statement to President Bush ... caused respondents to be less receptive to the message'. A leading civil society activist Evgenii Zhovtis (2008: 25) explained: 'the notion of democracy has been significantly discredited. It is often identified with anarchy, chaos, robbery, the cancellation of social guarantees'.

In the same interview and in reply to whether September 11 led to security being prioritized over human rights promotion, Sestanovich (2002) sees 'very strong continuity in U.S. policy in Central Asia'. By contrast, Jones Luong and Weinthal (2002: 61) note that 'Washington's marriage of convenience to Tashkent ... would actually exacerbate a key source of Central Asian instability: the domestic political repression that fosters the radicalization of Islamist movements and galvanizes popular support'. Others also worry about double standards. Zhovtis (2008: 38) elaborates again:

> During the Soviet time, the population was, metaphorically, trained to believe that $2\times2=25$ in the social and political sphere of our region. ... Over 15 years after the Soviet Union's collapse, ... the authorities sometimes cite the US or a European country as an example of where they also from time to time say that for the reasons of political expediency it is temporarily necessary to consider that $2\times2=4.15$....

Democracy promotion can occur 'by accident' where states such as Kazakhstan's, which sought legitimacy through international engagement, unexpectedly enabled democracy promoters on its territory. Most of all Edward Schatz's (2006: 278–9) argument shows that legitimacy matters: 'The domestic political climate fell well short of the elite's rhetorical commitment to international standards, but the need to keep up appearances was the result of watchdogs that sought to prevent the worst kinds of authoritarian abuse'. Commenting on the EU's Strategy for Central Asia, Melvin (2008: 139) says the EU 'cannot be a status quo actor in Central Asia'.

International democracy promotion has led to the financing of domestic political parties in the region, notably in the Kyrgyz Republic and in the early years of Kazakhstani independence. Turkmenistan and Uzbekistan have effectively closed possibilities for the West to engage in such activities in their states. Democracy promotion has involved not only financial support of opposition groups but also, primarily, input into election running and observation. The OSCE notably has become a key observer of post-communist elections and advisors of electoral reform.

Much is being written on how, by contrast, Russia and China are status quo powers, and how they push agendas of authoritarianism through the Shanghai Cooperation Organization (SCO). As written in the Declaration establishing the SCO, the Shanghai Spirit has six components: 'mutual trust, mutual benefit, equality, consultation, respect for multicivilisations, [and] striving for common development'. In July 2006, SCO heads of state held a summit in Astana,

Kazakhstan after Andijan and the Tulip Revolution of 2005. Then Secretary-General Zhang Deguang said that 'recent events' in Central Asia have:

> once again shown that terrorism, separatism and extremism still remain to be [sic] the most serious threat to peace, security, stability and development in the region. The summit made the right evaluation and properly reacted to the situation in the region. It adopted a decision, which says that the member states will continue to strengthen unity and interaction in their counteraction against 'the three evil forces'. Maintaining peace, security and stability is a matter of top priority to the Central Asia [sic].

Ambrosio (2008: 1336) writes: 'Stability is one of the most important values of the SCO, seen as necessary for progress on social or economic goals....While this may appear both obvious and innocuous, this notion takes on a strongly anti-democratic meaning in the context of the loose definitions of stability and instability'.

The politics of (dis)order: descent into violence and the restoration of order

In two notable cases, such stability has proven elusive for Central Asia: the Tajik civil war (1992–7) and Kyrgyzstan's Osh and surrounding region in 2010. For Pétric (2010), 'international organizations and NGOs in Kyrgyzstan are also indirectly responsible' for the descent into violence in June 2010 in Osh after Bakiev's removal some two months prior. He continues:

> These organizations have been present in the country for over 20 years promoting a certain conception of society and political system. Their role in co-producing a policy that has exacerbated and strengthened ethnic differences instead of producing a common social contract should be questioned. ... Roza Otunbayeva, the muse of the Tulip Revolution and now President, seems unable to restore order. ...But we should question whether Kyrgyzstan is still a state or the incarnation of a new kind of political arena, which emerged in the last decade in different parts of the world. I propose to call this new political arena a globalised protectorate, where the governance of the political system is strongly embedded within transnational economic networks, NGOs and international organizations.

In June 2010 hundreds of Uzbek and Kyrgyz inhabitants of the Kyrgyzstani city of Osh were killed in inter-communal violence. Writing back in 1997 Olivier Roy (143–4) remarked that '[T]hese two cases apart [Uzbeks and Tajiks in their respective states and Russians and Kazakhs], the areas of ethnic tension nowadays are the border regions, especially the border between Uzbekistan and Kyrgyzstan in the district of Osh. But, precisely for this reason, they are manageable as long as there is a consensus between the ruling regimes, as is the case at

Timeline 4 Osh Kyrgyzstan (June 2010)

12–14 May 2010: in Batken, Jalalabad and Osh, pro-Bakiev demonstrators briefly take over several government buildings (Najibullah and Abdraimov 2010).

19 May 2010: Rosa Otunbayeva is named interim president until December 2011 by the interim government (Najibullah and Abdraimov 2010).

11 June 2010: A fight breaks out among local Kyrgyz and ethnic Uzbek youth in Osh; the fighting soon escalates followed by rioting and the looting of the city; 49 people are reported dead and a state of emergency is declared (Najibullah 2010a).

12 June 2010: Violence continues as Kyrgyz troops are sent into Osh; the death toll numbers at least 79 with more than 1,000 injured; ethnic Uzbeks flee for the border as reports indicate targeted killings of ethnic Uzbeks by Kyrgyz groups (Najibullah 2010b).

17 June 2010: Estimates indicate that close to 60 per cent of the 250,000 citizens in Osh have fled the city, with many ethnic Uzbeks now in overwhelmed refugee camps in Uzbekistan; as aid finally enters the region and the situation begins to stabilize, reports of targeted rapes, murders and beatings toward ethnic Uzbeks emerge; reported death toll is 190 with over 2,000 injured (Najibullah 2010a, 2010c).

22 June 2010: Thousands of ethnic Uzbek refugees begin returning to Kyrgyzstan (NA 2010b).

26 June 2010: The declared state of emergency and accompanying curfew end (Najibullah 2010d).

3 May 2011: After an extensive investigation, the Kyrgyzstan Inquiry Commission, led by a Finnish politician named Kimmo Kiljunen, concludes that the attacks on Uzbeks in June of 2010 could amount to crimes against humanity; the final death toll is placed at close to 470 people with approximately 400,000 displaced because of the violence (including in nearby Jalalabad); Kiljunen also highlights the imbalance of finding that 80 per cent of the prosecutions following the attacks were targeted at ethnic Uzbeks while 74 per cent of those killed were also ethnic Uzbek (Najibullah 2011).

present'. Roy (1997: 141) was correct to have singled out Osh but sadly 'a consensus between the ruling regimes' proved insufficient to stave off violence. Writing at that time on whether the Tajik conflict might spread to other republics, he concluded that factors which provoked the civil war in Tajikistan – Islamism, ethnicity and localism – exist everywhere in Central Asia to varying degrees, but in Tajikistan they have been aggravated by the weakness of the state apparatus and the national identity. Elsewhere, they could set off local troubles but do not risk leading to general conflicts. The only area of comparable fragility is Kyrgyzstan.

What Roy (1997: 141) terms 'localism' he argues exists everywhere in Central Asia but only in 'Kyrgyzstan are there warning signs of a stark division of the state apparatus according to the rival regions'. Writing in the aftermath of Osh, Heathershaw (2010b) contends that '[t]he comparison which should be made is not with regard to the prospects for war but to the opportunities for conflict resolution. Such opportunities were lost in Tajikistan in the tumult of events over 1990–1992, but can still be seized by cool heads in Kyrgyzstan today. Kyrgyzstan is not yet at the point of state breakdown'.

Within Pétric's narrative, June is explained as a direct consequence of April. The April 2010 removal of Bakiev and the resulting power vacuum enabled political manoeuvring to occur that would have been far less easy under a functioning, if imperfect, government. Madeleine Reeves (2011) points out that the rhetoric of nationalism became possible in this context, and was also a continuation of the ethnicization process of April in which the deaths of some 86 ethnic Kyrgyz citizens became a primarily Kyrgyz national tragedy. Unlike March 2005 which had few ethnic overtones, 2010 very soon was associated with interethnic disputes over land-grabbing in Bishkek and the wider region.

Why 2010 as opposed to 2005 could become ethnicized is partly a consequence of the different national ideologies of the Akaev and Bakiev regimes. Under Akaev's early years, his policy of appointing primarily individuals from the north meant that the competition between the Uzbeks and Kyrgyz in the south was tamed: both were omitted and, relatively therefore, were not in a security dilemma. The inclusive rhetoric offered by Akaev also ensured that at least symbolically the Uzbeks felt as included in the project as the Kyrgyz. Bakiev, by contrast, promoted southern Kyrgyz, accentuating the Uzbek disadvantages. The absence of ideology under Bakiev heightened the sense among Uzbeks that they were being neglected by Kyrgyzstan's state-builders and their consequent insecurity. In this context any action by one group would be interpreted as an encroachment on the other group, resulting this time in a security dilemma.

While a power vacuum enabled Osh 2010, a power struggle defined the 1992–7 Tajik civil war. On a cold winter's day on 12 February 1990 demonstrators crowded in Dushanbe to protest rumoured plans to give Armenian refugees preference in receiving housing. Many were still homeless after an earthquake in the Hissar Valley west of Dushanbe, and many young people from Hissar joined Dushanbe townsfolk in the demonstrations. Among the crowds were also members of the Tajik intelligentsia pressing for liberalization.

Timeline 5 The Tajik Civil War (1992–7)

Early September 1989: The *Rāstokhez* Movement forms, committed to a modern, liberal Tajik state.

12 February 1990: Demonstrators in Dushanbe protest a plan to give Armenian refugees housing as many Tajiks remain homeless after an earthquake. The protestors quickly expand beyond to include younger government officials and the Tajik intelligentsia (Brown 1998).

August 1990: The Democratic Party of Tajikistan is founded.

23 August 1991: The Democratic Party of Tajikistan, on the heels of the coup in Moscow and the resignation of President Makhkamov, demands republican leadership and multi-party elections for a new parliament (Brown 1998).

September 1991: Demonstrators continue to gather in Dushanbe, numbering close to 10,000; the Supreme Soviet declares a state of emergency (Brown 1998).

29 November 1991: Former Communist Party Secretary Rahmon Nabiev is elected president of Tajikistan.

Early 1992: President Nabiev and Safareli Kenjaev, the leader of the parliament, attempt to force from power the Interior Minister, a Pamiri; public demonstrations form as opposition groups unite in calling for the resignation of Nabiyev (Lynch 2001) and the banning of the Communist Party (Brown 1998).

Mid-April 1992: In response to the large opposition protests, a pro-government protest grows in Dushanbe as well (Brown 1998).

2 May 1992: Nabiyev establishes the National Guard, a militia in his direct control (Kilavuz 2009), to quell the growing protestors; fighting begins as the National Guard confronts the opposition groups (Lynch 2001).

11 May 1992: Under pressure from opposition demonstrators, Nabiev forms a Government of National Reconciliation which includes the major opposition parties; however, the new government is unable to control the growing conflict quickly spreading across the country (Grotz 2001).

1992–3: With Russian and Uzbek support, conservative, pro-government militias dominated by the Kulyabi and Khojent clans (loyal, respectively, to Tajik security forces and President Nabiev), clash with the Pamiris and Garmis of the democratic-Islamic opposition movements; over this period an estimated 50,000 people are killed and another 500,000 made refugees (Horsman 1999).

7 September 1992: Nabiev is captured by the opposition and forced to resign (Grotz 2001).

23 September 1992: Documentary filmmaker Arcady Ruderman is killed amidst the fighting (*RFE/RL* 1992).

27 November 1992: The Government of National Reconciliation collapses; speaker of the parliament Imomali Rahmonov becomes the Head of State as well as the leader of the Popular Front, an alliance of conservative pro-government groups (Grotz 2001).

30 November 1992: CIS members agree to a CIS peacekeeping force for Tajikistan (O'Prey 1996).

June 1993: Under Rahmonov's growing power, the Supreme Court bans all political parties outside of the Communist Party (Grotz 2001) – the Islamic Renaissance Party, the Democratic Party, the nationalist Rāstokhez movement and the Lali Badakhshan separatists (Brown 1998).

17 September 1994: United Nations, Russian and Iranian mediators convince leaders of pro-government and opposition groups to agree to a ceasefire (O'Prey 1996).

November 1994: A new constitution outlining a powerful executive is allegedly approved via popular referendum; Rahmonov wins the non-competitive presidential elections (Grotz 2001); the United Tajikistan Opposition (UTO) is formed as an alliance of various opposition groups (*START* 2011).

1995: The formal ceasefire is violated by both pro-government and opposition groups (O'Prey 1996).

23 May 1996: The Inter-Tajik Dialogue, a Track II diplomacy effort, meets in Tajikistan; participants establish that 'the primary obstacle to peace in Tajikistan is the absence of an adequate understanding on sharing power among the regions, political movements, and nationalities in Tajikistan' (Imomov et al. No date).

27 June 1997: Rahmonov and opposition leader Said Abdullo Nuri sign the 'General Agreement on the Establishment of Peace and National Accord in Tajikistan', a UN-brokered peace accord; the Commission of National Reconciliation is formed as a part of the accord (Lynch 2001).

20 July 1998: Four members of the United Nations Mission of Observers to Tajikistan are killed in an ambush by unidentified assailants (Inoue no date).

22 September 1998: Otakhon Latifi, a former leader in the UTO and now a member of the Commission of National Reconciliation, is murdered outside his home (*RFE/RL* 1998).

30 March 1999: Safarali Kenjaev, former commander in the Popular Front, is killed outside Dushanbe.

November 1999: The UTO withdraws from the 1997 peace accord in protest to Rahmonov's election rigging in advance of the November 1999 elections (*HRW* 1999); Rahmonov is re-elected with 96 per cent of the vote (*BBC News*, 2011).

Comparative accounts of civil wars around the world point to various reasons. Park (1997) writes about 'the effect of unfreezing' with democratization bringing 'long-suppressed animosities' to the fore. Minogue and Williams (1992) put forward the 'swing theory' whereby the 'force-fed universalism' of Soviet communists led to the reaction of particularist nationalism. Gellner (1983) similarly focuses on the effects of a system of repression but he pinpoints the suppression of civil society as the reason behind its inevitable revenge. As a further reason Tadjbaksh (1993), for example, suggests that the actions by poorer regions were inspired by resentment. Others place the emphasis on a weak state (Woodward 1995; Rubin 1998). Focusing specifically on Tajikistan, Collins (2006) identifies an armed struggle among clans, while others emphasize the economic and political inequalities between regional groups (Tadjbaksh 1993; Jawad and Tadjbaksh 1995).

In her comparison of Tajikistan and Uzbekistan, Tunçer-Kilavuz (2011: 280) places primacy on the role of elite perceptions and points out that 'consistent with bargaining theories of war, a disparity between the distribution of power and distribution of benefits seems an important factor in the eruption of civil war in Tajikistan. Nabiev chose the war option in order to maintain the support of the hardliners but in so doing the elite apparently overestimated their own strength, and thought that the opposition would be unable to resist militarily. On the other hand the opposition chose to resist militarily, reasoning that their power was not weak'.

Dov Lynch (2001: 49) also explains the outbreak of the Tajik civil war as 'not a conflict over the "idea" of Tajikistan but over power', but in the Tajik case ideology increased the stakes and provided the means for the grab of power. Lynch (2001) also emphasizes how the so-called Kulobization was unacceptable to other regional factions. This included the UTO, the 'fundamentally moderate' opposition group that marked an alliance between the IRP (later recreated in the Movement for Islamic Revival in Tajikistan) based in northern Afghanistan and led by Said Abdullo Nuri, and the secular opposition based in Moscow, around the Democratic Party of Tajikistan and Rāstokhez under the umbrella of the 'Coordinating Center of Tajik Democratic Forces'.

Similarly to the Uzbeks in the Kyrgyz Republic groups felt sufficiently disadvantaged to lobby for power (Lynch 2001). Rubin (1998: 132) rightly faults narratives that claim '*how* Tajikistan broke down explains *why* Tajikistan broke down'. Such a narrative attributes causality to the cleavages and may thus attribute too much importance to the autonomy of identities and ideologies. Instead, political manipulation of those identities and ideologies is key and certain polities lent themselves to that more than others. The legacy of Soviet institutions had a peculiar regional dimension in the Tajik case, writes Dudoignon (1997a: 57):

> [S]ince the mid-1970s, the Ismaili communities of the Pamirs have made up the bulk of medium-level officers in the security forces (not surprising, given their religious particularism and phobia of fundamentalism); more over, they harboured an instinctive animosity towards the black market networks which had been developed, under cover of the Party, by provincial officials in Kulyab, in the south of the Republic – a region entirely overlooked by Soviet industrial investment.

What do Tajikistan and the short history of Kyrgyzstan post-Osh tell us about what sort of peace follows the descent into violence? The notion of legitimate power-sharing underpins much writing on the post-war situation, and that effective and meaningful representation in government would be essential to 'peace-building'. As Heathershaw (2005) notes, the term most frequently used in Tajikistan is 'mirostroistvo'. Lynch (2001: 68) emphasizes the 'fragility of the process', pointing to how 'the exclusion of Khujant and other minority groups from the process raises the prospect of a new challenge to the fundamental "idea" of the Tajik state as it has emerged since 1997'. This point is similarly raised by R. Grant Smith (1999: 249, 243) who points to both how the northerners 'found themselves pushed out of key positions' and how also 'the Uzbeks feel left out', concluding that 'instability will continue unless the northerners and the Uzbek community are brought into the process'. Similarly, the Open Society

Institute (1998: 9) reports that 'Officially, Tajikistan may no longer be in a state of war, but it is ever ready to erupt in armed conflict'. The IISS Strategic Comments (1997) noted 'The signing of the peace accords is thus just the first step on a long and uncertain road'.

Overall, the international community is found to have failed in its objectives to build a liberal peace. 'Was the exercise akin to prescribing a placebo treatment for a make-believe malady?' asks Najam Abbas (2010: 222). R. Grant Smith (1999: 247) admits that barring 'persuasion and appeals to both sides to consider the future of the country, the international community has few resources with which to persuade the government and the UTO and their component parts of the benefit of peace'. The World Bank and IMF credits, while quickly mobilized, 'flowed to or through the government, and they did not include post-conflict related performance criteria tied to their disbursement'. Similar to this last point, Sumie Nakaya (2009: 259) finds fault with the way development aid has focused on economic liberalization and not the implementation of the agreement, empowering 'a particular group of elites who have privileged access to state assets at the time of civil war settlement, allowing them to establish institutional frameworks that will consolidate their personal and monopolistic control of resources'. Heathershaw (2005: 27, 34) by contrast takes issue with the very aim of establishing a liberal peace, deconstructing the narratives and understanding how other means, however, currently imperfect and potentially unsustainable this might be, have led to 'the existence of institutionalized forms of compromise'. He further points to the erroneous characterization of Tajikistan as a failed state as this has been based on the assumption that violence will necessarily be followed by democratization attempts. Furthermore, 'for institutions to become embedded in post-conflict societies they must serve the longer-term interests of a broader range of political actors'.

Shahram Akbarzadeh (2000) writes that stability in Tajikistan is 'at the mercy of the perpetuating politics of patronage'. Davlat Khudonazarov (1995) shows how Tajik politics until the 1940s sought to maintain just such a balance of regional representation in the distribution of political power and administration positions. That balance was disrupted, however, by the appointment in 1946 of Babajon Gafurov as First Secretary of the Tajik Communist Party who dominated the party with people from Leninabad. Regionalism ('localism' or *mahalgaroi*) was introduced into the heart of Tajik politics. Bess Brown (1997: 86) writes that the war 'may be ultimately attributed to the removal of Soviet-era constraints that kept regional and ethnic frictions under control'. According to Dudoignon (1997a: 72), '[the] Tajik Communist Party was soon to extricate itself, at the close of the war which would pit the citadels of the opposition (Dushanbe, Hissar and Garm) against the provinces of Khojent and Kulyab, respectively the richest and the most impoverished provinces in the country; and would make a battlefield of the cotton-growing plains of Kurgan-Tyube, which had been since the 1930s the site of immigration by the mountain-dwelling populations of the foothills of the Pamirs, who recreated in this region the conflicts which had riven the leaders of their communities for generations'. The aftermath is also a 'perpetuating politics of patronage': the degree to which political stability has been restored in Tajikistan continues to be debated. In the immediate aftermath, doubt was cast as to whether the representativeness had gone far enough. Although by late 1999 the UTO had received 30 per cent of government posts, it remained excluded from many positions at lower levels of administration.

Commentators differ over which outside parties they see as most crucial to the signing of the peace accords between the government and the UTO. Payam Foroughi (2002), for example, cites the UN, OSCE and the governments of Russia and Iran. External factors, such as instability in neighbouring Afghanistan, September 11 and consequent Great Power competition shaped action. The Tajik civil war demonstrated the importance of Afghanistan to the development particularly of this republic's political trajectory. After all, the Tajik-Afghan border 'was never watertight' (Poujol 1997: 104). Lynch (2001) shows how, until late 1992, the Russian government had largely stayed outside the Tajik civil war and how Russia's support of Rahmonov enabled him to consolidate and centralize his power. At the same time, Russian pressure placed on Rahmonov was critical in forcing the government back to the table, along with five other factors (UTO successes at advancing around Tavildara and Gharm; rise of internal challenges to Kulobi rule from non-UTO forces; tensions that erupted in Khujant; collapse of law and order and the decline of the Tajik economy). The Peace Agreement ('General Agreement on the Establishment of Peace and National Accord in Tajikistan' on 27 June) was signed, notably, in Moscow.

In turn, domestic configurations have affected these states' ability to negotiate outside actors and their foreign policies. Ability is in part determined by the state to maintain its upper hand in agenda-setting; Jonson (2006: 181) observes that the 2002 'open-door policy' was made possible by 'the high degree of "autonomy" of the state in relation to society on domestic issues'. Taking issue with the view that Uzbekistan was 'taking the lead in Central Asian security' (citing Kangas 1996), Horsman (1999: 41–2) argues that in Tajikistan and Afghanistan Uzbekistan has consistently interfered and undermined neighbouring security. He explains the inconsistency of rhetoric and practice as serving the Karimov regime's 'domestic political objectives', seeking 'to portray Tajikistan's democratic and Islamic movements as radical, inherently unstable and ill-suited for Central Asia in its transitional period'.

Conclusions: symbiosis between in and out

In all the above discussions we see how internal politics cannot be understood without reference to the outside world. External factors have influenced domestic politics, be it in the construction of a new polity, the descent into violence or the establishment of peace thereafter. We have seen how authors differ on the degree and nature of that influence. The 1992–7 civil war saw actors involved both at the outbreak and also in the perpetuation of violence. Few would disagree that the communists would not have perceived their power as great had they not been assured of Russian backing. Uzbekistan, like Russia, aided pro-government forces but also since 1993 publicly urged the Rahmonov government to enter into dialogue with the UTO, with Rahmonov conversing with the IRP and democratic movements from 1995. Neighbouring Afghanistan, in turn, provided a safe haven and weapons sources for the opposition, also funded by US action in reaction to the 1979–89 Soviet invasion.

The zeitgeist of liberalism (to which we return in Chapter 6) and the attempted export of that ideology also had lasting effects. Whether one agrees or not with the damning conclusions made by Pétric of Western intervention, conditionality (economic or political) did undoubtedly play a role in the Tulip Revolution and Andijan. Andijan was in part provoked by new IMF regulations and the need to sustain a cross-border community. Lewis argues that the Tulip Revolution was provoked by a unique confluence of the domestic and the international. While mobilization in 2005 was elite-led and not the result of overthrow by leadership of an urbanized civil society in line with the previous two colour revolutions, the role of actors that had been funded and promoted by the West cannot be ignored.

But in many ways it is Russia's role in and its attitudes to the region in the 1990s that have shaped the ability of other actors and influences to matter in the Central Asian states. Irina Zviagelskaia (1995: 37) writes how in the early independence era Russia was more worried about NATO enlargement in Central Europe than about the South, suggesting that the 'ideal scenario for Russian politicians would be one that enabled Russia to develop contacts with Central Asia and maintain stability in the region at very little cost'. Jonson shows how for Tajikistan, September 11, and increased US engagement, created a window of opportunity for the regime to enact an 'open door policy' to begin in 2002. Despite Russia's 'involuntary disengagement' (Jonson 1998) in the 1990s, Yeltsin still viewed the Tajikistan–Afghanistan border as 'in effect, Russia's' (Brown 1997: 92). Russia has remained the single most important external actor to have influenced domestic and external foreign policies.

As Sherman Garnett remarks, 'For Russia, there are many different peripheries, not a single "near abroad."' Tajikistan and the Kyrgyz Republic have remained highly dependent on Russia throughout this period. Brown (1997: 95) writes 'By the end of 1993, Tajikistan was the only former Soviet republic to still be using Soviet roubles as its only currency. Dependent on Russian military aid and with the Tajik economy virtually destroyed by the civil war, the country's leadership believed that it had no alternative but to join Russia in a new rouble zone that had been spurned by other CIS states'. Gretsky (1997: 34) argues that 'Russian intervention in Tajikistan and subsequent developments in other parts of the former Soviet Union demonstrate that the Russian military has won the contest with other centers of power over the right to determine and execute the near abroad policy'. Jonson (2006: 196) refers to a January 2005 opinion poll where, on a question asking which countries people felt most sympathy with, 51 per cent answered Russia, 26 per cent Iran, 25 per cent India, 19 per cent Germany, 18 per cent Japan, 14 per cent US, 12 per cent France and 10 per cent China.

The single biggest element of these configurations is the incumbent regimes' desire to maintain power. All other goals, such as the pursuit of national ideology, state-building or the role as regional hegemon, become secondary. Sabit Zhusupov's (1998) conclusion for Kazakhstan can be applied to all of Central Asia: 'the emphasis on the strategic can in many ways explain the specifics of the way the Kazakhstani political system is functioning, indeed the sovereign state as a whole'. On Central Asia generally Roy Allison (2004a: 469) writes that:

> the preoccupation of local governments with regime security has also been an important factor encouraging Central Asian states to bandwagon with Russia. This concern has been sufficiently strong for them to be prepared to delegate some of their decision-making prerogatives to accommodate Russian preponderance.

As this chapter has shown, some Central Asian countries have been better than others at this regime security. Whether Central Asian societies mobilize is at least partially answered in Huntington's 1968 classic work, *Political Order in Changing Societies*. If institutions fail to reflect or keep up with societal aspirations they are likely to be unable to harness those aspirations. Menon and Spruyt (1998: 113) argue that 'an imbalance between institutionalization and social mobilization' led to a breakdown of state authority in Tajikistan. They proceed to show how elites can deal with mobilization in one of three ways, each practiced in Central Asia: use examples of other states' instabilities to justify repression at home or intervention abroad (Tajikistan about Afghanistan, Uzbekistan about Tajikistan); co-option by institutionalizing popular protest (repeatedly attempted by Kyrgyz leaders and successfully achieved in the early 1990s in Kazakhstan) or simple repression (Turkmenistan and Uzbekistan). The latter strategy 'may work indefinitely, particularly if citizens remain passive, if an economic crisis does not occur, and if the ruling group avoids internecine conflict. But the danger – as illustrated by the ongoing civil war in Tajikistan – is that festering problems (economic deterioration and a political opposition that feels disenfranchised) can culminate in instability. Worse still, to the extent that state formation creates systems that allow for little or no within-system participation, instability can produce extra-systemic, revolutionary movements' (Menon and Spruyt 1998: 114). Rubin (1998: 153) states: 'The descent into civil war mainly resulted from the breakdown of social control due to the dissolution of Soviet institutions. In the resulting insecurity, competitive mobilization led to escalation of conflict among patronage networks defined by the contours of elite recruitment in Soviet Tajikistan. But the loss of Union subsidies channeled through the Khujandi nomenklatura, combined with political and military mobilization for the civil war in southern Tajikistan, shifted the center of power to the south for the first time since the 1920s'.

These three techniques of power maintenance are mutually supportive. Of note is how Kyrgyzstan's presidents have been less able to sustain corrupt behaviour than their Central Asian counterparts, and this is partly a function of the degree to which all three techniques have been used at the same time. It seems that formal power can continue in a corrupt system when compensatory behaviour occurs. This has been observed in one of three ways. First, although not sustainable over the long term, corruption can continue if leaders have enough repressive power to curb dissent. Second, corrupt systems are easier to sustain if leaders can give carrots to other elites critical to their survival, such as strong economic factions or the security services. Neither Akaev nor Bakiev managed to keep the support of key elites; by contrast, Nazarbaev has been exceptionally adept at co-opting them, as we saw above. Finally, if at the same time as pillaging the state the leaders make attempts at state-building and craft broader legitimating programmes, then they are also likely to maintain their power for a longer period of time. One notable omission of the Bakiev regime was its failure to build anything – institutionally or ideologically. State legitimation is a central concern of the next chapter which looks more broadly at how identity and belief have shaped the political order.

5   Islam, nation and multiple identities in Central Asia

Two Tajik Ph.D. students at Moscow's Institute of Asian Peoples asked a fellow Central Asian in a Moscow restaurant in the latter half of the 1960s why he was eating pork: "After all, you are a Muslim". Most Muslims were thought to see in this a cultural and social, rather than a religious, issue, and there is evidence of Uzbeks and Tajiks living in mixed areas of Central Asian cities expressing resentment at having to inhale pork fumes from their neighbours' kitchens.

(Ro'i 2000: 464)

In response to the view that pork-eating is in any case 'hardly a sign of religiosity' (Ro'i 2000: 464) DeWeese (2002: 320–1) replies: 'But that is exactly what it is, if we cease strangling "religiosity" to the verge of lifelessness' continuing that:

pork has for centuries been a central marker of religiously defined communal identity, and remains so today, often becoming (along with circumcision) the pre-eminent divide between Muslims and non-Muslims, whether the latter are Kalmyks, Chinese, or Russians. Is it the chief concern of the most deeply spiritual? Perhaps not. Is it the cultural inheritance of many who never perform other 'religious' rites and would not profess any level of 'belief' in religion? Of course. The 'Muslim reality' is that '"Islamic tradition" itself was full of such compromises'.

(DeWeese 2002: 321)

The consumption of alcohol by Muslim Central Asia has come under similar scrutiny. Writes Adeeb Khalid (2007: 1):

Waiting in line at a cafeteria in Tashkent one day in 1991, in the last months of the Soviet era, I fell into conversation with two men behind me. ... A few minutes later, my new acquaintances joined me unbidden at the table, armed with a bottle of vodka, and proceeded to propose a toast to meeting a fellow Muslim from abroad. Their delight at meeting me was sincere, and they were completely unself-conscious about the oddity of lubricating the celebration of our acquaintance with copious quantities of alcohol.

To which Johan Rasanayagam (2007: 159) replies: 'the argument that Central Asian Muslims relate to Islam simply as national heritage is deeply flawed'. It fails to recognize that 'customary practices, such as shrine visitation and the celebration of life-cycle events, can also constitute and express personal engagement with the divinity and moral reflection. ... Islam in Central Asia is far from being *mere* national identity'.

In turn, I recall a conversation I had enjoyed with a fellow academic back in 1994 on nationalism and belief in post-Soviet Kazakhstan. Not having long returned from fieldwork, I had noted the altogether pragmatic worldviews of an emerging younger generation of Kazakh entrepreneurs and state officials. Only a handful of those interviewed had given any significant cultural or religious content to how they defined themselves in their newly independent and secular-defined state, but nevertheless Muslim society. My interviewees represented only a snapshot of the population, and a closed one at that (Cummings 2005). But if a comparable sample had been interviewed in other republics, would I have received similar answers? And what do such answers tell us?

Positions and paradigms: post-Soviet Islam

The study of post-Soviet Islam, probably more than most research areas of post-Soviet Central Asia, has encouraged questions about who is doing the research and how the topic is being researched. To a degree this applies also to the whole area of identity more generally. In other chapters, debates have also arisen about the application of set models or external perspectives to this unique region with its own set of actors, contingencies and ideas. The problem expressed in those chapters has been one that would arise from the application of any external framework without taking account of local knowledge and practices. Here the concern expressed is of a different order, namely that in both the Soviet and post-Soviet eras the study of Islam and ethnic belonging has been monopolized by what DeWeese (2002: 298, 299) terms 'Sovietological Islamology' or, after Soviet collapse, by area studies specialists who have little training in the 'history or religious culture of the regions of "Soviet" Islam, let alone of the broader Islamic world' (see also Khalid 2003; Rasanayagam 2006; Epkenhans 2011). Consequently, some argue that the conclusions that are drawn about what Islam is and how it is measured are coloured by the ontological, epistemological and methodological assumptions of such work.

The problem relates partly to the (non-)availability of reliable evidence. Sovietologists were highly constrained by their access to particular data, most of which was official. Statistics on ritual, mosque attendance or observance of religious scripture, for example, could only be semi-reliable. Yacoov Ro'i (2000: ix) pointed to these shortcomings in the Preface of his *Islam in the Soviet Union*, explaining how even though Soviet archives are now open, 'the material is singularly one-sided and presupposes certain ideological perceptions which permeate almost every sentence'. Similarly today, since authorities pursue their own ideological agendas, we can only rely so much on officially produced data on Islamic observance.

But data access and reliability is only part of the expressed concern; how scholars then choose to categorize, interpret and analyse information is potentially more serious. Four challenges particularly are stressed (some echoing concerns voiced in the previous chapter for the Soviet era). The first is how we capture the essence of what is religious belief. DeWeese (2002: 305) 'in connection with a religious system such as Islam in which "orthopraxy" traditionally trumps "orthodoxy"' helpfully refers to Islam 'as a focus of communal affiliation, as a lifestyle and set of practices, and as a worldview'. Further (2002: 309): 'To restrict what is "Islamic" to the Qur'an and a limited body of Hadith may be the business of contemporary Muslim fundamentalists and the medieval jurists they cite, but it was never the business of the majority of self-defined Muslims over the centuries, or even of most medieval jurists'. Thus explained, if it so happens that more people know scripture in the Middle East than they do in Central Asia this does not make the Middle East the standard or Central Asia any less Islamic or a place of 'less good' Muslims. So, the Soviet, or post-Soviet Muslim, drinking alcohol or eating pork may still be a believer.

Linked to these concerns is the larger discussion about the relationship between religion and nation in Central Asia. The same vignettes about pork and alcohol may be taken to illustrate one of a number of ways that we might interpret the relationship between religion and culture. We may see religion as subsumed to culture and as part of the nation-building process. In this view talking about the weather or going to pray would be considered as traits of national belonging or praxis. Khalid (2007: 121) writes how '[p]ride in Islam as national heritage can coexist with complete lack of observance or indeed any belief at all, let alone a desire to live in an Islamic state'.

At another extreme, religion is altogether taken out of its national (or any other) context, reifying it and confining it, in Abramson and Karimov's (2007: 331) view, mistakenly, to matters of 'purity of intention'. In between are positions that view religion and culture as coexisting, sometimes intertwining, sometimes not, but definitely mutually dependent and able to influence how either is transformed. Certainly the Soviet regime succeeded in 'linking religion with honour for traditions and customs' (DeWeese 2002: 326). But this is hardly surprising or difficult, argues DeWeese (2002: 326) 'since religion had been at the core of pre-national communal identities, and remained so outside the elites'. There is no national identity free of religious identity, it is a false dichotomy, nor is national identity necessarily the bigger construct within which religious identity fits.

Third, is the unhelpful tendency to slot observations into pre-existing, binary opposites. The divide between official and unofficial is often blurred. Akiner (2003) proposes that Muslim practice be placed on a continuum of shades of belief from the affective (for example, the wearing of protective amulets) and integrative (celebrations which foster communal solidarity) to a spiritual and intellectual relationship with God. Mark Saroyan (1997) made the important observation that Soviet mullahs did not use Muslim practice as a form of subversion (tradition getting back at the Soviet modernizers) but worshipped within the framework of the Soviet project (in the way that Jadids had hoped the modernizing project would be in their favour). He explains that '[b]y reworking state discourses of the "new Soviet man" into the new Soviet Muslim citizen they attempted to subvert the state's hegemonic argument that religion only served to hamper human progress'. So, official is not always the same as state-controlled Islam. Muslim belief was not seen as a way for tradition to subvert authority. Rasanayagam (2006: 223) notes in the post-Soviet era these binary opposites have simply acquired new labels, with 'official' becoming 'traditional' Islam, and 'parallel' becoming 'fundamentalist' Islam.

A final challenge is the oft misunderstood relation between politics and Islam. 'That Islam would appear in politics is only natural', writes Aleksei Malashenko (1994: 117). But, as Khalid (2007) among others argues, such a view is borne of a broader misconception that Islam is always politicized. Thus, it is to recognize that what we are witnessing today is wrongly described as a 'resurgence of Islam', implying either some indomitable force or that it had disappeared in the Soviet era, or, still again, that it had only temporarily become separated from the national intelligentsia. Already the Jadids (Khalid 1998), keen to adapt religion to the demands of a modern lifestyle, had begun to attempt to bring forms of modernity into Islam. Overall, in matters of both identity and religion, writers aim to distance themselves from the essentializing nature that marked both in the Soviet nation-building project.

Taking on board these (by no means exhaustive) paradigmatic discussions, the remainder of the chapter is organized into three sections: the view from below and the multiplicity of identities that have come to characterize the region's post-Soviet period; the state's uses of identity (especially pan-, ethnic and sub-ethnic in its attempts to consolidate power and build authority); and the links between societal mobilization (violent or non-violent) and identity.

The lived experience of identities in Central Asia: the view 'from below'

Everyday Islam

When we talk about religion in Central Asia we are, of course, not just talking about Islam. As Chapter 2 emphasized, the region historically is multi-confessional, the post-Soviet era is only the most recent to have witnessed a new religious influx. Christianity has now become the region's majority minority religion and 'Orthodoxy remains the most established of the Christian denominations' (Peyrouse 2008). The relative isolation of the region in the prior Soviet era has added prominence to the contemporary arrivals. This multi-confessionality notwithstanding, the emphasis in this chapter is on the dominant religion of Islam.

These Muslim societies and secular states have practised, contemplated and used Islam diversely in this early independence period. We begin here with a few remarks on how Islam is observed before looking further from the perspective of national, ethnic, regional and sub-ethnic identity. In terms of historically inherited forms of Islamic identification, Central Asian Islam is of the Sunni Hanafi school which is often described as tolerant and adaptable. In the Gorno-Badakhshan Autonomous Region of Tajikistan all Tajiks, with the exceptions of the Lazgulems and Vanchtsy, are Ismailites (Shi'a trend).

With the collapse of communism, writers refer in general to 'an Islamic revival' (Khalid 2003: 583) among ordinary people of this region but what they choose to emphasize varies. Some stress the continuation of types of Islam already practised, such as Sufism, including, for example shaykhs recruiting openly or the increasing popularity of shrine worship. Others review the importing of Muslim models, the revival of scripture, and still others the practice of the Five Pillars. In Uzbekistan the school system remains secular and religious instruction is an entirely private matter not within the remit of the education system. *Otins*, women who instruct children in basic faith, have experienced a revival (Fathi 1997). Typical of writing on the Five Pillars, Safronov (1999) refers to how knowledge of Islam in Turkmenistan was undeveloped. A further study (that excludes Turkmenistan) finds that the Five Pillars (*shahada* (testimony); *namaz* (five daily prayers); *zakat* (almsgiving); *hajj* (pilgrimage), *Ramadan* (fast) and their observance are not perceived in Central Asia as the exclusive markers of Muslimness. The researchers found that the *zakat* was the most widely practised of the Five Pillars, that residents of the Ferghana Valley seemed more religious than those elsewhere in Uzbekistan, for example, and that differences between rural and urban were not as great as expected. Young people and academics 'are at the forefront of Islamic affiliation and observance' (Ro'i and Waigen 2009: 318). Some six years earlier, a survey commissioned by the International Crisis Group (ICG) (2003b) had found 92 per cent of Uzbek citizens consider themselves Muslims and that just under two-thirds (64.5 per cent) of those considering themselves to be Muslims claim to observe Ramadan. Tajiks in the ICG's Kyrgyzstan survey considered themselves Muslims, as did 94.1 per cent of ethnic Kyrgyz, though religious beliefs are generally considered to be relatively shallow among the Kyrgyz (even if less so among the southern Kyrgyz who reached Central Asia and converted to Islam long before the northern Kyrgyz).

In these varied depictions the tensions between local and imported forms of education and worship are stressed, particularly by local writers. According to a Kyrgyz scholar, the religious establishment is generally uneducated, only a few having a command of Arabic or understanding the hadith (Tabyshalieva 2000: 30). Kanatbek Murzakhalilov, Kanybek Mamataliev and Omurzak Mamaiusupov (2005) write in the early twenty-first century of a risk of tension if Kyrgyz Muslims are educated abroad 'in radical religious institutions' that 'try to spread their ideas in Kyrgyzstan'. Soviet-trained ethnologists continue to view the defence of local forms of Islam as traditionalism which, for Poliakov (1992: 4) 'does not simply battle novelty; it actively demands constant correction of the life-style according to an ancient, primordial, or "classical" model.... The only thing that is important is that society must depart from its "ideal form". In his study of healing, Rasayanagam (2006: 390) finds that '[a]lthough scripturalist interpretations of Islam are becoming more influential, and men who attend worship at the mosque are influenced more directly by them, in constructing themselves as Muslims both men and women combine multiple ideas of Muslim selfhood and practice'. Popular Islam is also observed in 'new weddings' and faith-healing (McBrien 2006; Rasnayagam 2006) and Sean Roberts (2007: 340) describes, among other rituals, the *neka*, the religious marriage ceremony between an Uighur couple there.

In the same ICG (2003b) survey, belief in, and veneration of God's *avliyo* (saints) comes across as one of the most important aspects of popular Islam in Central Asia. Central Asia was the birthplace of several Sufi orders, most notably the Naqshbandiya. Writing on Tajikistan, Oumar Arabov (2004: 346) refers to the *zikr* ('remembrance of god' through either chant and dance or silent rituals) and to Sufi pilgrimages, concluding that 'Orthodox Islam and Sufism are very intermingled in Tajikistan and the majority of believers are not able to make out the difference'. This may be because, as DeWeese (2002: 317) underscores, 'the reality that Islamic literature alone, not to mention actual practice over the centuries, is replete with defences of pilgrimage to saints' shrines'. Historian Robert McChesney (1996) explains how mosques do not occupy the same importance in Central Asia as they would in other Muslim areas of the world because only shrines are viewed as evoking passage to another life. The discussion over forms of worship reminds us of one of the paradigmatic debates with which we opened this chapter.

Maria Louw (2006: 321) describes how Muslims in Uzbekistan re-establish a sense of 'normality' and moral direction in a situation where previous certainties and securities have been shattered, and in which they feel helpless and dislocated. She uses the phrase 'morality in the making' to convey the sense of how 'Muslimness', a local way of being Muslim, is an ongoing process of exploration and negotiation rather than a distinct and reified Uzbek version of Islam. Rasanayagam (2011) also emphasizes the process of becoming and the centrality of morality in the Uzbek religious experience.

Many, however, view the Islamic revival as inseparable from the national revival. This elaborates the third of the paradigmatic debates outlined at the chapter's start, the relationship between religious and national identity, 'an axiom in the study of the peoples of Soviet Central Asia' (Atkin 1992: 46). 'The Islamic revival remains largely a phenomenon of cultural rediscovery which shows little sign of affecting everyday life. ... Islam, nation, and tradition coexist happily in Uzbekistan' (Khalid 2003: 586). Chris Hann and Matthijs Pelkmans (2009) see Islamic and national revivals as going hand in hand, with the result that an unintended consequence of Soviet policy was that Muslim identity became fused with the static, primordial notion of national identity so that, tautologically, Kyrgyz and Uzbek national dress, dishes and holidays became Muslim as well because the Kyrgyz and Uzbeks were Muslim. Deniz Kandiyoti and Nadira Azimova (2004) report how: 'The "return" to authentic Uzbek culture was most evident in increased interest in Islamic learning (through a revitalized madrassa system) and the performance of religious obligations. The official reaffirmation of Uzbek identity also involved an articulation of national values that explicitly targeted women as an important repository of their expression'.

Mariya Omelicheva (2011: 246), like Hann and Pelkmans (2009), confirms that '[f]or Kazakhs, ethnic identity is a Muslim one: being Kazakh means being Muslim'. Cholpon Chotaeva (2003) notes how the degree of Islamization is dependent on region, the Bishkek and Chu regions with many Europeans is one region and the northern regions of Issyk-Kul, Talas and Naryn another. Writers on Islam in the Kyrgyz Republic tend to stress less the 'national' dimension of Islam than do their Kazakh counterparts. Islam does not seem to provide a unifying platform among Kyrgyz as, for example, Bruce Privatsky (2001: 238) suggests it does for the Kazakhs. Writing that 'Kazak religion is a local or popular contextualization of Islam, affectively experienced in the collective memory', he suggests that 'religious minimalism' is a feature of being a Kazakh Muslim, in other words, Islam is practised similarly by all Kazakh Muslims.

Rasanayagam (2006: 225) questions Privatsky's portrayal of 'the existence of coherent, localised formations of Islam, so that there is a distinctively Moroccan, Indonesian or Kazakh Islam'. Joma Nazpary (2002: 171) in his study of urban Almaty similarly negates the portrayal of Islam as an overarching identity for the Kazakhs which is less important than concerns about power and access to resources, asserting that Muslims in Kazakhstan will not necessarily support Muslims over non-Muslims and that 'notions of an umbrella Islamic identity are an illusion'. Also Kazakhs are internally fragmented: urban and rural, or northern and southern identities, for example, may create additional conceptions of self that override a simply national one. Fragmented, identities cut across each other in all sorts of ways, so that particular identity ascriptions are not automatic prescribers for the way an individual may think or act. In other words, essentialist accounts of ethnicity work as unreliably as do overarching Islamic ones. The suggestion in this quote is that all sorts of other factors shape identities, including urban versus rural settings, opportunities and power distribution. As Atkin (1992: 46–7) writes, 'Central Asians also have other [not just religious and national] loyalties that do not fit tidily into the equation between religion and nationality' and that 'the religious-national linkage ... may even have helped legitimate the comparatively recent political emphasis on national identity'.

The trials of economic independence might also contribute to a rise in religiosity, particularly in the poorer, more rapidly liberalized framework of Kyrgyzstan that has also seen a marked rise in unemployment with few prospects of improvement. In this context Julie McBrien (2006: 343) offers the important observation that the 'turn of the millennium' rather than the early 1990s marked the point 'at which the change in religiosity in their town became palpable'. The addressing of 'ordinary human needs' (DeWeese 2002: 319) is as much a religious act.

Everyday nations

The collapse of communism for the ordinary Central Asian citizen came suddenly, and generated responses on levels additional to the religious. The only regional grassroots movement in the Gorbachev period promoting a Baltic-type Central Asian front was the Uzbek group *Birlik*. The idea of pan-Central Asian unity or pan-Turkism did not resonate with the Central Asian people as much as the idea of gaining greater cultural autonomy within a larger Federation continued to. Soviet identities, on the one hand, and individual titular identities, on the other, still seemed to gain the best of both worlds – accommodating large non-titular populations while giving increased cultural and linguistic rights to local Kazakhs, Kyrgyz, Tajiks, Turkmen and Uzbeks.

Quite far into the post-Soviet period, the idea that somehow these titular groups were still part of the Soviet whole persisted. In part, as we shall shortly see, this resulted from the initial absence of iconography and statecraft tools: for example, the Kazakh *tenge* was not the most widely used currency for the Kazakhs until 1995, the rouble operating in many northern parts of the country. Some communities found themselves also now cut off by national borders, like the Kazakh diaspora (Svanberg 1999). Writing on the everyday effects of the introduction of a fourth alphabet change to Turkmen in 100 years, Victoria Clement (2007: 267) remarks on an elementary school teacher's continued use of Cyrillic over the new Latin script because 'in their personal lives they privileged comfort over national symbolism'. The former only nominal intra-Soviet borders also better suited cross-border communities who were linked either ethnically or economically, such as between Uzbekistan and Kyrgyzstan or Kyrgyzstan and Tajikistan, or 'the transformation of places once familiar, once "ours," into sites which remind of changed status – comrade into alien, fellow-citizen into foreigner' (Reeves 2007: 283). It was also a generational question, those socialized and educated in the Soviet period still feeling more comfortable in that identity, and seeing continued interests and benefits from promoting and investing in that identity.

The lived experience of titular national unity seemed particularly elusive for the Tajiks, who for some continue to struggle with national identity as a meaningful concept. Already in the Soviet era, '[t]he designation of Tajiks or other Central Asian peoples by ethnic names did not mean that a majority of them perceived such categories as the proper basis for constituting states when the Soviets first reshaped the region into nationally defined republics. However, decades of Soviet rule in Tajikistan, entailing both the institutionalization of national identity and transgressions against national feeling, made national politics important there' (Atkin 1992: 64–5). Dudoignon (1997a: 70) points out that the 'national and Soviet identities were inseparable to the point that the national intelligentsia, the usual promoter of independence, saw its future not without the Soviet state but with it, rather like the Jadids had done'. The Tajik civil war also showed that '[w]hile the Soviet solution had seemed to offer a form of national identity, Moscow had also, perhaps intentionally, built localised power structures that worked against national unity' (Bergne 2007: 134).

For the titular nations, ethnicity and language, on the one hand, and ethnicity and territory, on the other, became linked (Kolstø 1999). As ethnic cousins, the Kazakhs and the Kyrgyz are often compared in discussions of the historic and cultural contents of their national selves. A difference often highlighted is the absence of a unifying national epic for the Kazakhs enjoyed by the Kyrgyz in the form of the Manas, the epic named after the leader who united the forty Kyrgyz tribes. William Fierman (2009: 1218) writes that the 'extent of linguistic nationalisation in Uzbekistan and Kyrgyzstan has been somewhere between the pole of Turkmenistan on the one hand and Kazakhstan on the other'. Fierman (2009: 1224) continues that 'with the possible exception of Turkmenistan, Russia has continued to maintain a high symbolic niche everywhere'. This would seem to confirm in-country studies and surveys. Gulnara Dadabeva and Aigul Adibayeva (2010) point to the different positions of the 'Kazakh nationalists' who wanted Kazakh as the sole state language and Russians who wanted to retain the status quo and reject Kazakh. Matthias Koenig (1999: 57) similarly points to competing group claims and proposes 'multiculturalism as practised in some countries of immigration, such as Australia'. Chotaeva (2004) concludes from a 2003 poll conducted by the Center for Social Studies at the Academy of Sciences of the Kyrgyz Republic that 'even though the Kyrgyz language is fairly widely used, Russian still dominates many spheres due to the fact that it is not merely the tongue of the local ethnic Russians but also one of the channels that helps the republic join the world information process'.

Sub-national, regional and ethnic identities in ordinary lives

The discussion so far has, on the one hand, attempted to problematize the relationship between Islam and nation and, on the other, to deconstruct national understandings of the self to show how identities are varied, contingent and in flux. At the personal level national understandings have often been quite unrelated to grand narratives about cultural authenticity. Our discussion of how titular nations have experienced their identities in a new sovereign political container sit alongside, and are often intertwined with, other processes and levels of identity formation. These may relate to discoveries about other aspects of their identities, such as region or sub-ethnicity, or they may relate to how different communities in their polity make sense of independence.

In the early independence years, many argued that there was no such thing as, say, Kazakh national identity, but rather sub-Kazakh identities in the form of tribes and clans. We saw in the previous chapter how varied understandings of clan and tribe have fed into discussions of patronage and mobilization. Here the focus is instead on meanings attributed by titular nations to kinship. As already noted, a distinction between kinship on the one hand, and patron-client relations on the other, is necessary; in Atkin's (1992: 39) words, fusing families and clients 'is problematic, since the latter is explicitly tied to a political and economic inequality that trades political support for public goods. That relationship dissolves when its economic cause disappears'. In her reference to 'an informal organization built on an extensive network of kin and fictive, or perceived and imagined, kinship relations', Kathleen Collins (2006: 25) explains her choice of 'clan' over 'tribe': the latter 'often has negative and "primordial" connotations, and in any case was destroyed by the Soviets'. By contrast Edgar (2004) in her study of the Turkmen nation shows how the use of the term 'tribe' is appropriate, as it refers to an organization based on patrilineal descent. Still again, Saulesh Esenova (1998: 452, 457) conflates the terms 'clan' and 'tribe', and finds in her fieldwork in Almaty and Karaganda that due to Soviet sedentarization, rapid urbanization and emigration, 'the notion of the clan structure is not at all relevant to present-day Kazakh society as a social phenomenon, but it seems that there are some special fields – such as politics – where the tribal identification does still probably have an effect'.

A further implication is voiced by David Gullette (2007: 156) who suggests that '[b]y employing outdated and flawed depictions of social organization, Collins fails to explore different conceptualisations of political and social life'. Using instead the term 'factionalism' to describe major ethnic and clan cleavages, and the Russian terms 'rod' for a narrower group, 'clan' and 'plemya' for the broader 'tribe', he suggests that 'in everyday usage these terms are used almost interchangeably'. During his fieldwork in Kyrgyzstan Gullette (2007: 381, 383) noticed that 'clan' identities 'were predominantly asserted during life-cycle rituals' and proposes the term 'genealogical imagination' 'to describe relatedness as constructed through a process of personal and collective forms of memory and representations of history, and expressed through various deployments of scale (temporality, spatiality, local and national, etc.) and (politicised) formations of descent'. Writing on Turkmen tribal policy in Soviet Turkmenistan, Edgar (2001: 269) writes how:

> Turkmen identity was itself rooted in genealogy. 'Turkmenness' was under-stood in terms of patrilineal descent, with all those who called themselves Turkmen claiming origin in a single mythical ancestor named Oghuz-Khan. Each of the major Turkmen tribes – Tekes, Salïrs, Sarïks, Yomuts, Chodïrs, and Ersarïs – was thought to descend from one of Oghuz's grandsons. ... On this tree of lineal descent, only the smallest branches tended to represent 'real' or biological kinship; most Turkmen knew their own genealogy and their relationships to other individuals going back five or seven generations.

In post-Soviet Turkmenistan the same author (2004: 264) posits that 'genealogy remained an important aspect of identity'. And Shokhrat Kadyrov (2003: 112) writes that '[e]ven today, the Turkmen are still a nation of tribes'.

Radnitz (2005: 417) says that:

> People do have a tribal identity and everybody I asked was able to name his/
> her tribe without hesitation, yet it is not politicized. There is, however,
> *zemlyachetstvo*, support for people who originate from the same region. As
> mentioned earlier, one's village of origin remains with a person for life and
> people readily assume that somebody from their region who gets elected will
> represent their interests. Yet both tribal and village identity are usually
> ignored in daily life and marriage between different tribes and sub-tribes is
> common.

And also Tunçer-Kilavuz observes (2009a: 324):

> More recently settled nomadic Turkmen, Kyrgyz, and Kazakhs have tribes
> and clans with names which are kinship-based, and are defined by descent.
> Clans are connected under a larger structure. Only Uzbek tribes such as the
> Loqays or Kongrats have that kind of structure. Unlike the Turkmen, Kyrgyz
> and Kazakhs, the vast majority of Uzbeks and Tajiks – members of
> Central Asia's sedentary societies – either never had, or do not remember, a
> tribal past.

The challenges of creating a sense of Kyrgyz national belonging are often
presented less in tribal than in regional terms. Regional identities usually refer to
Soviet administrative regional divisions but are sometimes also specified in
broader geographic terms such as northern or southern. These regional differences in the case of Kazakhstan, Kyrgyzstan and Tajikistan are emphasized as
reinforced by ethnic differences, and sometimes also by religious differences, for
example, between the Slav-dominated Kazakhstani north and Kazakh dominated
south, or the Kyrgyz Russian Orthodox North and the Kyrgyz Uzbek Muslim
south. Olivier Roy (2007: 96) refers to 'regionalist factions' produced by original
provenance, Soviet territorialisation, and forced population transfers. He concludes
that the:

> administrative structure imposed by the system crystallises and politicises
> former solidarities deriving from history and geography ... In Kyrgyzstan,
> the country's geographic fragmentation has meant that the imposition of a
> tight administrative framework has solidified and institutionalised very long-
> standing oppositions between the more Islamized south and a north that was
> closer to Kazakhstan – a kind of north-south split that one also finds in
> Tajikistan.

As in the Kyrgyz case, Tajikistan's regionalism is defining the process
of national consolidation and in 'the course of the civil war, regionalism gained
in importance as the basis for society's polarization. The fact that different
provinces were controlled by rival political groups and that an armed force

composed of Kulobis and Uzbeks spearheaded the neo-Soviets' drive for victory in the civil war reinforced the significance of regional identity' (Atkin 1994: 615).

Jones Luong (2002) explains how this strengthening of regional identities was furthered by Soviet-era policies of economic specialization and *korenizatsiia* (Chapter 3). Coupled with regional recruitment and resource distribution patterns, kinship became regional in nature, clans were left intact in the same region and tribal affiliations were subsumed to administratively defined regional identities. A 'tribe', Jones Luong (2002: 54, n.7) explains, is 'an ethnically homogeneous socio-political unit based on kinship, often composed of several clans. It is thus distinct from clan in that it is much larger and often serves an explicitly political purpose'. The process thus 'reinforced regionalism rather than nationalism or tribal affiliations' (2002: 68).

This discussion of everyday belonging must, finally, also include lived experiences by non-titular ethnic groups. Nationality is not ethnicity. As pointed out by Atkin (1992) ethnicity does not necessarily have a political commitment where nationality does. While all ethnic groups have had to come to terms with the challenges of independence, additional issues face minority groups, and different minority groups differently. A member of a titular nationality is likely to have awaited independence with less trepidation than a national with former first-class about to be relegated to second-class status (Russian) or than a member of a minority with prospects of returning to homeland (German) or with prospects of carving out a niche in the home country in which they found themselves residing on collapse (Koreans in Central Asia, Uzbeks in Central Asia). Space does not allow us to go into any of these groups in detail here but two particular minorities have caught the attention of analysts, Russians and Uzbeks.

Given their relatively larger numbers, minority groups in Kazakhstan, Kyrgyzstan and Tajikistan were particularly affected. The Kyrgyz in 1989 accounted for only 65 per cent of the total population and the Kazakhs would not cross the majority threshold until the 1999 census. Even if Russians had begun to leave the region well before the collapse of the Soviet Union (as a result of Brezhnev's *korenizatsiia* policies from the 1970s and perceived poor economic prospects), nevertheless on Soviet collapse more than one-third of the some 25 million Russians outside Russia resided in Central Asia, in 1989 making up nearly 20 per cent of the total population of these five states.

Unsurprisingly, then, the status of Russians and the future of the lingua franca Russian, exercised much writing in the early independence period. With Soviet collapse and in the absence of Russian intervention to protect their rights:

> [T]he Russians of Central Asia often employ the dual terminology *otechest-vo-rodina* to clarify their identity. Russia is certainly the country of their fathers, to which one does not cease belonging even if one does not emigrate there, while the motherland remains the republic in which one was born, and Russians 'thus find themselves in a paradoxical position: a discriminated

minority seeking to profit from a new rapprochement with Russia in which they are neither principal actors nor principal beneficiaries.

(Peyrouse 2008: 9, 1–2)

This 'paradoxical position' was perhaps most acutely felt by the Russians in Kazakhstan who on independence nearly outnumbered the Kazakhs (42–44 per cent according to the 1989 census) and who were physically most proximate to Russia. The creeping authoritarianism and the persistent refusal to federalize the country heightened the perception by some that Kazakhstan was heading for 'trouble', with 'two potentially explosive factors that may impact democracy's fate: the Kazakh economy and the influence of Russia' (Bremmer and Welt 1996: 195). But instead a partly self-regulating situation resulted in which, simplified, Russians in large numbers out-migrated. Russia did not intervene but facilitated their homecoming through the Simple Exchange of Citizenship Agreement, the Kazakh economy has on the whole shown double-digit growth (Chapter 6) and those remaining in Kazakhstan stayed out of politics and found an economic niche. This is by no means to conclude that the problem of Russian rights or a sense of belonging has been solved, simply that it became less acute.

The Uzbeks, by contrast, have generally not chosen to return to their fatherland where political and often economic conditions are considerably inferior. They represent the largest Central Asian diaspora community abroad and in one case, the Kyrgyzstani, have become the largest minority. They are, in Rogers Brubaker's (1996) triadic nexus, facing similar problems as Russians abroad. Like mother Russia, mother Uzbekistan has not intervened to defend their rights, seeming to prefer to view this group as a fifth column. In the Kyrgyz republic the issue under Akaev and Bakiev's rule was how their cultural rights, or at least sense of belonging to the Kyrgyz state, might be enhanced (Chapter 4) (Fumagalli 2007).

Legitimating statehood at home and abroad:
the role of identity and belief

These multiple experiences of belonging and becoming continue to be strongly influenced by state policies. As authoritarian regimes, ruling elites have considerable potential to influence agenda-setting and legitimation practices. Legitimation strategies, designed to increase the power and authority of the ruling elites, involve both foreign and domestic audiences.

Representing and portraying who you are to the outside world anchors independence and legitimates interaction. Erica Marat (2009) has termed these external images 'branding'. These narratives stressed neither pan-Central Asian, nor pan-Turkic identities. The Uzbek government refers not to Central Asia but a particular Timurid heritage that they make their own. The Tajiks and Turkmen have also nationalized their regional provenance. Nazarbaev's Eurasian strategy is regarded with suspicion by Uzbek cultural and political elites. 'The independence of each Central Asian country will be more valuable based on the principle of cooperative development; otherwise there will be greater risk of losing more and finding oneself on the periphery' (Tolipov 2006). By contrast, Nazarbaev has invested much in the portrayal of his country as Eurasian, this stemming from his country's

> geographic position at the cross-roads in the Eurasian region. The process of globalization of world economic and political processes [sic] elevates this factor as a key one. Our ancestors as a part of a united family of Turkic peoples [narody] used this important strategic factor to their advantage: along the legendary Silk Road as wide trading corridor between European and Asiatic countries was organized. Today, we are beginning to restore it in cooperation with other countries of our region and with the support of the world community. Of course, in the future the trading system, financial currents and migrations of people between Europe and Asia will grow. ... For this very reason, to say nothing about the many politically stabilizing factors, I issued forth and will develop the idea of Eurasianism [*evraziistvo*], which has, I am convinced, a strategic future.
>
> (Nazarbaev 1997: 104)

In this spirit, Nazarbaev's daughter Dariga (2003, 2006) explains that 'Kazakhstan borders on Central Asia, but it is not a Central Asian country. Ours is a Eurasian state strongly influenced by Europe and Western values. Contrary to what certain politicians and journalists assert, we are not another *stan*. Saudi Arabia is not our historical landmark: we look to Norway, South Korea, and Singapore'.

Nor have pan-Islamism or pan-Turkism captured the imagination of Central Asia's rulers. In the context of weakly Islamized national ideologies (below) the attraction of transnational Islam was understandably low. Sultan Abdul Hamid II had attempted to foster Pan-Islam since the late nineteenth century. While countries belonged to organizations such as the Economic Cooperation Organization (ECO) alliances with other countries were not struck on the basis of Islam. By contrast, writes Murat Laumulin (2007), 'the restrained and moderate policy conducted by Iran, which for the past few decades has been accused of exporting Islamic revolution, arouses our respect'.

Neither did the leaders view independence as an opportunity to develop strong ties with the broader pan-Turkic world. For a start, this would not greatly interest the Tajiks. Second, the links with the Turkic world were historically weak. In the dying days of the Ottoman empire, official Pan-Turk propaganda was primarily directed against Russia and was largely a response to Pan-Slavism; 'the arrival of Enver himself in Central Asia in 1921, his command of the Basmachi forces and his assumption of the title of "Emir of Turkestan" appeared to many as the realisation of the Pan-Turk ideal .... Several local and foreign observers agreed at the time that although the Central Asian population may not have shown excessive interest in Pan-Turkism after all, there was no doubt concerning Enver's own sincerity in the matter' (Landau 1995: 55–6). And, when these countries gained independence, Turkey was neither a beacon nor a provider of much needed financial assistance. Regime security and pragmatism (Chapters 4 and 7) have instead shaped the foreign policy direction of Central Asian states. A Kyrgyz NGO leader commented:

> The West should stop seeing us as Muslims and recognise us as Europeans, not only as Asians and Muslims. Many of the elites do not want [our country] to be identified as a Muslim country or as an Islamic state and are strongly opposed to this categorisation. How you [the West] identify us will become a self-fulfilling prophecy. You need to develop the same standards for us as for Eastern Europe. If we're compared to Eastern Europe, we'll become like it, but if we're compared to Afghanistan, then we'll become like that.
>
> (ICG 2003: 19)

As an adviser to Tajikistan's president said: 'The West should recognise us as European states, but with Muslim cultures'. This position is occasionally expressed by government officials wishing to gain acceptance by the West while maintaining their legitimacy at home (ICG 2003: 19).

All five Central Asian leaders have declared their states secular and their constitutions enshrine strict separation between church and state. *Sharia* has no official status in any of these countries (ICG 2003: 20). But within this framework they have sought, very carefully, to use Islam both as a tool of legitimation and as a way of striking out to other Muslim countries abroad. James Critchlow (1991: 196–9) notes that already prior to Soviet collapse 'the year 1989 witnessed a dramatic volte-face in official policy toward religion'. Funds were redirected to refurbish holy places, such as 'Mount of Suleiman' in Osh and 'the Soviet state airline Aeroflot promised help in delivering one million copies of the Koran' donated by Saudi Arabia. Muhammad Sadiq Muhammad Yusuf, who as Mufti of Tashkent heads the Religious Board for the Muslims of Central Asia and Kazakhstan, became a prominent figure. Critchlow continues: 'The new deference to religion also pursues practical ends.' As Gorbachev began to speak more favourably of Islam (punctured by warnings of 'Islamic fundamentalism') Islamic commandments were corresponding to 'communist morality'. Already under Gorbachev, the Central Asia-wide spiritual board SADUM was splitting along national lines, the Kazakh wing already seceding in 1990 and 'by 1992 each of the five had their own religious administrations which continued, however, to function as an organ of the state, firmly under the control of the regime' (Khalid 2003: 587).

These similarities notwithstanding, the five leaderships have integrated Islam to different degrees in their legitimation toolboxes, and these differences stem largely from how Islamic content relates to the broader content of state ideologies. In Kyrgyzstan and Kazakhstan there has been much less interest in ideologies that challenge secularism. But non-traditional Muslim tendencies have appeared in both, and there is debate over the role of religion in society and in politics and over the limits to state interference in religion. President Akaev liked to stress that the Kyrgyz were less Muslim, partly as a way of keeping a distance from extremism, partly as a way of strengthening his country's Western reform path. Instead, he stressed the ideology of Manas, and that Manas, not Islam, would provide moral and spiritual guidance (Marat 2008). Schoolchildren were taught about the seven lessons or commandments of Manas: patriotism, unity of the nation international cooperation, defence of the state, humanism, harmony with nature and the aspiration to obtain knowledge and skills (Van der Heide 2008). Referred to also by Akaev, President Bakiev supported the idea of Tengrism, a syncretic religion practised before the peoples of the region converted to Buddhism, Manichaeism or Islam, as a basis for a new national ideology (Laruelle 2007; Murzakulova and Schoeberlein 2010). Nazarbaev has exercised similar caution in his deference to Islam, celebrating in parallel his nation's multi-confessionality by visiting the Vatican the same year as going on a hajj. Celebration of Islamic holidays or Islamic prayers at the start of public rituals serve a broader Kazakhisation policy (below).

While the Tajik president refers officially to Zoroaster as the 'first prophet of the Tajiks' (Laruelle 2007: 51–70), the country's early independence history demanded a careful appraisal of Islam in state-building and its state mismanagement was viewed by some as a contributory factor to the outbreak of civil war in 1992. The Islamic Renaissance Party (IRP) led opposition to the former Communist regime but failure on both sides to compromise produced bitter fighting that continued until a peace accord was reached in 1997. That agreement legalised the IRP 'but in practice President Rahmonov has gradually undermined [the IRP's] position in the political system' (ICG 10 July 2003).

Both Turkmenistani and Uzbekistani state creeds have contained more public references to Islam but only insofar as they serve their presidents' broader, secular ideologies. In Turkmenistan, in a pseudo-Islamic spiritual creed which focuses on his own personality, Niyazov required that his *Ruhnama* – his self-authored 'Book of Spirit' – be displayed in mosques beside the Koran and that prayers be said in his honour during Friday services. In Uzbekistan the government has staged several lavish jubilees marking the anniversaries of such Islamic figures as al-Bukhari, al-Marghinani and al-Maturidi, all of whom are claimed as Uzbek national figures. Andrew March (2003) argues that Karimov's national legitimation has been successful partly because it makes references to an Uzbek pre-political consensus.

The national has featured much more strongly in top-down legitimation strategies than Islam. Could leaders easily draw on national identities as sources of claimed difference and cultural authenticity that have been so helpful in legitimizing other emerging sovereign leaders around the world? We noted at the close of Chapter 3 how communists had to find new formulae on which to base their new-found sovereignty and ruling in the name of the nation seemed the most obvious successor strategy. But how has this been achieved and what sorts of problems have been encountered?

Five main such legitimation techniques have been used: historiography; visual symbolism; language – official/state and script issues; indigenization of power; and various forms of indigenizing associations with territory (e.g., denial of land privatization or census numbers). All five speak to a form of 'nationalising by stealth' (Bohr 1998a) by elites.

Legitimation strategies vary in the degree to which they deny or incorporate the Soviet past. The state sponsorship of historiography, and the introduction of new textbooks in the classroom, generally frames the nations as the logical culmination of a long process of statehood that began well before the arrival of the Soviets. Even in the more pro-Soviet state ideology of Kyrgyzstan, the Kyrgyz state is celebrated as long in formation. New constitutions enshrine titular nations as the rightful owners of the state. Kazakhstan's 25 October 1990 declaration of sovereignty within the Union affirmed ethnic Kazakhs as the 'constituent nation of the state'. Another striking example of continuity with the Soviet era was the emphasis on the Turkmen 'homeland' in the new state's nationalist ideology (Edgar 2004: 264). Uzbekistan's national ideology partly celebrates the country's 'golden heritage' (*oltin meros*). The regime has also acted to 'nationalize' the state and make it 'more' Uzbek.

New visual symbolism involved public celebrations (Adams 2010), the nationalizing of monuments and the renaming of streets and national heroes. This process of hero celebration spawned unintended consequences in the Kazakh case (Schatz 2005). As noted, the Kazakh nation had no equivalent to a unifying popular hero of the Manas, and its Kazakhization process by default spawned the celebration of all sorts of local heroes at the regional, rather than national, levels. New monuments and symbols (such as the swastika) celebrate an officially sponsored Aryan past of the Tajiks. The revolving statue of Niyazov fuses the personal and national in Turkmen state ideology.

Language issues mobilized societies already in the Gorbachev era and into the post-independence era issues became one of language and script choice. As noted, Russian remains the language of communication for the majority of the population of Central Asia. In 1989, all five established their indigenous languages as state languages. In the 1990s, three – Kazakhstan, Kyrgyzstan and Tajikistan – agreed to recognize Russian as the interethnic language of communication. The 2001–2010 Language Programme in Kazakhststan promulgates further development of the Kazakh language. In April 2004 a new language law obliged all civil servants to demonstrate their knowledge of the Kyrgyz language. In Turkmenistan, Russian lost all official status upon promulgation of the Constitution of 1992. In December 1995 Uzbek legislation stopped Russian being used as the interethnic language of communication and in 2005 the government replaced Uzbek's Cyrillic with a Romanized script.

Already well underway in the Soviet period, indigenizing rule provided a fourth way of legitimating an ethno-national state ideology. This provided titular elites with power and also anchored their sovereignty externally, as most local diplomats were of the titular nation. Turkmenistan went to the extreme of establishing a pragmatic national preference policy that forbids any non-Turkmen from competing in presidential elections. The Kazakh diaspora until the 1995 Constitution was given the right to dual citizenship and special rights if it returned home to Kazakhstan.

One of the key issues that occupied Russian communities in Central Asia was whether their Central Asian governments would grant them the right to dual citizenship. Uzbekistan has maintained its original position which was firm denial of that right. For Russians in Kazakhstan, the issue became less pressing with the introduction of a simple citizenship agreement as a result of these countries' participation in customs and economic unions. Kyrgyzstan, similarly involved in such agreements, went a step further in 2006 by including a provision for dual citizenship in its new constitution (with restrictions, but a pragmatic move designed to ease Kyrgyz migration to Russia). Tajikistan's dependence on Moscow encouraged the introduction of dual citizenship already in 1994/5, but importantly only one-third of those taking up this possibility have been 'ethnic' Russian. While Turkmenistan was the first to instigate dual citizenship in 1993 – partly because it had the smallest ethnic Russian minority – in 2003 this was revoked, with the stipulation that Russians in Turkmenistan had to decide between one or the other with the result that by 2007 'approximately 50,000 citizens of the Russian Federation remain in Turkmenistan, deprived of their rights and regularly harassed by the authorities' (Peyrouse 2008: 13).

Leaders have faced challenges in their emphasis on ethno-national content in legitimation strategies. These challenges have been greater in multi-ethnic Kazakhstan, Kyrgyzstan and Tajikistan, where elites were faced with the tasks of simultaneous narratives of exclusion and inclusion. The Kazakhstani elite in the early independence years faced what it perceived as an existential crisis, particularly in its northern regions that held a Russian majority and bordered on mother Russia. Such concerns drove the decision to relocate the capital from south to north in 1998 (Schatz 2004). Nazarbaev's legitimation strategy has thus involved a dual policy of Kazakhization and internationalism.

A second challenge for rulers has been to successfully decouple themselves from the Soviet past. 'Despite the new Turkmen rulers' efforts to distance themselves from the Soviet era, the discourse and institutions of independent Turkmen nationhood were profoundly shaped by the Soviet experience' (Ochs 1997). While the Karimov regime has sought to anchor its legitimacy in Uzbek nationalism and statehood, its form is very much in the Soviet mould and the 'regime's policy toward Islam is best understood in this context. It celebrates the Islamic cultural heritage of the region and invokes the moral and ethical values stemming from it. Sufism has been adopted as an example of the humanist traditions of the Uzbek nation, just as old mosques are celebrated as "architectural monuments"' (Khalid 2003: 587). Adams (2010: 33) captures the complexity of selective choosing in a nation's collective memory: 'Some of Uzbekistan's shared memories provided a solid basis for national identity, while others were cast in doubt either because of the suspicion of Soviet repression or because of the uses to which they were being put by the current government'.

State-builders in Turkmenistan and Kazakhstan have sometimes engaged in a collective amnesia about their nomadic and tribal pasts. Some scholars even go so far as to deny the nomadic heritage of the Turkmen. The nomadic past was rejected in favour of a narrative that stressed longer pasts as states and thoroughly modern futures. Turkmen state officials and historians spared no effort to prove that the Turkmen had inhabited their current territory since time immemorial. A similar attitude to their nomadic pasts was found by state officials in the early years of Kazakhstan's independence, although as national confidence has grown so has their embracing of this past to the point of a government-sponsored film called *Nomad* (admittedly partly in reaction to *Borat*). Furthermore, several ethnic Kazakh political elites have commented that their country must escape their tribal past and that intra-Kazakh cleavages were a greater obstacle to achieving national unity than interethnic ones (Cummings 2005). Likewise in Turkmenistan '[t]he president spoke out strongly against those who would elevate tribal loyalties above national patriotism' (Edgar 2004: 265).

Finally, legitimation does not occur in a vacuum; top-down and bottom-up narratives often compete. Krisztina Kehl-Bodogri (2006) shows how shaykhs' claims on tombs are shaped by local struggles and debates. McGlinchey (2007: 316) refers to 'a threat of competing legitimacy, of local religious leaders who enjoy growing grassroots support and of a central leadership whose one power is its promotion of an environment of fear'. Berna Turam (2004: 353, 365) aims in a study of the Gülen movement 'to challenge the binary thinking that juxtaposes politics against culture and dichotomises the ethnic and state-framed base of nationalism and nationhood, observing how the sympathisers of the Gülen movement in Almaty were not touched by the transnationalisation of Islam'. Also, while authorities 'use these monuments as secular tourist sites in their endeavour to promote nation-building – "chronotropes of national monumental time"' (Louw 2006: 326), ordinary citizens often see them as profoundly spiritual. Aurélie Biard (2010: 323) illustrates the paradoxes involved in the Kyrgyz case when the state, failing itself to deliver basic public services, uses Islam to reemphasize its nationhood but 'in the process, it becomes the subject of a drive towards territorialization that aims at erasing any transnational and/or pan-Islamist dimension from this universalist religion'. Legitimation amounts, in sum, to the process that Paul Geiss (2003: 245) traces as the relationship between political community and normative order, and how 'enduring political stability within the republics will also depend on the ability of the political elites to relate communal commitment to the political culture of these states'.

Islam and identity: force of stability or cause of violence in Central Asia?

Such 'communal commitment' has exerted various impacts on political order and stability in Central Asia. While elites have used Islam to legitimate their rule and have even enshrined religious freedoms in their constitutions (Geiss 2003: 245), their overriding practice has been hostility, control and repression. President Karimov has declared that '[S]uch people [Islamic extremists] must be shot in the head. If necessary, I'll shoot them myself'. Leaders have seen how cultivating a discourse of danger (Heathershaw and Megoran 2011) around Islam can help them justify blanket repression and silence opposition. The 'threat' is then portrayed by local and international actors as operating throughout the region.

Such threat manufacture has occurred even in countries that have seen less Islamic revival, such as Kazakhstan (Omelicheva 2011: 254) and even after visible signs that threats have diminished, 'spurred on by both developments in the global arena and local attempts to control and define Islam'. Fundamentalism is mistaken for extremism or jihadism (Yuldasheva 2002). These portrayals occur in a narrative of a 'clash of civilizations' (Huntington 1998) and the assertion that Central Asia is 'almost certain to become the new global battleground' (Rashid 2002: 4).

While threats from Islamist and jihadist groups have been unhelpfully conflated, the existence of extremist or militant groups (Chapter 7) requires explanation and deserves discussion. Most observers do not deny that such organizations exist. The question, however, becomes one of how they emerged, who supports them, and whether they are likely to grow stronger. The two main extremist organizations in the region since independence have been the Islamic Movement of Uzbekistan (IMU) and the Hizb ut-Tahrir al-Islami (popularly known as the Hizb ut-Tahrir and here shortened to HT). Some have highlighted the links of al-Qaeda and the IMU to Wahhabi and neo-Wahhabi ideas, particularly the Wahhabism that was reported to have resulted from its spread by Saudi missionaries in the early independence years (ICG 2002). The situation is further confused by the tendency of officials to label strong religious figures that they consider potential threats as '*Wahhabis*' in an attempt to discredit them with little if any discussion about what constitutes Wahhabism. Real *Wahhabism* invalidates many traditions and customs indigenous to Central Asia, such as shrine worship and so does not have widespread appeal.

The ideologies and membership size of the IMU and HT differ considerably. If the IMU's Islam 'derives largely from Saudi Arabia's Wahhabism and the interpretation of Deobandism by the Taliban' (Rashid 2002: 95), 'to a striking degree, the IMU was motivated by simple hatred of Karimov and his regime' (Khalid 2007: 157). By contrast, the HT in Central Asia has urged the peaceful overthrow of governments across the region and the establishment of an Islamic caliphate throughout the Muslim world. While the IMU was largely wiped out in late 2001 in anti-insurgency operations, with the help of Western forces (Chapter 7), the HT since the late 1990s has reportedly expanded 'dramatically' (ICG 2002: 6), operating in all five countries. The same report quoted an HT female member explaining how, to recruit, she approaches 'people eating pork or drinking alcohol in restaurants and cafés and starts talking to them about how to live properly according to Islam'. Writing on the HT's attraction in Kentau, South Kazakhstan, Igor Savin (2003) refers to how the HT becomes 'a mechanism of successful socialization; it turned uneducated young men with no hopes for a higher social status and a successful career into people with what they perceived as a life worthy of respect and a great future'. This, he adds, is in the context of an ethno-national state ideology that fails to give meaning to the republic's multi-ethnicity. Zanca (2004) argues that religious movements in Uzbekistan can be seen as part youth rebellion and part opposition to the current monolithic Uzbek political system.

Writers distinguish these extreme groups from the more moderate Islamic Renaissance Party (IRP), the only officially registered Islamic party in the FSU. Ahmed Rashid (2002: 95) writes how the 'Tajik Islamicists – heirs to the Basmachis – are unique amongst militant Central Asian Islamic groups. The movement brings together the various strands of Central Asian Islam, a grounding that gives it a legitimacy far beyond that of other extreme radical groups operating in Central Asia today'. Akçali (1998: 267) argues that between the Afghan mujahidin and the Tajiks the 'bond of Islam was the most important and decisive identity that transcended other identities in the region, such as nationalism and ethnicity'. As explained in Chapter 3, the IRP had already been prominent in February 1990, after the Dushanbe housing riots. But their aim in Tajikistan was not to establish a caliphate but rather, in alliance with two other organizations, to wrest power from the incumbent regime. Their inclusion in government after the 1997 peace accords marked a decline in their appeal, Rahmonov's regime successfully undermining their effectiveness and the party leadership unable to offer a competitive economic or political plan for the country's revival (Rashid 2002: 113) and facing rigged elections by the incumbent regime.

Societal insecurities are fed by rapid change in environments that are poorly institutionalized and therefore, paradoxically, some argue that liberal policies can end up with the same result as repressive ones. This is the argument often made about the Kyrgyz Republic which has the most liberal of religious policies. Hann and Pelkmans (2009: 1538) argue that the Kyrgyz state 'has been no more successful in charting a viable religious path than it has been in the political and economic spheres. Attempts to forge a distinctively Kyrgyz identity on the basis of a "liberal" Islam appear to be failing and the country remains vulnerable to internal factional forces and destabilizing transnational forces'. From a different angle Rashid (2002: 130) also argues that 'Kyrgyzstan is the only Central Asian country where a variety of Christian evangelist movements are allowed to proselytize, a concession the HT finds humiliating'. Anara Tabyshalieva (2000) writes how '[t]he process of Christianization of the northern part of Kyrgyzstan competes with the Islamicization in the southern part'. Babajanov (2008) fears that if Islamic parties participate in political life they will radicalize what are fundamentally highly conservative societies. Abdullo Khakim (2005) writes that this very same conservatism requires overhaul and modernization. The requirement, it seems, is pursuing simultaneously a policy of liberalizing and institution-building, so that old organizations do not feel disadvantaged and old and new movements find legitimate channels for expression and change.

The alternative policy of repression currently practised by most Central Asian presidents is very likely to be self-defeating (Abdullaev 2010). Pushing voices underground has shown to radicalize (Peyrouse 2007b). 'Despite its apparent success, repression has not succeeded in eliminating the Islamist threat in Central Asia but instead has served as a short-term coping mechanism'

(Trisko 2005: 386). The appeal of militancy is likely to grow if elites continue to block legitimate and formal channels for voice and dissent. This raises the interesting and important question of the degree to which legalization of Islamic parties can help in this process. Rashid (2002: 134) argues that 'legalizing the HT would make it less likely to forge links with other radical Islamic groups that do advocate violence'. Others invoke the 1992–7 civil war as the necessary price to allow such legalization to become accepted.

In a post-imperial perspective and all things considered, Central Asia has seen comparatively few outbreaks of violence. Two notable exceptions are the Tajik civil war (1992–7) and Osh/Jalalabad (June 2010). As in the discussions about the general link between identity and regime type in Chapter 4, however, there was nothing inevitable about such identities leading to the break-out of conflict. While the Tajik civil war was not about Islam (Chapter 4), the role of belief and ideology in mobilizing the population cannot be discounted altogether. More precisely, to continue from Chapter 4, we continue to respect the important distinction made by Barnett Rubin (1998: 132) who berates narratives that claim '*how* Tajikistan broke down explains *why* Tajikistan broke down'. Chapter 4 concentrated on the 'why' and assessed domestic and external factors in state or regional breakdown. Here we focus on *how* Tajikistan and the Kyrgyz republic divided. In the Tajik case the *major* fault-line was regional, in the Kyrgyz, ethnic. By following Rubin's distinction we insist that identities and ideologies do not have autonomous force separate from the leaders who promote them. This did not constitute a Balkanization of Central Asia. Instead both illustrated classic cases of societal insecurity in which identities were successfully mobilized and, as stated for the Tajik case, under 'incompetent leadership' (Akbarzadeh 1996: 1126).

At its inception, the Tajik civil war pitted a neo-communist nomenklatura against moderate Islamists, democrats and nationalists. Ideology was only part of the story, however, and in time decreased in importance. Opposition groups were driven by the desire for genuine Tajik national sovereignty. The loss of Bukhara and Samarkand in the Soviet delimitation process of 1929 made it hard for the regime to establish a nationalist credibility (Akbarzadeh 1996: 1126). For Walker (2003) ethnicity also mattered in that Uzbeks, who made up a quarter of the population, were concentrated in the more industrialized and wealthier northern oblast of Leninabad (later Khujand, now Sughd province, which extends into the Ferghana Valley) and ethnic Russians, most of whom lived in the north or in Dushanbe, were disproportionately represented in the Tajik government. 'The strongest cleavage, however, appeared regional in nature, with an alliance of Leninabadis and Tajiks from the southern province of Kulyab pitted against an alliance of Tajiks from Garm province and Pamiris from the remote highland of Gorno-Badashkhan'. Expands Olivier Roy (2007: 121):

The drama of Tajikistan was that it was created without the historic Tajik cities, and on the basis of a rural and mountain-dwelling population that lacked elites and also lacked a sense of nationalism. There was a fundamental division between the Tajiks of the cities, Samarkand and Bukhara, who were interested in fighting for a Greater Uzbekistan or a Greater Turkestan, even Turkified, and the Tajiks of the foothills and mountains, who were known as Ghalcha and who saw themselves landed with a republic that they had not asked for, but which regionalist factions then tried to appropriate for themselves. The events of 1992 in both camps were the retribution of the peasants and mountain peoples against an intelligentsia that had no localist rooting.

By contrast, for some time it seemed that successful framing in the Kyrgyz case had helped assuage the localist concerns of the Uzbek community in southern Kyrgyzstan. Between 11 and 14 June 2010, however, an explosion of violence, destruction and looting in southern Kyrgyzstan killed many hundreds of people, mostly Uzbeks, destroyed over 2,000 buildings, mostly homes, and deepened the gulf between the country's ethnic Kyrgyz and Uzbeks (ICG no 193: i). Most of the violence took place in Osh with violence also in and around the region's other main city, Jalalabad. Osh and Jalalabad oblasts (regions) account for 44 per cent of Kyrgyzstan's population.

The ICG (2010: i) offered the following societal-based explanation:

Many features of the 2010 violence strongly resemble the last round of bloody ethnic clashes, in 1990. At that time there was no attempt to address the root causes of the problem, and the same phenomena burst to the surface in an even more virulent form twenty years on. During the intervening two decades, state neglect and economic decline have deepened social deprivation, increasing the pool of poorly educated and mostly unemployed young men who, in 2010 as in 1990, proved particularly susceptible to destructive violence.

This state neglect and economic decline had been brought on by the disappearance of major Soviet industrial and agricultural enterprises that had provided tens of thousands of jobs. The region slipped into an increasing reliance on subsistence farming and labour migration, cross-border trade and narcotics smuggling. On 8 April, the day after Bakiev's overthrow, local Uzbek leader Batyrov addressed a celebratory rally of some 5,000 Uzbeks. Batyrov emphasized the moderation of Uzbek demands, denying any interest in an autonomous Uzbek region in the south and noting that he had proposed to a commission discussing a new constitution that the Uzbek language be given legal status in majority ethnic Uzbek areas of the south.

In societal-security dilemmas, actors may be uncertain as to whether the other is employing either a cultural-nationalist (cultural autonomy) or political-nationalist (political autonomy/secession) strategy. Assuming the worst can lead to a spiral of nationalisms and, finally, violent conflict. Both the Tajik and Kyrgyz cases pointed to such security dilemmas, with tragic results. Cultural-nationalist and political-nationalist strategies can be used to defend societal security

(Chapter 4). A societal-security dilemma occurs when the actions taken by one society to strengthen its identity cause a reaction in a second, which is perceived to, and may actually weaken the position of the first. Inspired by the democratic claims of the regime that overthrew Kurmanbek Bakiev in April 2010, and by the fact that many provisional government leaders were from the north and thus traditionally more sympathetic to the Uzbek minority, Uzbeks once again were tempted to propose greater linguistic and political representation. They underestimated a strong feeling within Kyrygz society that any concessions on linguistic and cultural grounds to the Uzbeks threaten Kyrgyzstan's own cultural survival as a state. Crucially, they underestimated the readiness of many Kyrgyz politicians to make an anti-Uzbek position part of their political platform.

Conclusions

It is multiplicity not uniformity of identities, within and across the five states, that has characterized this region's early independence years. The Tajik and Kyrgyz experiences shed some light on the rest of Central Asia's absence of violence, but also the uniqueness of each country. Neither case confirms Islam as the major cause or the conflicts' ensuing narrative. '[T]here has been an Islamic revival, yes, but its political implications from the beginning have been misconstrued and exaggerated' (Khalid 2003: 583). Both however appear to confirm the salience of leadership and imagination in state-building strategies. The Tajik leadership has often been accused of a dearth of imaginative nation-building strategies and the Kyrgyz for lacking meaningful ideologies. By contrast, Nazarbaev's effective continuation of the Soviet rhetoric (and in part policy) of 'dual assimilation' seemed to help assuage fears in the context of an otherwise largely self-regulating mechanism. The degree to which populations have found meaning in the ideologies of Karimov and Niyazov and his successor Berdymukhamedov is difficult to assess in the context of their repressive regimes.

The Kyrgyz and Tajik republics were the first to politically liberalize: the former, for the early independence years, from above; the latter, for a few months, from below. While regime liberalization was welcomed and actively promoted by some sectors of their populations, it was not accompanied by sufficient state- and institution-building to accommodate changing ideas, beliefs and identities. This led to widespread popular and often also elite disaffection. Profound societal insecurities and uncertain belonging were exploited by leaders for their own ends.

This and the preceding chapter seem therefore to confirm the observation that regime security and power maintenance trump strong nationalizing ideologies. Cengiz Sürücü (2002: 386) argues that 'the desire for and positioning along the political power and cultural hegemony more than ethnic boundary markers, captures the dynamics of the struggles of the elites'. Dzhenish Dzhunushaliev and Vladimir Ploskikh (2005) add that '[t]he more than 70-year effort to promote and assert class consciousness among the Kyrgyz has failed to achieve its aim'. Annette Bohr's (1998a) expression, 'nationalisation by stealth' captures the altogether less discriminatory policies pursued by Central Asian governments so far than elsewhere in the post-Soviet space; Peyrouse (2008:14) further argues that 'one cannot view discrimination against the Russians of Central Asia as part of an official policy, as was the case in the Baltic States'. These dynamics of regime maintenance and societal insecurities have been further fed by economic change and broader security challenges, the subjects of the final two chapters.

6 Economics and political transformations

In the context of Soviet collapse, three main economic puzzles are assessed in this chapter. The first introduces the economic reform programme promoted by the international community and some insights into how the introduction of a 'market' is negotiated from below. The second looks at the policies in greater detail: why they were chosen, how they have fared and what is sustaining them further. As Richard Pomfret (2006: 2–3) writes, examining these different trajectories is 'intellectually exciting' because of their similar origins. The role of natural resources, both in their effects on initial policy directions and in reform sustainability, is the central element of this discussion. Finally, in common with the political (Chapter 4) and security (Chapter 7) realms, the economic realm is not in a vacuum and Central Asia's economic challenges are set in a broader regional and international context.

A manager of a large US-based transnational oil company in the early 1990s coined the memorable, if somewhat ungrammatical, phrase 'Multiple pipelines is multiple happiness'. It encapsulated the dilemma of a region attempting to escape the orbit of its erstwhile centre, Russia. During the Soviet period, to ensure Central Asian dependency on the centre, all raw materials in the periphery were refined in Russia; thus, upon independence, all oil and gas pipelines ran through Russia. Finding ways to bypass Russia and yet anchor economic sovereignty became a top reform priority for at least three of the newly independent Central Asian states (Kazakhstan, Turkmenistan and Uzbekistan).

During the shooting of the 1966 Kyrgyz film, *Pervyy Uchitel* (First Teacher), Director Andrei Konchalovsky wanted to recreate the authenticity of a 1916 landscape unspoilt by signs of mechanization. He travelled miles into the mountain valleys to find locations that had no electricity pylons (Cummings 2009). The difficulty of this task reflects the degree to which the Kyrgyz republic had become mechanized in just some 20 years.

Soviet economic legacies loomed large on independence. To recall, the Soviet command-administrative system, which involved communal ownership of production and bureaucratic management of the economy, administered prices and had external economic relations only with other socialist states (CMEA). While all of the Soviet economy shared these features, Central Asia had its specificities. Central Asia was the breadbasket and the key natural resource provider of the

Soviet Union. All five republics emerged in 1991 with economies that had been profoundly politicized, mis-developed as resource economies and highly dependent in terms of personnel, markets and routes on Russia. As a region of the Soviet Union, Central Asia was economically the poorest upon independence.

Despite these commonalities, each of the five faced its own unique set of challenges, which stemmed largely from variations in income level, geography and resources. Energy grids and transport infrastructure connected four of the Central Asian states but economic organization enforced a divide with Kazakhstan, whose industrial core was integrated into Southern Siberian networks. By 1991 Kazakhstan was the only republic to have more than half of its population residing in urban areas (Wegren 1988: 164). Kyrgyzstan and Tajikistan emerged as the poorest and most peripheral of all the Soviet republics, with Tajikistan also remaining culturally and politically embroiled in events in neighbouring Afghanistan. Turkmenistan's closeness to Iran and its relative isolation from the economic reforms of the Gorbachev period also created its challenges.

Macro- and everyday economic transformations

The international community had its own vision of what a transition from plan to market economy would necessitate. Over the years, this consensus, led by the World Bank and the International Monetary Fund, had led to the formation of a set of policy prescriptions that had informally become known as the 'Washington Consensus'. A priority would be to liberalize, deregulate and convert currencies, given the politicization of the Soviet economy through the preponderant role of the Communist party and its 'soft budget constraints' (Kornai 1992). Economic reform strategy would involve also: macroeconomic stabilization and a new role for the state; the blurring of the distinction between state, party (nomenklatura) and the replacement of the command economy by separate state and private sectors; the turning of planners into shareholders, by liberalizing prices and creating markets via, for example, the formation of a legal code and competition policy; the change from 100 per cent state ownership to majority private ownership, which would have to be followed by privatization and corporate governance; industrial restructuring, which would allow consumers' preferences to replace planners' preferences; the creation of labour market institutions by replacing wage fixing with labour markets; the creation of financial and capital markets to further overcome the soft budget constraints; and trade liberalization and exchange rate convertibility to replace autarchy, non-convertibility and import substitution with integration into world markets.

The 'Washington Consensus' was strongly promoted in Central Asia as a universal blueprint for development by an increasingly co-ordinated set of actors – public and private international financial institutions (e.g., the IMF, World Bank and private banks). Domestic state factors were seen as the cause of mis-development. The main task was to downsize the large communist state, and the state was redefined as the enabler of the private sector. But the result of rolling back the state was the throwing into greater poverty of a large number of Central Asian citizens. Debt remained a serious problem. To date, trade has benefited the richest, not poorest. Social problems have increased as access to basics, for example education and healthcare, have declined. Basic state infrastructures have declined (ICG 2011). More and more criticisms have been heard within the IMF and World Bank, and have resulted in significant resignations (e.g., Joseph Stiglitz).

After communism, liberal markets by populations in the region have paradoxically often become associated with fewer freedoms than their socialist predecessors, as 'the political liberties many people of the Soviet Union have acquired do not compensate for the greater economic hardships they now face'. Capitalism 'has brought neither repetition nor boredom to Central Asia .... Now most economic activity falls within the private realm, where state welfare guarantees are largely absent' (McMann 2007: 233, 245). This is because these economies remain highly politicized (Chapter 4) and access to them has remained tightly controlled but also because citizens continue to expect a high degree of public services from the state.

Further on this, Nazpary (2002: 55–6) wrote how in his qualitative interviews: 'People identified the Soviet era with security in two senses: economic security and social security in general. Economically, the collapse of the welfare state was described as the main source of insecurity....The social dimension of this loss of security was related by people to the disintegration of the state and the destabilization of their networks'. When we talk about 'markets' and their introduction in the post-Soviet space, we must bear in mind that 'this version of "the market" did not land on unoccupied ground' and was being 'introduced into societies where there were already a variety of entrepreneurial or profit-oriented practices of one kind or another' (Humphrey and Mandel 2002: 2), which might be legal or illegal.

The issue of morality in economic life has been a rare dimension in analyses of the economic reform process but it has been taken up by cultural anthropologists and sociologists. In interviewing professionals, Balihar Sanghera (2008: 658) writes that most 'excuse bribes because economic inequalities push professionals to make compromises. ... "Gift-giving" has become a social institution to ease ethical tension and conflict between professional and economic values, as doctors, lecturers and others seek both to obtain appreciation and gratitude, and to make ends meet'. Not only professionals but also entrepreneurs face substantial moral concerns related to the triple effects of 'social status anxiety, daily moral dilemmas and guilt and the moral vacuum of post-Soviet materialism' (Özcan 2010: 193).

Conditionality of reform was accompanied by, and sometimes linked to, development aid. Despite this marked social stratification, development programmes have shown that this region is not a Third World region, but instead home to industrialized countries with high rates of literacy and education and a sizeable professional class of doctors, teachers and scientists. Catapulted from the 'Second

World' that 'vanished' with the collapse of the Soviet Union, representatives from international aid agencies often 'alienated local representatives by comparing their concerns to those of Third World countries' (Schoeberlein 2000: 56, 60). At the same time, although on many scales these countries would be considered 'highly developed', the recently socialist societies remained undeveloped in the structures characterizing a market economy (Mandel 1998: 632). Despite development programmes to assist in such necessary restructuring, Central Asia has substantial pockets of poverty.

Vertical inequalities (income-dependent) and horizontal inequalities (e.g., differences across geographical regions or social groups) have both increased across all of Central Asia. "'You go to Uzbekistan or Kyrgyzstan and there are a few very rich people", Baurzhan said. "Richer even than our rich – and we have half a dozen billionaires listed in Forbes. But in these other countries it's unbelievable. Crazy rich. But they have no middle class. People have no hope for a better life. Ever. So it's a mess. A middle class was made here [Kazakhstan]– you make a middle class, you make a country' (Robbins 2007: 71). Focusing on Uzbekistan, Alisher Ilkhamov (2001: 33–4, 53) argues that in parallel with 'the appearance of a small class of the nouveau riche (the "new Russians", the "new Uzbeks", etc.) a large class of the so-called "new poor" has been formed, including budget workers (*budjetniki*), ordinary farm workers and industrial and construction workers', concluding also that '[t]he natural leaders of the "new poor" will be those who can formulate slogans that will strike a chord amidst this mass of unfortunates. It is evident that both Islamist slogans and left radical catchwords could be successful'.

In a study of rural Kazakhstan, Rosamund Shreeves (2002: 227–8) concludes that '[T]he political science approach to the public/private dichotomy fails to capture the specific ways in which the introduction of the market is intertwined with public (state) and private (kin, domestic) spheres'. Despite challenges to the rural economy, she continues, 'the "rural gender contract" is perpetuating the association of men with the "outside" and women with the "inside" economy, with men primarily linked with market production and women with the domestic/ subsistence domain'. In Central Asia as a whole, women 'have been the chief victims of the shrinking labour market' and that '[e]ven in Kyrgyzstan, where official attitudes to working women are still generally favourable, it was estimated that by mid-1993 almost 70 percent of the unemployed were women' (Akiner in Buckley 1997: 288).

Kinship and social networks are central ways that all of these societies are coping with growing poverty. Howell's (1995: 361) study of household coping in Kyrgyzstan concluded that households used 'a combination of four key strategies to ride the crisis, namely reducing consumption and variously depleting, maintaining and regenerating their resource base'. Cynthia Werner (1998) also shows how daily survival relies on gift exchange and networking in Kazakhstan. Kandiyoti (1998: 576) demonstrates how in Uzbekistan rural households in Andijan draw on Soviet and reconstituted post-Soviet networks to make ends meet, concluding that 'one of the more enduring legacies of the command economy will be the tendency to develop informal methods and strategies of coping, especially when other avenues for participation appear to be blocked or non-existent'.

Government reforms appear to have strengthened the economic importance of network relations, not just in Inner (Humphrey and Sneath 1999) but also Central Asia. This strengthening has not always come in the ways expected. Gift exchange has, indeed, often been in place of otherwise failing market mechanisms. But money has also become an important element among the wealthier. Sometimes money transactions work within social or kin networks, sometimes irrespective of them. Research in Kyrgyzstan, for example, suggests that 'money has become a key means of establishing and mobilizing networks' (Kuehnast and Dudwick 2004: 4) and transactions among the non-poor involve money even if they are kin. Similarly in his analysis of how individuals compete to obtain a position as a *shirkat* (collective and state farm) manager in Uzbekistan, Kai Wegerich (2006: 127) argues that 'money as transactional content becomes more important than family and friendship ties'.

Policies, performances and pathways: explaining variations

Policies

Ordinary citizens were thus experiencing tumultuous economic change as a result of domestic and international processes well beyond their control. Despite this change and economic orthodoxy, not all Central Asian leaders embraced economic reform to the same degree. Discussions in the early 1990s centred on shock therapy being contrasted with gradualism. Kandiyoti's writing on Andijan (Chapter 4), shows how communities were hard hit by the government's decision to go, finally, for currency convertibility in 2003. The contract with authorities was being broken: 'I broke my back on these cotton fields. And now they think they can fob me off with a tiny parcel of bad land to grow a few carrots and sunflowers. The farm manager sells all the good, irrigated land to the rich. Some of them even come from outside. Are we to starve?' (Kandiyoti 2005).

Uzbekistan and Turkmenistan opted for the gradualist paths. In September 1996 in Uzbekistan restrictions were introduced on the use of foreign currency, leading to substantial currency over-evaluation. Gleason (2003: 119) refers to the 'Uzbek Path' and 'self-reliance' which 'emphasized establishing self-sufficiency in energy and food grains, developing manufacturing for domestic consumption, creating an internally oriented services market, and exporting primary commodities, particularly cotton and gold'. At the time of writing a dual-exchange policy was still in operation to hoard hard currency and only make it available to prestige industries. Turkmenistan's economic policy was similarly gradualist; in late 2001 the EBRD singled out Turkmenistan as the only former Soviet republic to have gone back in economic reform (Synovitz 2001: 25).

A large debt financed import-substitution projects, especially in petrochemicals and textiles. As the fourth largest gas producer in the world (after Russia, the

US and Iran) and with substantial oil reserves, Turkmenistan set out to maintain as much distance from Russia but at the same time maintain access to its markets; self-interested policies with southern neighbours; and to attract maximum foreign investment (Cummings and Ochs 2002). While gas is the largest revenue earner, agriculture remained the largest employer. Because of the procurement of new investors, there was less talk of stagnation. Like Niyazov, Berdymukhamedov continued to keep the leading sectors of the economy, notably hydrocarbons, in state hands and invested large amounts in prestige construction projects and infrastructure.

By contrast, the earliest and most far-reaching reformers were Kazakhstan and Kyrgyzstan. In Kazakhstan's 1992 'Strategy for the Formation and Development of Kazakstan as a Sovereign State', the country opened its doors to foreign direct investment. It signed 'the deal of the century' with oil giant Chevron and launched an export-led, foreign direct investment path. This involved a mass privatization programme (1994–7) with substantial input from foreign investors. In its scope and speed the privatization was regionally unrivalled and some even say globally unsurpassed. According to Sander Thoenes (1996) in an article entitled 'Kazakhstan's sale of the century', '[s]peed differentiates Kazakhstan's privatization more than anything. One company asked a consultancy to submit a proposal for a three-week legal and commercial investigation for a bid. Two days later the consultancy found that the company had already won the bid'. In addition to the establishment of four major banks and the consolidation of the large Samruk-Kazyna conglomerate, the government continues to press for better terms with foreign companies, as they relate to both taxation and stakeholder percentages. The 2010–14 programme also pressed for industrial diversification.

Kyrgyzstan's reforms were enacted differently and in a different context. In 1999 President Akaev wrote that 'the most recent liberal reform was the amendment to the constitution introducing private ownership of land' (Goskominvest/UNDP 1999). In the absence of comparable hydrocarbons to offer potential foreign investors, the Kyrgyz government in the 1990s liberalized the economy as part of a conditionality package for further economic aid by the Bretton Woods institutions. In line with World Bank recommendations, for example, the regime economically decentralized, making regions financially responsible and somewhat autonomous of the centre. 'In foreign trade liberalization efforts, Kyrgyzstan's record of achievement has been unmatched' (Gleason 2001: 173).

In the midst of civil war, Tajikistan's early economic reform efforts were overshadowed by questions of existential security. Gleason (2001: 174) says that it 'is probable that Tajikistan would have moved decisively in the direction of structural reform initially if the country had not fallen prey to an internal contest for power in the first years of independence' and already by 'March 1992, the Tajikistan parliament had approved land reform legislation'. Price liberalization had taken place soon after Soviet collapse. In all aspects, Tajikistan's leaders were to introduce their economic reforms later, only establishing a national currency in 1995 for example. Since the 1997 peace agreement, the Tajik government has partly followed the international community's recommendations and remains reliant on international aid to tackle food supply issues, infrastructure and capacity-building. It is a three-prong process: improvement in legal infrastructure (1995–7); privatizing large-scale infrastructure (1998–2000); and, modernization of the economy (2001–3). In the early twenty–first century the leadership began to be in a position to think about its energy and mineral development but it did not set out to attract new economic partnerships in the same way as it did in the security sector (Chapters 5 and 7). Twenty years into independence the economy is based on foreign aid, subsistence agriculture, some barter agreements with neighbours and the commercial export of a few commodities.

Performances

In the mid-1990s some segments of Kazakhstan's and Kyrgyzstan's populations looked on enviously at their southern neighbours, wishing their governments also had taken reform more slowly and retained a larger role in their economies. In the Kyrgyz Republic particularly, the failure of reform to kick-start the economy or provide meaningful alternative economic benefits set in the beginnings of resentment by a population that market economies brought chaos and little else. These were also not just perceptions; by 2001 Uzbekistan was the first post-Soviet republic to regain its pre-1991 GDP level. Pomfret (2006: 25) refers to this performance 'puzzle' as 'one of the most enigmatic of the thirty-plus economies in transition'. Gradualism thus 'did not mean no change' (Pomfret 2000: 734). Similarly Anders Aslund (2003: 75) remarked that '[f]or years, the state-controlled Uzbek economy attracted attention because of its limited output decline'. Stuart Horsman (2003: 47, 55) by contrast writes that 'the "gradualist" agenda is simply a pretence for the continuation of the status quo, avoids expedient reform and masks stagnation' and that the 1990s was a period of 'economic inertia'.

Pomfret (2006) subsequently argued that however much of a puzzle in the 1990s the ever-tightening control, particularly its introduction of exchange controls between 1996 and 2003, was not going to be sustainable. According to the Economist Intelligence Unit (2011 – EIU Uzbekistan Country Report March 2011: 14), the subsequent dual exchange rate policy has presented its own disincentives for foreign investors and possibilities for corruption. Already in this short period, Uzbekistan has had cycles of reform and non-reform. Brad McAllister and Julie Khersonsky (2007: 449) warned that 'current indicators suggest that Uzbekistan needs to begin shifting to export-oriented development in order to head off economic and ecological deterioration that would destabilize an already economically depressed region and augment the ranks of terrorist organizations'.

As a result of the dual exchange rate policy, foreign investors are often denied immediate access to hard currency. Also, firms with government connections can cheat by importing goods at the official rate and selling at the black market rate, converting back into hard currency the local currency they receive (EIU Uzbekistan Country Report March 2011: 14). Peter Craumer (1995: 44), moreover, argues: 'Farms have been superficially transformed, but without any structural change; life for the farmers goes on much as before'. Pomfret (2000: 733) concludes that Uzbekistan's experience ultimately 'sheds little light on a debate framed in terms of rapid reform versus gradualism'.

On Turkmenistan, Gleason's opinion (2003: 115) is that '[N]one of these goals of Positive Neutrality were achieved by the end of the first decade of independence'. Some analysts say that as much as 90 per cent of economic activity by 2003 continued to be under the direct or indirect control of the government. Aslund (2003: 75): 'Turkmenistan's economy is erratic: in 1999 and 2000 it enjoyed record growth of 17 percent per year and official growth rates continue to be more than 10 percent a year. This increase was caused by Russia's repeal of its previous commercial embargo against Turkmenistan's exports, which allowed the country to export its abundant natural gas to Russia through its pipeline system, as Russia's own gas production has proven insufficient'.

The other extreme of economic liberalization did not seem to have led to better economic performance either; even if the Kyrgyz republic was the first Central Asian economy to bring down hyperinflation and in 1998 became the first Soviet republic to accede to the World Trade Organization (WTO) few seemed to experience the economic benefits of either.

The unmitigated success story has been Kazakhstan. In 2008 Kazakhstan's GDP had become 'almost two-thirds that of the entire Central Asian region' (Dave 2008: 57). Its Caspian offshore waters were also the site of the most significant new global oil discovery in recent years (Kashagan in 2000, commercially viable by 2002). The oil sector dominates the economy, accounting for 25 per cent of GDP, 65 per cent of total exports and 40 per cent of total budget revenues by 2011. In the twenty-first century Kazakhstan is experiencing an oil-led boom and its economic growth is far outpacing other Central Asian economies. By 2002 the US government had already designated Kazakhstan a market economy. Kazakhstan has become the only regional investor and also the only magnet for labour migrants. In Uzbekistan, Kyrgyzstan and Tajikistan remittances from migrant labourers, largely to Russia, account for between 8 and 50 per cent of the legal national income (Marat 2009).

Pathways

Four main explanations have dominated the discussions that have led to these policy choices and performances. The varying pathways along which the five republics have travelled are the result of differences in their leadership, their initial starting points, the interplay of economics and politics as reforms have been undertaken, and resource endowments.

Given their preponderance in the system, presidents have been held to account for their countries' major economic policy directions. Thus, Akaev's preparedness for risk-taking and his gamble that his resource-poor country needed to attract, above all, foreign aid was pivotal in the country's early economic liberalization. Or, again, Niyazov's conservatism influenced his country's gradualism and isolationism. Sixty per cent of the country's GDP was in Niyazov's personal Foreign Exchange Reserve Fund (Bohr 2003: 15). Nazarbaev is the only post-Soviet president to have had an advisor who has been tried for corruption abroad. Karimov's national ideology and proclivity to strong control tally with his country's practices of autarchy and import substitution. Gleason (2001: 178): 'In Uzbekistan the political leadership played the key role in the determination of policy'. On Sub-saharan Africa Robert Bates (1981: 3) asked: 'Why should reasonable men adopt public policies that have harmful consequences for the societies they govern?' The more the policy system became personalized and de-institutionalized, the greater the harm, it seemed, on economic policy and performance. On Tajikistan Rafis Abazov (2003: 66) writes that the 'consequences of the civil war, however, offer only a partial explanation for the country's economic difficulties. The government's inability to conduct major macro-economic reforms, encourage private entrepreneurship and attract direct foreign investments have all contributed significantly to Tajikistan's failure to achieve full economic recovery and boost productivity'.

Initial starting points and broader security environments also framed economic reform choices and their fates. Possessing on independence the third largest nuclear weapons arsenal in the world, Kazakhstan, at an early stage, benefitted from substantial Western interest. Gleason (2001: 169) writes: 'Uzbekistan and Tajikistan, however, inherited the legacies of lawlessness and underdevelopment that resulted from a decade long civil war in Afghanistan'. The Alma-Ata declaration of 1991 legally ended the USSR and established the community, 'Commonwealth of Independent States' (CIS); 'Kazakhstan was thus symbolically the resting place of communism and the birthplace of the post-communist order' (Gleason 2001: 171). In these early years, the Kyrgyz republic was less concerned than Kazakhstan about security issues which only really began to be of importance with the Batken events of 1999 (Chapter 7). Turkmenistan's inglorious isolationism helped it to pursue its gradualism (Cummings and Ochs 2002).

While all sharing the Soviet experience, these countries' different economic starting points seem to have mattered in both policy choices and subsequent trajectories. GDP levels in 1991 seem to have mattered, with the two poorest remaining the two poorest in 2011. Notably Tajikistan, by 2000, with a national income per capita of $180, was poorer than most of sub-Saharan Africa or the poorest countries of Asia. Kyrgyzstan and Tajikistan were also resource-poor and landlocked, and a significant percentage of the better-educated were from ethnic groups who were likely to emigrate. But at the same time structural factors cannot present the whole picture. Uzbekistan's economy was more diversified on independence and yet its performance levels were not on a par with Kazakhstan's, whose Soviet experience had been primarily one of extraction rather than industrialization or diversification. Kazakhstan remained linked to the former Soviet Union's centralized energy grid, making Kazakhstan's northern factories and cities dependent upon Russian energy supplies.

As reform has proceeded, it has existed in mutual symbiosis with broader political and legal reform. Pamela Blackmon (2007: 367) puts Kazakhstan's success down to its good laws and banking reform: 'While the Kazakh government implemented this type of legislative framework to encourage outside investment and business, the Uzbek government did not'. In reverse, economic reform has strengthened political authoritarianism. Patron–client relations and patronage systems have co-opted opposition members and ensured loyal clients. Despite quite different reform strategies and performances, Asel Rustemova (2011) points out, the effect in Kazakhstan and Uzbekistan has been the same. Both systems have encouraged the preservation of the status quo: in Kazakhstan foreign investors and small- and medium-sized enterprises (SMEs) with a degree of independence and in Uzbekistan where state financing dominates, business elites also support the incumbent regimes. But these regimes are different and, since this so-called 'varieties of capitalism' approach 'does not theorize the economy behind these practices', she promotes the notion 'governmentality' to explain the influence of Kazakh managerialism versus Uzbek paternalism in ensuring these outcomes. Martin Spechler (2007) shows correlation between economic reform and improved human rights. However the relationship is viewed, in none of the Central Asian economies has there been a notable bifurcation of political and economic elites.

The Kyrgyz Republic seems to provide a powerful example of a country where political and institutional reform failed to keep up with economic reform. 'The general problem in the 1990s was the lack of preparedness for the transition to a market economy' (Pomfret 2006: 77). If the political system does not produce institutions that support a fledgling economy then the economy cannot sustain itself. 'Were it not for foreign aid, Kyrgyzstan's domestic reform efforts might not have been politically sustainable' (Gleason 2001: 174). As noted in Chapter 4, this was an argument formulated back in 1968 by Samuel Huntington in *Political Order of Changing Societies* when he spoke about institutional decay and the praetorian politics that resulted. The Kyrgyz state in the 1990s was increasingly torn between two tendencies: reformist and rent-seeking. By the close of the first decade of the twenty-first century, the Kyrgyz state had become almost nothing about reform and almost everything about stagnation and corruption. Writing on agricultural restructuring, Malcolm Childress (2003: 139) concludes that the Kyrgyz '[g]overnment has not adjusted itself to the role of a regulator and promoter of private sector activity. Instead it plays a role which sometimes competes with the private sector, and far too regularly uses state authority to skim off rents from private activity'. Economic growth is 96.3 per cent the level of 1990 (Kudabaev 2009a), and 'privatization of state power' has been 'the main cause of failure of all the [economic] reforms' (Kudabaev 2009b).

Fourth, and finally, initial reform choices and trajectories relate to these countries' resource endowments. For some writers the link is general. Thus, the poorly endowed Kyrgyz Republic sought to compensate by attracting foreign aid and interest through a liberal reform programme. The Tajik economy's reliance on its Tursunzade aluminium factory and hydro-electric plants has encouraged its governments to seek investment in those two sectors, a path followed by the Kyrgyz Republic in gold and hydro-plants once the liberal economic reform project was perceived to have failed. The significant hydro-carbon reserves of the remaining three have encouraged policies that either boost these countries' interdependence or dependence.

How exactly resources matter and with what effect is, however, disputed. For Jones Luong and Weinthal (2010: 367) the oil-resource rich countries of Kazakhstan, Turkmenistan and Uzbekistan did not restructure their industries in the same way and the divergences were a factor of two things: '(a) the availability of alternative sources of export revenue and (b) the level of political contestation. Where leaders enjoy a high degree of access to alternative export revenue and a low level of contestation, they choose to nationalize their energy sector and to minimize international involvement'. While both Turkmenistan and Uzbekistan also inherited an alternative source of export revenues to the energy sector – cotton – Kazakhstan did not. While the former's governments faced few potential contestants for power and ideology since they were less multi-ethnic and more centralized, Kazakhstan's government was faced with a polity in which titular Kazakhs were outnumbered by minorities and where effective power was more regionally decentralized (Chapter 4). Thus, Turkmenistan and Uzbekistan, both less reliant on the international community, could afford to nationalize industries and consolidate. By contrast, the attraction of foreign investors in Kazakhstan's case 'provided the necessary means to bolster the position of regional leaders as well as to address the demands of potent nationalist groups' (Jones Luong and Weinthal 2010: 387). The authors conclude that Kazakhstan's elite 'initially chose privatization not because they considered this a better long-term economic strategy but because the transfer of ownership provided them with the means to alter the status quo distribution of resources to either incorporate or counter rivals to their preferred power base' (Jones Luong and Weinthal 2010: 394). Through a careful mix and balancing of international, corporatist, informal and regional networks, the Kazakh political elite thus still managed to keep control over its economic resources (Cummings 2005; Ostrowski 2010).

While resources give countries leverage domestically and internationally, their effects on economic performance and political transformations have often been couched negatively. A so-called 'resource curse' (Karl 1997) is traced which leads to economic problems such as the Dutch disease effect or the political challenge of emerging rentier states. As rents (income) from resources flow into the economies the exchange rate rises and economies are overheated. Kutan and Wyzan (2005) find evidence of Kazakhstan's foreign exchange rates showing such a Dutch disease effect. Resources 'curse' countries into a dependent trajectory of similarities in 'property rights, tax structures, vested interests, economic models, and thus frameworks for decision making across different governments and regime types' (Karl 1997: 227). Overreliance on the resource sector leads to unbalanced growth with little diversification: light industries are not developed, an indigenous bourgeoisie that might develop the SME sector is kept tightly in check and agriculture in still often largely rural economies is sorely neglected. In the process, income is used to enrich elites and sustain authoritarian regimes by giving money to buy off oppositional elites and keeping alive elaborate patron–client networks.

Wojciech Ostrowski (2011) traces such path dependency for all five Central Asian states by expanding the term to include 'semi-rentiers without oil' (Beblawi 1987: 59). In this he incorporates, for example, income from illegal commodities such as drugs along with the remittances earned by migrant workers abroad. As these remittances only in part, however, go to the state, Giancomo Luciani (1990) argues these are therefore semi-rentier economies. For the conventionally regarded full rentier states of Kazakhstan, Tajikistan and Turkmenistan, Ostrowski marks a direct correlation between pre-Soviet and post-Soviet patronage networks and external income from the sale of hydrocarbons as providing the necessary finance to maintain those networks. According to a report by the International Crisis Group, money obtained from the sale of cotton circulates within a small elite, and rarely, if ever, enters the agricultural financing system: '[o]ne estimate is that as little as 10 to 15 per cent of the income generated by the sale of cotton goes back into agriculture thus to the farmers' (ICG 2004: 4–5).

Jones Luong and Weinthal (2010), by contrast, argue that there is nothing inevitable about the effects of oil on a country's economic and political performance. Key intervening variables are ownership structure, source of rents and policies enacted. Thus, to follow on from their findings above, they (2010: 261) conclude that 'Kazakhstan has managed both to redistribute the benefits of foreign investment from the petroleum-rich to the petroleum-poor regions and to institutionalize limits on expenditures that has at least created the possibility for the government to make better spending decisions'. Furthermore if Turkmenistan and Uzbekistan both decided to keep oil and gas in state hands, their different policies have had quite different impacts. While Turkmenistan 'launched an ambitious ten-year development plan in 1993 which was designed to achieve the country's potential as a "second Kuwait" as quickly as possible' (Auty 1997: 30), 'Uzbekistan', write Jones Luong and Weinthal (2010: 79, 81):

> did not. In sharp contrast to Turkmenistan, in the early 1990s Uzbekistan focused its efforts on self-sufficiency in energy, which it achieved by 1995, prioritized oil and gas production from existing fields, alongside the increased use of hydropower, to satisfy internal demand, and sought international financing to build or upgrade local refineries rather than to discover and exploit new reserves

and its decision 'to consume rather than to export its petroleum wealth has neither engendered positive socioeconomic outcomes in the short term nor improved its long-term development prospects'. Max Spoor (2005: 54–5) in relation to Uzbekistan's 'white gold' also does not see its cotton necessarily as a curse, having helped 'to avoid the dramatic contraction' experienced elsewhere in the FSU, and 'that the cotton crop can (with necessary and appropriate institutional reforms) become the engine of agroindustry-led growth and development'.

In a broader discussion about the absence of an inevitable link between resources and development Tunçer-Kilavuz (2011 264–5) takes issue with the economic grievance argument behind the Tajik civil war, suggesting that the 'economic indicators were also very similar in Uzbekistan and Tajikistan, and both were heavily subsidized by the Centre'. Instead it is important 'to study the adversaries' perceptions of power in relation to the actions that led to the civil war and how the perceptions of the distribution of power are influenced by structural, process and network-related variables'. Earlier the same author (2009b: 693), concentrating on the 'how' rather than 'why' of Tajik civil war, suggested that 'the mechanisms of network activation by the elites, together with the establishment of local militias and their involvement in the war through the activation of violence specialists, were important factors in bringing about the eruption of violence'. Atkin (1997) has also emphasized how stability in the Soviet era had been aided by a careful balancing of different regions in personnel policy.

The international political economy of Central Asia and the new Great Game

These actors in Tajikistan, like their Central Asian counterparts, now negotiate their economies in a broader, globalized world. On the one hand, they are variously able to influence the terms of foreign investor engagement and choose those partnerships and regional and international organizations that they assess as best suiting their political and economic goals. On the other hand, as peripheral, landlocked and economically highly dependent states they are beholden to the forces of globalized markets and the interests of outside players who may compete or collaborate in the provision of economic infrastructure, agreements and norms.

Central Asia's economic potential continues to be strongly shaped by its geography. Geography would appear to offer huge incentives to Central Asian states to co-operate among themselves. Uzbekistan is one of a few landlocked countries in the world to be bordered by countries that in every case are themselves landlocked. Kazakhstan, also landlocked, is positioned between two great powers and Turkmenistan has the region's longest border with the Greater Middle East. Furthermore, two major natural resources, water and fossil fuels, are distributed in such a way as to make co-operation potentially mutually beneficial, particularly in the form of water and fossil fuel swaps, and 'Central Asian borders do not represent "natural" jurisdictions if one bears in mind that the area's natural resources are inherently international' (Gleason 2001: 1091).

Despite sharing these challenges of geography, Central Asian countries have, among themselves, failed to co-operate economically, a point we also encounter in the realm of security (Chapter 7). This is not for want of trying. Uzbekistan, Kazakhstan and Kyrgyzstan formed the Central Asian Union (CAU) in 1994 with a view to forming a 'common economic area' (Ushakova 2001), with Tajikistan joining in 1998 (Uzbekistan having effectively vetoed this previously). Turkmenistan consistently declined invitations to join the CAU. In 1998 the CAU acquired a new name of Central Asian Economic Union (CAEU) and then in 2001, the Central Asian Cooperation Organization (CACO). In reality, however, the organization 'has not come close to harmonizing customs, taxation or anti-dumping policies. An interstate system of payments has not been created, no mechanism for the resolution of disputes exists, and no efficient mode of compensation from gainers to losers has been formulated' (Bohr 2004: 487). By 2004, member states were trading only 4 per cent among each other, compared to 15.6 per cent some 10 years previously (Ushakova 2003: 122). Instead, national protectionism has defined CACO interstate practice encouraging discussions about the viability of such co-operation, or how leaders and people imagined the region, or the degree to which they were committed to it.

The specific examples of electricity and water further illustrate this 'virtual regionalism' (Bohr 2004; Allison 2008). The unified regional energy grid signed in August 2001 was 'rewarding lengthy international efforts to foster such cooperation' (Gleason 2001) but, it seemed, as the countries were left to themselves, less than a decade later the grid was severely compromised as Uzbekistan withdrew on 1 December 2009. This withdrawal provoked national responses by both Kyrgyzstan and Tajikistan to finish Soviet-era begun hydropower stations and to build new ones (Kambarata-1, 2 and Rogun, respectively). With regard to water, the Aral Sea Basin encompasses nearly all of Kyrgyzstan, Tajikistan, Turkmenistan and Uzbekistan, the southern Kazakhstani oblasts of Qyzylorda and Shymkent, and parts of Afghanistan and Iran (O'Hara 1998; Micklin 2000; Horsman 2001). The single biggest reason for the failure to co-operate on water is that 'certain states have much more interest in water management issues within the basin than others' (Micklin 2000: 3). Tajikistan and nearly all of Uzbekistan's territory are within the basin, compared with Turkmenistan (80 per cent), Kyrgyzstan (70 per cent), Kazakhstan (13 per cent) Afghanistan (40 per cent) and Iran (2 per cent). In the Soviet era, the All-Union Ministry of Water Resources based in Moscow had established water quotas for each republic (Dukhovny 2005). In return, the downstream states provided the upstream with gas, oil, coal and electricity. In February 1992 this was replaced by an Interstate Commission on Water Coordination (ICWC) [*Mezhgosudarstvennaya koordinatsionnaya vodokhozyaystvennaya komissiya*]. The two upstream states, Tajikistan and Kyrgyzstan, have complained, amongst other things, that although generating 80 per cent of the flow, they receive only a fraction of what is allocated to the three downstream states where 85 per cent of the irrigated lands are located (Yuldasheva, Hashimova and Callahan 2010). The upstream states have tried to increase the compensation they receive, Kyrgyzstan in 2008 even announcing its intention to sell water, some say a delayed reaction to Uzbekistan's reduction in natural gas deliveries to Kyrgyzstan, compounded by the severe winter of 2007–8 and also 2008's serious drought. Valentin Bogatyrev (2009) writes that 'the notion that Central Asia's water problems are transnational problems is simply an illusion given that one set of countries' interests are directly at odds with other countries'.

These examples underscore both domestic reasons for the absence of co-operation and how the involvement of external powers, at least temporarily, can assist economic co-operation. Quite apart from the asymmetries of power and the non-complementarity and frequent competitiveness of their goods (Green 2001; Spechler 2002), Central Asian countries are structured in such a way as to disfavour sharing. Intra-state co-operation is marred by individual states' frequent absence of trust in their neighbours' intentions (especially as young sovereign states), so states bandwagon against what they view as, for example, Uzbekistan's bid for regional hegemony. Domestic economic policies discourage trade (Spechler 1999; Gleason 2001). The 'vested interests' associated with presidential neo-patrimonialism (Chapter 4) 'have opposed economic regionalism that would threaten their personal and family fortunes or their clients' economic interests' (Collins 2009: 267).

By contrast, the involvement of external powers has shown how, at least temporarily, these problems can be mitigated. The management of water resources is a case in point. Weinthal (2002: 35) argues that in the Soviet era '[b]ecause Moscow was able to mitigate conflicts among the Central Asian republics over water, and hence act as a mediator, Moscow solved the problem of collective action among the Central Asian states'. Under the specific conditions of transformation, these dynamics are altered as both domestic and international conditions are changing and highly dependent on each other. This creates its own paradoxes since, continues Weinthal (2002: 218) '[t]he international community replaced Moscow as a supplier of resources without being able to meet its objective of environmental protection in addition to regional cooperation'.

Central Asian countries have, furthermore, joined alternative economic groupings, the involvement of powers outside of the five countries again seeming to improve co-operation chances. In 1995 Kazakhstan, Russia and Belarus signed an agreement on the formation of a CIS customs union, which was subsequently joined by Kyrgyzstan (1996) and Tajikistan (1999), and refashioned in October 2000 into the Eurasian Economic Community (EAEC). As OSCE chair, Kazakhstan emphasized security and co-operation over human rights and democracy. It was able to play a role in formulating ideas for peace brokership of Caucasus conflicts at the OSCE summit meeting in December 2010. In the same year, Kazakhstan, Belarus and Russia launched the Single Economic Space and their Customs Union. The EAEC and tripartite Customs Union seem to have been altogether more successful at realizing their goals. Bohr (2004: 492) suggests this represented 'the gravitation of the centre of regionalism in Central Asia to the north'.

The politics of on the one hand domestic, and on the other international, economics thus influence each other. In addition to the sorts of domestic structural forces elaborated on in the previous section, as a landlocked state, it is in Kazakhstan's interest to conduct friendly relations with its contiguous neighbours of which two, Russia and China, are great powers. But rather than depending on one or the other or even both, Kazakhstan, in line with its multi-vector foreign policy, has also sought new partners further afield, notably in the Middle East

Table 6.1 Economic organizations in Central Asia

Organization	Kazakhstan	Kyrgyzstan	Tajikistan	Turkmenistan	Uzbekistan	Description
ADB	x	x	x	x	x	To promote regional economic co-operation
EAEC	x	x	x			To create a common economic and energy policy
EBRD	x	x	x	x	x	To facilitate the transition of seven centrally planned economies in Europe (Bulgaria, former Czechoslovakia, Hungary, Poland, Romania, former USSR and former Yugoslavia) to market economies by committing 60% of its loans to privatization
ECO	x	x	x	x	x	To promote regional cooperation in trade, transportation, communications, tourism, cultural affairs and economic development
FAO	x	x	x	x	x	To raise living standards and increase availability of agricultural products; a UN specialized agency
G-77	x		x	x		To promote economic co-operation among developing countries; name persists in spite of increased membership
GCTU	x	x	x			To consolidate trade union actions to protect citizens' social and labor rights and interests, to help secure trade unions' rights and guarantees, and to strengthen international trade union solidarity
IBRD	x	x	x	x	x	To provide economic development loans; a UN specialized agency
IDA	x	x	x	x	x	To provide economic loans for low-income countries; UN specialized agency and IBRD affiliate

Continued

Table 6.1 Cont'd

Organization	Kazakhstan	Kyrgyzstan	Tajikistan	Turkmenistan	Uzbekistan	Description
IDB	x	x	x	x	x	To promote Islamic economic aid and social development
IFAD	x	x	x			To promote agricultural development; a UN specialized agency
IFC	x	x	x	x	x	To support private enterprise in international economic development; a UN specialized agency and IBRD affiliate
ILO	x	x	x	x	x	To deal with world labour issues; a UN specialized agency
IMF	x	x	x	x	x	To promote world monetary stability and economic development; a UN specialized agency
ISO	x	correspondent	correspondent	correspondent	x	To promote the development of international standards with a view to facilitating international exchange of goods and services and to developing co-operation in the sphere of intellectual, scientific, technological and economic activity
ITSO	x	x	x		x	To act as a watchdog over Intelsat, Ltd., a private company, to make sure it provides on a global and non-discriminatory basis public telecommunication services
ITU	x	x	x	x	x	To deal with world telecommunications issues; a UN specialized agency

Continued

Table 6.1 Cont'd

Organization	Kazakhstan	Kyrgyzstan	Tajikistan	Turkmenistan	Uzbekistan	Description
MIGA	x	x	x	x	x	Encourages flow of foreign direct investment among member countries by offering investment insurance, consultation, and negotiation on conditions for foreign investment and technical assistance; a UN specialized agency
UNCTAD	x	x	x	x	x	To promote international trade
UNIDO	x	x	x	x	x	UN specialized agency that promotes industrial development especially among the members
UNWTO	x	x	x	x	x	To promote tourism as a means of contributing to economic development, international understanding and peace
WCO	x	x	x	x	x	To promote international co-operation in customs matters
WFTU	x	x	x	x	x	To promote the trade union movement
WIPO	x	x	x	x	x	To furnish protection for literary, artistic and scientific works; a UN specialized agency
WTO	observer	x	observer		observer	To provide a forum to resolve trade conflicts between members and to carry on negotiations with the goal of further lowering and/or eliminating tariffs and other trade barriers

Source: (2011) *The World Factbook*, Washington, DC: Central Intelligence Agency

and the West. As in domestic politics, Kazakhstan's foreign policy has been multifaceted, straddling various interests, its direction devoid of strong ideological content. In April 2007 Nazarbaev reiterated that 'pure pragmatism' drives foreign policy decision-making. By contrast, Turkmenistan's policy of positive neutrality has coexisted with aims of regime security and engagement with Russia (Anceschi 2008). Kyrgyzstan's initial embracing of the Washington Consensus enabled it to join the WTO in 1998 and its subsequent derailing from that path propelled it to seek economic answers more through bilateral relations and economic groupings that involve China and Russia.

The new Great Game

Russia, indeed, remains central in its role and overall influence in the region. By way of a bridge to the book's penultimate chapter, we ask whether outside economic interest in this region, popularly referred to as the new Great Game, has overall stabilized or destabilized these countries' emerging statehoods. On the latter, recall the point made that the nineteenth century game over territory has been replaced by many authors with a great game over oil (Chapter 1) and that its fundamentals affect security architectures and provision (Chapter 6).

The possession of oil and gas, and access to water resources, continue to be viewed as essential to state power in Central Asia. The Soviet period developed a successful water management/distribution system which collapsed with independence. The question for this chapter becomes whether resources have become a source of intra-state animosity and we can say that both gas and water have been used as tool for intra-state posturing. For example, southern electricity grids tie Uzbekistan to southern Kazakhstan and Kyrgyzstan and the Uzbekistani elite has used its power over these resources to cajole neighbouring states. Resources have increased regional tensions but fallen short of provoking outright conflict.

The extent of the Caspian basin's reserve base is still unknown in that the era of post-Soviet exploration is only just starting. Writing at the beginning of the twenty-first century, John Roberts (2003) estimates the Caspian region as having 7–10 per cent of world-proven gas and 4–6 per cent of world-proven oil reserves. He also writes that international production has been focused on the further development of three existing giant reserves (Tengiz and Karachaganak in western Kazakhstan alongside the Azeri-Chirag-Guneshli complex) and two new ones (Kashagan in 2000, declared commercially viable in 2002 and Shakh Deniz off Azerbaijan).

In a landlocked region transport is key to the successful development and export of these hydrocarbons. Rosemary Forsythe (1996: 44) writes that '[g]etting Caspian oil out of the region and into the international markets is a key issue that will ultimately deeply affect the political and economic fate of the countries concerned'. In regional and outside actors' attempts to diversify routes

Table 6.2 Hydrocarbon resources in Central Asia

Country/Region	Oil (thousand million barrels)	Share of total (%)	Gas (trillion cubic metres)	Share of total (%)
Africa	132.1	9.50	14.7	7.90
Asia Pacific	45.2	3.30	16.2	8.70
Europe and Eurasia	139.7	10.10	63.1	33.70
Middle East	752.5	54.40	75.8	40.50
North America	74.3	5.40	9.9	5.30
South and Central America	239.4	17.30	7.4	4.00
Kazakhstan	39.8	2.90	1.8	1.00
Turkmenistan	0.6	insignificant	8	4.30
Uzbekistan	0.6	insignificant	1.6	0.80

Source: BP Statistical Review of World Energy June 2011: *BP* avaliable at: http://www.bp.com/ statisticalreview (last accessed on 06-Dec-2011).

away from Russia, various pipelines have been developed or planned in these first independence years, and Map 1 provides a status summary.

As part of its continued 'pure pragmatism', in March 2009 Kazakhstan insisted on a controlling stake in a new venture designed to funnel oil into the Baku-Tbilisi-Ceyhan route (BTC), and the precise percentage – the Kazakhs not accepting below 51 per cent – being disputed with foreigners. The opening of a new route in late 2005 to the People's Republic of China and some shipment through Azerbaijan have increased export opportunities, and Kazakhstan continues to embrace all pipeline routes with pragmatism. The strong rise in commodity prices in 2010 allowed the Eurasia region's hydrocarbon-rich states to emerge from the global economic slowdown. Like his Kazakh counterpart, Berdymukhamedov has sought to diversify Turkmenistan's economic partners notably after the halting of gas exports to Russia during most of 2009. 'China started importing Turkmen gas through the new Central Asia-China gas pipeline in late 2009, with levels set to rise in 2011–12, and Iran is also expected to increase its purchases' (EIU January 2011: 9).

In addition to the challenges of these old and new routes, the Caspian continues to throw up legal questions around its status. In greatly simplified and diluted terms, the Soviet Ministry of Oil Industry in 1970 divided the Soviet part of the sea according to the median line principle, in which the four Caspian Union republics (Kazakhstan, Russia, Azerbaijan and Turkmenistan) were granted the right to develop fields in their own sectors (Kondaurova 2008). Upon independence, Iran has pressed for a different view that instead gives everyone, including itself, 20 per cent in a condominium arrangement. Azerbaijan, Kazakhstan and Russia have consistently pressed for continuation of the median line principle.

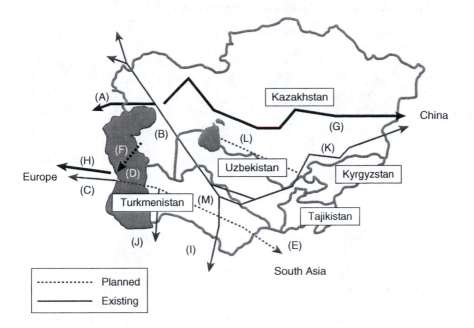

Map 2 Major pipelines in Central Asia, existing and planned, with oil pipelines in thick lines
and gas pipelines in thin lines: (A) the Caspian Pipeline Consortium, which connects the Tengiz oil field in Kazakhstan to Novorossiysk, Russia on the Black Sea;
(B) the Central Asia-Center system (CAC), which begins in Turkmenistan
and carries gas to Russia; (C) the South Caucasus Pipeline (SCP) from
Azerbaijan to Turkey, which could possibly connect to the Nabucco pipeline
system from the Georgia/Turkey border to Austria or to other proposed pipelines
intended to carry Azerbaijani gas to Europe; (D) the proposed Trans Caspian Gas
Pipeline (TCGP) from Turkmenistan to Azerbaijan; (E) the proposed Turkmenistan-
Afghanistan-Pakistan-India (TAPI) gasline; (F) option for oil and/or gas pipeline
from Kazakhstan to Azerbaijan; (G) the Western Kazakhstan-Western China oil
pipeline, which connects China to the Caspian Sea; (H) the Baku-Tbilisi-Ceyhan
oil pipeline; (I) the Dauletabad-Sarakhs-Khangiran pipeline and (J) the Korpezhe-
Kurt Kui Pipeline, both of which carry gas from Turkmenistan to Iran; (K) the
Trans-Asia (sometimes 'Central Asia – China') Gas Pipeline, which primarily
carries Turkmen gas to China, although eventually Kazakhstan will connect into
the pipeline and become an export state along with its current 'transit state' status;
(L) Kazakh link to Trans-Asia Gas Pipeline; (M) Turkmenistan's East-West
Interconnector (EWI), construction of which has officially started and is due
to open in 2015, enabling gas produced almost anywhere in Turkmenistan to be
exported in any direction.

Sources: (2006) 'New export routes on stream', Petroleum Economist, 1 July,
available at: www.petroleum-economist.com/Article/2732864/New-export-routes-
on-stream.html
(2008)   'China, Turkmenistan: Natural Gas and Regional Geopolitics', *Stratfor*,
22 January.
(2009)   'China's President Hu Jintao opens Kazakh gas pipeline', BBC News,
13 December, available at: http://news.bbc.co.uk/2/hi/8410369.stm
(2010)   'Country Analysis Briefs: Kazakhstan', *Energy Information Administration*, available at: www.eia.gov/cabs/kazakhstan/pdf.pdf
(2011a) 'Energy Report: Turkmenistan', *IHS Global Insight*, 8 June.
(2011b) 'Energy Report: Kazakhstan', *IHS Global Insight*, 20 May.

What, finally, are the economic interests, successes and strategies of the three main great powers in the region, the US, China and Russia?

First, an observation on Table 6.3 below: one Central Asian country in this period has itself become a regional investor and also a magnet for migrant workers – Kazakhstan. In 2010, for example, the Kazakh-Tajik Private Equity Fund boasted $30m, promising a potential growth to as large as $80m, especially tapping into Tajikistan's hydroelectric power sector. The Kazakhstan Hong Kong Development Fund will focus on the oil and gas, minerals and related sectors, and Kazakhstan has become the Kyrgyz Republic's key trading partner and by the early twenty-first century effectively owned its banking sector.

While the US interest in Caspian energy predated September 11, some doubt the extent of US economic interest in the region. In his speech back in 1997, the Clinton administration's chief architect of policy toward the former Soviet Union, Deputy Secretary of State Strobe Talbott (1997), indicated plainly that the US was not interested in planting its flag in Central Asia as a player in another Great Game. The title of his speech was *Farewell to Flashman*, referring to a fictional character who had ostensibly played an active role in the Great Game. Jaffe and Manning (1998–99: 112, 129) argue that 'the notion that Central Asian and Caucasian oil can be the panacea to long-term energy security in the West is misguided' and that in the long term, 'the priority is Russia's transformation into a normal, modern actor in Eurasia. That is the real "Great Game"'. Similarly Menon (2003: 187) downplays the importance of Central Asian hydrocarbons for US involvement, even with multinationals becoming involved, 'Central Asia was hardly becoming critical to the American economy'.

The newest power is China. As a net importer of oil since 1993 it continues to increase its trade and economic ties with Caspian countries. China has become Kazakhstan's top importer and China is not far behind Russia in exports to Kazakhstan. Swanström writes (2005: 577, 578): 'Oil and gas have emerged as the most important *financial* reasons for China to engage with Central Asian states to the degree that it has done'. Also important 'is the strategic linkage China can establish with the Middle East through a network of pipelines, which is in place or planned through its Central Asian pipelines'.

Despite China's growing economic presence, the strong economic continuation of Russia as an erstwhile imperial power has surprised many. In Tajikistan's case the trade figures show that Russia remains this republic's primary importer and exporter. Atkin (2011: 317) has characterized this changed status as one from '*de facto* colony to sovereign dependency', with Tajikistan primarily dependent on Russia but also on the wider international community in a more general sense with regard to its foreign debt, which had by 2005 reached 40 per cent of its GDP. Similarly, the 2004 agreement with the Russian aluminium company RusAl was criticized for disproportionately increasing Russian influence in Tajikistan.

Russia remains the preponderant economic power in Central Asia, not only in terms of trade but in terms of the continuing, and increasing, soft power that attracts Central Asian workers as migrants. With few prospects at home, migrant workers have sought employment in Russia. As many as 1.5 million as of 2009

Table 6.3 Central Asia: major export and import partners

Central Asia, exports (1995 and 2009) in millions USD (top three and totals)

Exporter	Importer	1995	2009
Kazakhstan	China	297.0	5502.5
Kazakhstan	Germany	171.1	2785.2
Kazakhstan	Russian Federation	2365.8	2299.9
Kyrgyzstan	Switzerland	0.0	358.7
Kyrgyzstan	Russian Federation	114.3	335.0
Kyrgyzstan	Kazakhstan	112.5	162.6
Tajikistan	Netherlands	255.2	11.1
Tajikistan	Turkey	8.1	97.5
Tajikistan	Russian Federation	95.3	154.8
Turkmenistan	Ukraine	460.3	653.0
Turkmenistan	Hungary	n/a	197.8
Turkmenistan	Turkey	149.6	300.7
Uzbekistan	Russian Federation	807.9	695.1
Uzbekistan	Ukraine	89.5	1491.6
Uzbekistan	Turkey	14.6	375.5

Central Asia, imports (1995 and 2009) in millions USD (top three and totals)

Importer	Exporter	1995	2009
Kazakhstan	Russian Federation	1899.7	9214.3
Kazakhstan	China	34.7	8727.2
Kazakhstan	Germany	196.7	2139.6
Kyrgyzstan	China	27.4	3190.1
Kyrgyzstan	Russian Federation	104.8	1084.1
Kyrgyzstan	Kazakhstan	66.8	332.6
Tajikistan	Russian Federation	136.0	672.5
Tajikistan	China	0.4	667.9
Tajikistan	Kazakhstan	26.5	252.3
Turkmenistan	Russian Federation	95.8	1033.8
Turkmenistan	Turkey	160.4	1039.4
Turkmenistan	China	7.7	1140.8
Uzbekistan	Russian Federation	906.5	1966.0
Uzbekistan	China	52.3	1687.7
Uzbekistan	Korea	269.3	1080.3

Source: (2010) 'Country Tables: Key Indicators for Asia and the Pacific (2010)', *Asian Development Bank*, http://beta.adb.org/key-indicators/2011/country-tables (last accessed on 06-Dec-2011)

have been estimated for Tajikistan alone, 'a strikingly large number for a country with a total population of under seven million' (Atkin 2011: 316). Russia enjoys the upper hand through its deeper knowledge of the business environment and its willingness to take risks in that environment, and is a vast source of investment capital. Allison (2004b: 277) traces Putin's overall 'more practiced, hard-headed and effective Russian policy in the Central Asian and Caspian regions since at least summer 2002'.

There is growing competition between Russia and China but as Niklasson (2008: 33) writes they use different strategic methods:

> China takes on the role of the major consumer and rapidly needs to find reliable partners for energy support to its booming economy. Russia wishes to control existing and new reserves of energy through both economic and geopolitical leverage, including pipeline systems with the continued possibility for energy to be transferred and exported from Russia to Europe.

Lutz Kleveman (2004: 8) asks: 'Is there a link between the quest for Caspian oil and the war on terror in Central Asia?' Some of the preceding has pointed to how outside powers have sometimes collaborated as well as competed in attempts to provide economic security. We can define the pursuit of economic security itself as safeguarding the structural integrity and prosperity-generating capabilities and interests of a politico-economic entity (for example, a nation state) in the context of the various externalized risks and threats that confront it in the international economic system. John Oneal and Bruce Russett (1999) declared that 'the classical liberals were right' in their study of the record in the post-war period. Can the economy become the new socializing experience in the FSU, many similarly ask. The Kyrgyz experience shows how in the context of prior fusion of economy and polity (communism), ignoring the political or depoliticizing the economy is not only flawed but impossible. The pursuit of economic security broadly determines how a nation state or other state-like define their foreign-economic-policy (FEP) objectives, and in the final chapter we look at the broader security setting in which such objectives are made.

7   Securing Central Asia

Introduction

Ask an onlooker of Central Asian affairs to name ten key security challenges that have confronted the region since independence and they are likely to include (in no particular order of importance): population density, land claims and possible irredentism in the Ferghana Valley; the Tajik civil war (1992–7) and post-conflict resolution; regime collapse in Kyrgyzstan (2005 and 2010); interethnic peace (explaining as much how violence was avoided, such as between Russians and Kazakhs in Kazakhstan as where violence has tragically occurred, such as in Kyrgyzstan's Osh/Jalalabad in 2010); environmental degradation; terrorism and extremism; drugs and people trafficking; nuclear and biological weapons; government repression; and, to refer back to Kleveman (2004), the intense competition between outside actors to gain access to Central Asia's massive energy reserves.

This chapter addresses the nature of the broader security threats to the region and the place of Central Asia in a larger international security order. The types of threat listed above are not by any means all specific to this region. At the same time we need to know what, if anything, is specific about Central Asian security. Neorealists, for example, based on their view of security as state to state interactions and relationships, argue that (in)security is fundamentally the same everywhere. A quick caveat, however: the chapter places various authors in particular theoretical camps but these authors may not necessarily agree with how they have been classified. This classification is intended to convey the riot of colours that now inform our understanding of the region's international security dynamics.

What is security?

The concept of security is much debated by both empirical and theoretical observers of the region. Definitions, as we shall see, are very much dependent on what an author thinks are the core values or referents to be secured, as well as the epistemological and ontological assumptions of their enquiry. The deepening of the security agenda, which we explore at the end of this chapter, has further complicated definitions, as exemplified by the contribution of critical theorist Ken Booth (1991: 319) who argues that 'Emancipation, not power or order, produces true security. Emancipation, theoretically, is security'.

While a contested term, security is often defined as the absence of fear that acquired values will be attacked (see e.g., Wolfers 1962: 150). Core values can refer to 'the quality of life for the inhabitants of the state' and this can appear to be threatened if something significantly narrows 'the range of policy choices available to the government of a state or to private ... actors' (Ullman 1983: 33). In the 1990s both the nature of threats and whom they affect have been broadened to include new issues and referents. Simon Dalby (2002) explains this evolution as a direct consequence of the end of the Cold War and the emergence of new dangers in a now unipolar world.

Simultaneously, security has been broadened and the referents expanded (Buzan 1991; Buzan and Wæver 2003). Previously, security threats were directed against the state, and the state is and should be about security; consequently the emphasis was on military and political means. Buzan (1991) defines threats to states in three senses: to the idea of the state (nationalism); to the physical base of the state (population and resources); and to the institutional expression of the state (political system). In the realist framework (below), societies and regimes are written about in terms of how they affect the state and national interest, 'defined foremost as upholding the physical, territorial integrity of the state against external military attack, but in reality often involving protection against internal fragmentation or challenge to the ruling elite' (Thomas 2000: 247). This consensus has now gone. As Brian Job (2004: 5) explains:

> In principle, four or more distinct securities may be at issue simultaneously: the security of the individual citizen, the security of the nation, the security of the regime, and the security of the state. For a society composed of communal groups, with distinctive ethnic or religious identifications, their perceived securities may also be at stake, making the interplay and competition among the various players even more complex and unresolvable.

An analytical expansion of the security agenda is profoundly apposite for post-independent Central Asia. For Weisbrode (2000: 62) non-traditional trump traditional threats, since '[t]he real state of affairs in Central Asia is not one of rival imperial interests. It has more to do with banditry, territorial or socio-economic dislocation and relatively small-scale contests for land and resources'. Niklas Swanström (2010: 36) argues that a new challenge faced 'is the intellectual separation between hard and soft security threats; a separation which has been almost total and in too many ways, artificial ... there has also been a failure to understand how traditional and non-traditional security threats overlap, and in many ways, reinforce each other'. Three non-traditional threats are discussed here: terrorist groupings; transnational criminal and drugs trafficking groups; and the depletion of and competition over resources and the environment.

Terrorism

Threats of international terrorism are often automatically associated with the region of Central Asia but instead they need to be placed in the broader context of politics, international and domestic. International terrorist groups such as al-Qa'ida and the safe haven of Afghanistan carry far-reaching international security implications but for a bordering region like Central Asia these threats become immediate. Afghanistan consists of 27 per cent of Tajiks, 9 per cent of Uzbeks and 3 per cent of Turkmen, and for Jonson (2006: 42) the country was a key reason behind the outbreak of the Tajik civil war, 'which provided inspiration and later weapons and a safe haven for the opposition fighters'. Operation Enduring Freedom (OEF) has internationalized the Afghan problem but if overall withdrawal of Western troops occurs, the country is perceived to be a Central Asian problem, which it might become. One particular spin-off and enabler of the Afghan problem has been the nurturing and transformation of a home-grown terrorism organization, the Islamic Movement of Uzbekistan, the IMU, which was declared around 1998 in Kabul but formed as a network essentially out of Uzbekistan with 'limited' goals of overthrow of the Uzbek government, and that had three training sites in Afghanistan: Rishkor (near Kabul), Kunduz and Mazar-i-Sharif. Some of their training procedures have become available for public scrutiny (Olcott and Babajanov 2003).

The emergence of the IMU prompted discussion about how serious a home-grown terrorist threat was becoming in Central Asia. Sub-state terrorists, as Paul Rogers (2008: 175) writes, 'can originate in very different societies and with highly variable motivations and underlying drivers'. He groups terrorist organizations into two loose types: a revolutionary movement seeking fundamental change in a state or society and often based on religious commitment versus a group seeking change for an identifiable community. Evidence suggests that the IMU at its strongest period was primarily an example of the latter. Growing out of the Islamic Renaissance Party and led by Tohir Yoldash and Juma Namangani, it split into the Adolat (Justice) Party in 1990. In 1992 Adolat was outlawed, the rest of the movement was evicted, and the leader of the 'more guerrilla-oriented and criminal part', Namangani, joining the United Tajik Opposition Forces as the Tajik civil war escalated in 1992. Meanwhile, Yoldash, who controlled 'the more religious part' (Cornell 2005: 632) looked to the Islamic world for support including from Osama Bin Laden whom he met in Kabul. Both leaders were seen as united in their goal to overthrow the Karimov regime.

In early 1999, a series of bomb explosions rocked the Uzbek capital Tashkent, injured hundreds and killed 16. President Karimov was reported to have narrowly escaped, although analysts regard this portrayal as exaggerated. The attacks intensified the debate over the IMU. Some speculated that Karimov himself engineered the blast to justify further crackdowns, and the IMU was publicly blamed but to date has still not claimed responsibility. Heathershaw and Megoran (2011) argue that Karimov's speech acts and repressive measures have fed a broader discourse of terror and insecurity. This discourse has fed popular and official perceptions of Central Asia. They have, as critical constructivists have done elsewhere (Doty 1993; Fierke 1998), set out to expose what Karin Fierke (1998) terms 'language games' and we explore this approach further below. It is a discourse that has been used also by elites within and outwith the region to maintain power or policies. Authors rightly point out that elites in the region have benefited from this representation. Stephen Blank (2010: 166) concludes that 'all the Central Asian governments have acted consistently upon the belief that all opposition to them is by definition Islamic, fundamentalist, and/or terrorist, and have therefore harshly repressed those phenomena whether that assessment is true or not'.

It is, however, hard to deny the destabilizing effects of the IMU's insurgencies in neighbouring Kyrgyzstan in the late 1990s. Having opposed the 1997 peace accords that ended the Tajik civil war, both Yoldash and Namangani decided to break with their former Tajik allies. Thereafter hundreds of IMU militants moved back into Tajikistan, in the Tavildara valley bordering Kyrgyzstan's section of the Ferghana valley. In August that same year, the IMU launched a first military incursion into the Batken region of Kyrgyzstan, catching the Kyrgyz military completely by surprise and prompting a mobilization of the Uzbek army. The relatively small IMU detachments took several villages and numerous hostages, including the commander of the Kyrgyz Interior Ministry Forces (Naumkin 2003). Namangani extracted a reported $2m ransom for four Japanese hostages, with assistance from and mediation by Kyrgyz parliamentarian and drug lord Bayaman Erkinbaev. This action was repeated in August 2000, estimates of between five and 100 men traversing the mountains separating Tajikistan and Kyrgyzstan, toward Batken and the Sokh (Tajik) and Vorukh (Uzbek) enclaves in Kyrgyzstan. Again, Namangani and followers eventually escaped to Afghanistan by helicopters belonging to the Tajik Ministry of Emergencies. These acts bore the hallmarks of terrorist organizations 'who employ violence designed to create extreme anxiety and/or fear-inducing effects in a target group larger than the immediate victims' (Wardlaw 1982: 16), and the aim still, it seemed, was to remove Karimov from power.

Namangani was reported killed when the IMU joined al-Qa'ida and Taliban forces defending Kunduz against the OEF and his death prompted further questions about how the organization would evolve. As Yoldash was now in command, some onlookers predicted a possible metamorphosis along the lines of Roger's first category of terrorist organization. But the accompanying heavy losses inflicted on IMU forces during OEF led many to predict that any remaining activists would be absorbed elsewhere. Momentarily, events in the Spring and Summer of 2004, including further Tashkent bombings, indicated that the IMU was 'alive but not well' (Weitz 2004: 522), although by 2006 'it is a legitimate question whether the IMU – as a coherent organization – even exists anymore, or whether its remnants have disintegrated and joined with other and diverse forces' (Cornell 2006: 59–60).

All three broad approaches to responding to sub-state terrorism have been adopted in Central Asia. The most common approach has been traditional counter-terrorism measures of policing, intelligence and security. Previously denying the presence of terrorists on its soil, Kazakhstan set up an Anti-Terrorist Centre in 2003 (Lester 2010: 4). The EU has played an important role in promoting border policing (Chapter 4) and Russia still has the best intelligence on the region. Omelicheva (2009) argues that Uzbekistan's response to terrorism has influenced how its neighbours, in particular the Kyrgyz Republic, have come to respond to terrorism, and that policy transfer of this kind has trumped its own domestic security concerns. OEF practised the second measure, direct military action against paramilitary organizations. In their study of Uzbekistan, Brad McAllister and Julia Khersonsky (2007: 445) address the 'socioeconomic feeders of radicalism while simultaneously dealing with the threat of political violence itself'. Tightening border and customs regimes is integral to their advocating trade-led countermeasures for Uzbekistan. This study reflects the third measure that concentrates on the underlying motivations of terrorist groups and the environment from which they draw support.

As a movement with specific domestic aims the IMU has prompted questions about whether it might more accurately be situated between a criminal and a terrorist organization. Phil Williams (2001) notes that transnational criminal networks generally are 'economic rather than political organizations; they do not pose the same kind of overt or obvious challenge to states that terrorist groups do; crime is a domestic problem; and law enforcement and national security are based on very different philosophies, organization structures and legal frameworks'. Similarly Interpol called the IMU 'a hybrid organization in which criminal interests often take priority over "political goals"', adding that 'IMU leaders have a vested interest in ongoing unrest and instability in their area in order to secure the routes they use for the transportation of drugs' (Mutschke 2000). The IMU may therefore provide a classic example of an organization in the grey zone between criminal organization and terrorist network.

The idea of a grey zone was developed by Tamara Makarenko with specific application to Central Asia and the IMU. For Makarenko (2004), three groups profit from the narcotics trade: drugs mafia, transnational criminal organizations and terrorist groups, the latter including the Taliban and IMU. A security continuum can be conceptualized which places pure traditional organized crime on one end of the spectrum, and armed ideological groups at the other (Makarenko 2002). A 'grey area' between these two extremes exists, including 'where organized crime and terrorism are indistinguishable from one another' and such an alliance is 'a terrorist group little known to most Westerners, but one in which 70% of Central Asia's drug trade is under its control, and is the true wildcard for stability in the region. Its name is the Islamic Movement of Uzbekistan (IMU)'. Several authors link the IMU and drugs trade, such as Martha Brill Olcott and Natalia Udalova (2000: 24) who argue that the narcotics trade 'has become one of the main sources of revenue for the existing criminal groups that are also involved in money laundering'.

Drugs and transnational criminal organizations

The degree to which the IMU is a security rather than criminal threat is partly, then, about the degree to which it feeds on the drugs trade. Three types of violent crime have been linked with the drug trade: crimes whose purpose is to protect drugs routes, those whose purpose is to get money to buy drugs, and those conducted by people under the influence of drugs. Cornell (2005: 629) points to how various 'aspects of the modalities of the IMU incursions suggest that they were in fact conditioned to a great extent by the drug trade. These include both the geographical areas targeted, the timing of the attacks, as well as the tactics used'. Weitz (2004: 508–9) also warned that the IMU 'might become so involved in trafficking illicit substances that it will evolve, like Columbia's main guerrilla movements, into more of a narcoterrorist entity than a messianic religious movement'.

In the twenty-first century, 80 per cent of heroin consumed in Western Europe originates in Afghanistan (World Drug Report 2009) and a large share travels through Central Asia, either via the Altayn-Mazar, Batken or Khujand routes (Olcott and Udalova 2000: 12). The curbing of the Osh route, the so-called 'Osh knot' (Osmanaliev 2003), became a primary aim. This had become Central Asia's first drugs trafficking route because it used the only major highway that linked up with Khorog on the Tajik-Afghan border. The Islamic Rennaissance Party of the United Tajik Opposition operated from bases in northern Afghanistan, chiefly areas controlled by the Shura-i-Nazar in the Takhor and Kunduz provinces (Gretsky 1995: 231). The Batken route travelled through Jirgatal and Tavildara, strongholds of the IMU during the civil war in Tajikistan. Drug traffickers also found safe havens in the political vacuums of Vorukh and Sokh enclaves, and also in smaller enclaves such as the Qalacha and Khalmion areas in Kyrgyzstan administered by Uzbekistan, as well as Chorku, administered by Tajikistan (Madi 2004: 10).

The drug problem in Central Asia has been presented primarily in these terms of trafficking but production is also a key challenge. Opium has long been culti-vated in the region, and records of opium poppy cultivation in Kyrgyzstan go back to the nineteenth century. Olcott and Udalova (2000: 9) write that some '98 state and collective farms in Kyrgyzstan's Issyk-Kul oblast produced 80 percent of the total illicit opium in the Soviet Union and 16 percent of the world's supply'. The challenge is thus twofold: to control the trafficking routes and to control home production. Drugs production and trafficking produce further multi-ple threats: social effects in terms of increased drugs use and the encouragement of organized crime in the region itself; political effects in its fuelling of corrup-tion (border guards and elites); economic effects in its skewing of production in favour of the opium trade over other agricultural crops (e.g., opium fields have displaced wheat fields, and sheep farmers prefer opium production), creating a form of Dutch disease effect.

This dual challenge is a product of the symbiotic relationship between state and transnational crime. On the one hand, a particular type of state is more prone to transnational crime and the evidence that Kyrgyzstan and Tajikistan are the primary states affected conforms to this pattern. As the economically weakest and politically most fragmented, they promote 'fewer control mechanisms' (Swanström 2010: 44), benefits to economic livelihoods, porous borders and the general instability favourable to criminals (Olcott and Udalova 2000: 10). Cornell and Swanström (2006) go further and make a direct link between drugs money and the Tulip Revolution. The geography is also in the criminal's favour, with mountainous regions difficult to patrol. Swanström (2010: 45) concludes that it is precisely the weaknesses of the Afghan, Tajik and Kyrgyz states that 'make them easy targets for the criminal networks, and [they] have emerged as three of the most corrupt states according to Transparency International'. On the other hand, this becomes a vicious circle as the drugs trade further weakens the state. Criminal groups seek to capture and corrupt the state (Shelley 1999).

The challenges to state legitimacy through this eventual failure to provide a secure environment to its citizens can be seen as a security threat, but to date counter-narcotics operations in Central Asia have fallen short of military operations. As with counter-terrorism, counter-narcotics measures have been primarily national or international rather than Central Asian ones. In 1996 the five Central Asian states signed a memorandum of understanding between them and the UNDCP, and in January 1998 they were joined as signatories by Russia and the Aga Khan Development Network. But funding problems exist for all these. Some personnel shake-ups and legislation have also followed. The UNDCP provides the main foreign assistance, principally through a large-scale programme for regional co-operation 'that includes border control, capacity-building, intelligence-gathering, demand reduction, and control of drug precursors' (Olcott and Udalova 2000: 21).

The environment: top guns and toxic whales

While transnational terrorism, crime and trafficking have been among the less controversial areas of broadening, the same cannot be said of the final threat analyzed here, the environment. Gwyn Prins' documentary film and accompanying book of the same name, *Top Guns and Toxic Whales*, points out that someone has to deal with the whale carcasses washing up on the beach but that fighter pilots and their expensive machines are not the best equipped to do so. Doing so would reinforce the state nationalism and militarization that has perpetuated many modern forms of insecurity (Klare 2004).

Previously this demonstrable connection was largely discussed in realist, state-centric terms as a relationship between the possession of natural resources and a country's growth and stability. Possession of, or reliable access to, important natural resources was often seen as central to the development and maintenance of state power. The new agenda adds more broad-based discussions about human-induced environmental degradation and scarcity. Some (e.g., Matthews 1989) insist that this broadening called for security to be redefined.

This 'new thinking' on the environment was contained in Gorbachev's more general 'new thinking' of the late 1980s, at a time when prominent think tanks such as the World Resources Institute and World Watch Institute in Washington D.C. were also focusing on ways to promote sustainable development. In the pages of its 1987 report on *Our Common Future* the authors had taken for granted that environmental degradation and shortage of resources would lead to political stability and conflict. In the 1990s Vice President Al Gore was influential in drawing attention to the matter of 'failed states' and the possible environmental causes of their political collapse, and this extrapolation was given particular prominence in Robert Kaplan's essay in the February 1994 issue of the *Atlantic Monthly*. One academic school at the University of Toronto under Thomas Homer-Dixon became influential in promoting this link between the environment and security.

Not everyone, however, is convinced that the environment is a legitimate security issue, including those writing on Central Asia. Libiszewiski (1992) and Levy (1995) argue that the environment as a national resource is more an economic than a security concern and that an environmental conflict is one 'caused by a human-sourced disturbance of the normal regeneration rate of a renewable resource' (Libiszewiski 1992: 6), with Levy stressing that there must be some identifiable link to national interest. Daniel Deudney (1999), perhaps one of the more notable sceptics, argues that environmental concerns and military matters were so different that confusing them was doing just that – causing conceptual confusion and the use of military solutions to non-military problems. The link between the environment and outbreaks of violence is thus contested and remains so when applied to Central Asia.

Central Asia faces substantial environmental challenges that are largely a product of mismanagement and over-irrigation. The environmental concerns include the desiccation of the Aral Sea, the depletion of river and irrigation waters, and the consequences of Soviet and Chinese nuclear testing at Semipalatinsk (now known as Semey) and Lop Nor, respectively. Population rises in the basin exert added pressures: 50 per cent of people in the Aral Sea basin live in 20 per cent of its territory. Tishkov (1992: 74) relates the Kyrgyz-Tajik violence during the 1980s to these land and population pressures. Water poses a threefold challenge in Central Asia: allocation, significance and attendant mismanagement.

The allocation problem stems from a mismatch between supply and use, largely between upstream and downstream states. The three downstream states of Kazakhstan, Turkmenistan and Uzbekistan currently receive 73 per cent of total withdrawals from the Aral Sea Basin while the two upstream states, the source of 90 per cent of all available waters, are allocated only 0.4 and 11 per cent. This mismatch becomes a source of national tension because for three of the downstream states water is key to the region's most important irrigation crop, cotton, and, as we saw in the previous chapter, the leading source of income and employment for Turkmenistan and Uzbekistan. With independence and the overnight collapse of water sharing agreements, Central Asian states were forced to rapidly develop management strategies and assume responsibility; by 1994 'over 300 agreements concerning the Aral Sea region had been signed' (Horsman 2001: 73). But these agreements are not legally binding. The global commons has not, therefore, provided incentives for co-operation or joint pooling of resources, but instead has become a tool for intra-state coercion and competition.

Horsman (2001: 77) considers Central Asia a 'potentially volatile water security environment', writing that regions 'that faced water-related conflicts in the late Soviet period – Batken-Isfara, Osh, the lower Zeravshan and the lower Amu Darya – remain potential flash-points'. Blank (2010: 168) writes that '[a]rguably Central Asia is one of those regions where a war breaking out over resource and environmental issues is quite conceivable'. Akiner (1996: 14) writes how elements in Tajikistan had discussed the idea of using the Syr Darya as 'an offensive weapon in any territorial dispute with Uzbekistan'. Authors of *Calming the Ferghana Valley* in a Homer-Dixonian sense argue that scarcity and degradation provoke economic decline which 'aggravates popular and elite grievances, increases rivalry between elite factions, and erodes the state's legitimacy' (1994: 42). Terriff et al (2000: 133) remind us that: 'Different conceptions of environmental security are based on different conceptions of security' and Christine Bichsel (2009) in her study of the Ferghana Valley shows the importance of combining ethnography, development and security perspectives for a holistic understanding of threats.

Theorizing security in Central Asia

Human security

This broadening of threats and referents has been captured by a concept which has also come to be applied to Central Asia, human security. The expanding UN agenda of human security concerns (among them war-affected children, racial discrimination, women's rights, refugees), coupled with former UN Secretary-General Kofi Annan's personal interest in and commitment to human security activism, catapulted these questions to the forefront of the scholarly and policy research agenda in the 1990s (see MacFarlane and Khong 2006). The individual is placed as the point of reference. Threats, therefore, are less about how they affect state sovereignty than about how they reduce an individual's sense of 'first, safety from such chronic threats as hunger, disease and repression. And second it means protection from sudden and hurtful disruptions in the patterns of daily life – whether in homes, in jobs or in communities' (UNDP 1994: 23). The unit of the individual, rather than region, state or system, is the critical factor that upholds or undermines international order.

Both of human security's major schools are locatable in Central Asia. The narrow school's focus on 'freedom from fear' from the immediate threats of violence has been seen particularly in writings on the effects of civil war on Tajikistan (including, e.g., the broader small arms report produced by S. Neil Macfarlane and Stina Torjesen 2007), the spill-over effects of the war in

Afghanistan, and the Andijan massacres of 2005 and the violence of April and June 2010 in Kyrgyzstan. The broader school's focus on 'freedom from want' (see Report of the Commission on Human Security 2003: 2) and its focus on the threats arising from underdevelopment again has Kyrgyzstan and Tajikistan, Central Asia's poorest states, as primary concerns for economic security (e.g., Glenn 1999). As Carole Thomas (2000: 244) remarks, 'poverty and human insecurity are in many respects synonymous. Both refer to a human condition characterized by the lack of fulfillment of a range of entitlements such as adequate food, healthcare, education, shelter, employment and voice'. In Uzbekistan and Turkmenistan the right to voice has been more of a human security concern than in the Kyrgyz Republic where media and association have remained relatively free. Diseases such as tuberculosis and HIV/AIDS have, by contrast, been human security concerns for the whole region.

The concept is not without its detractors, however. Roland Paris (2001) and Yuen Foong Khong (2001) and Andrew Mack (2001, 2005) express concern about including too much into a definition and thus making its investigation problematic and the concept then meaningless, not least as the evidence that a threat to individual security constitutes a threat to global security is often considered scant. The concept's application in Central Asia has highlighted what issues and which actors are making particular people or geographic areas feel more or less secure. It does not amount, however, to a theory that might better help us to understand why security problems have arisen in Central Asia (and therefore how they might be solved) or how these issues became security issues in the first place, thus ultimately questioning 'whether there is a distinctive value added in a human security approach to these problems. Such discussions bring us to the bigger field of international relations theory' (Hampson 2008: 237).

As recently as 1966 Martin Wight posed the question, 'why is there no international theory?', by which he meant an equivalent body of knowledge to that which comprised political theory. Wight argued that there was no body of international theory ('speculation about the society of states, or the family of nations, or the international community') to match the achievements of political theory ('speculation about the state') (Burchill in Burchill et al 1996: 7), but since then international political theorists have come to classify theories under two broad approaches: problem-solving and constitutive. The first refers to those sets of theories that test hypotheses, propose causal explanations, describe events and explain general trends and phenomena, while the second seeks to uncover the normative assumptions that underpin research. Cox points out how knowledge has a fundamentally different function in both cases. In the first approach, in which classical theories belong, the knowledge uncovered is used to make the existing order function better and thus, intentionally or not, to sustain; in the second approach, one non-traditional theory, critical theory, by contrast, 'unpacks that order by concerning itself with their origins and how and whether they might be in the process of changing' (Cox 1981: 1928–9). We begin with the application and relevance of the latter to Central Asia.

Constructivists: conventional versus critical

The need to come up with complex solutions to broader threats, coupled with the view that threats might become exaggerated, is reflected in the agendas of both the constructivist and critical theorist schools. Both schools deconstruct the process of understanding security, and aim to gain a better understanding of how threats emerge, and how issues become threats. Constructivism, a term first elaborated by Nicholas Oluf in his ground-breaking book *World of Our Making* in 1989, is a broad theoretical approach to the study of International Relations that has been applied to such a range of issues, from political economy (Blyth 2002) to international organization (Ruggie 1998: 41–130, Barnett and Finnemore 2004) and security (Katzenstein 1996).

Constructivists argue that these threats have become part of the security realm (broadly and in application to a region, here Central Asia) as a result of both agents and structures that are mutually constituted. This view is most neatly captured in Alexander Wendt's seminal 1992 article, 'Anarchy is What States Make of It', arguing that states can choose to support or undermine a culture of anarchy in the international system. Another popular approach by conventional constructivists has been to explore the conditions that favour the emergence and development of 'security communities', namely groups of actors (usually states) for whom the use of force in resolving disputes between each other has become unthinkable over time (Adler and Barnett 1998).

Constructivism does not mean 'constructed' in the sense of 'fake'. Rather, agents and structures are mutually constituted and norms, ideas and identity are central to this constitution. In Huysmans' (1998) terms, security is a site of negotiation (between political leaders and domestic audiences in particular) and contestation (between different actors elaborating different visions of 'our values' and how 'we' should act). Ted Hopf (1998) argues that political leaders designate other states as 'friend' or 'enemy' depending on how they formulate their identity (perceptions of who they are). Norms, or shared expectations about what constitutes appropriate behaviour, are another key determinant defining what or who is viewed as threatening (Finnemore 1996; Crawford 2003).

The Copenhagen School comes closest to offering a theory of constructivism, and chooses to focus on how 'speech acts' designate particular issues or actors as existential threats. The discourse of danger literature in Central Asia shows how such 'speech acts', 'enemies' and 'threats' are constructed.[1] Regional security complexes and sectors provide sites of danger where issues may become, through their removal from the political process, securitized. First outlined in depth by Ole Wæver in 1995, securitization may be defined as a process in which an actor declares a particular issue, dynamic or actor to be an 'existential threat' to a particular referent object.

The securitization process as applied to Central Asia throws up the approach's strengths and weaknesses. In her analysis of human and drugs trafficking, Nicole J. Jackson (2005: 18–19) illustrates how the Shanghai Cooperation Organization made a security concern by bunching in its speech acts the 'three evil forces' of 'terrorism, extremism, and separatism' as well as narcotics trafficking or again the UNODC's use of the term 'uncivil forces' in reference to 'drug traffickers, organized crime groups and terrorist alike'.

The process of securitization is not automatic, however, not least as Central Asian state actors are often ineffective in countering illegal practices, making their prolongation attractive. But whatever the process or agents, the effects of securitization will be substantively the same – the suspension of the normal rules of the game and the enabling of emergency measures. In his study of discourses of danger, Megoran (2005) showed how in Uzbekistan the main securitizing actor has been the government while in the Kyrgyz Republic, that role has been filled by civil society. Buzan, Wæver and De Wilde (1998) view securitization as implying a form of 'panic politics' and thus express a normative preference for desecuritization as this removes from the security agenda what should be simply handled as political issues.

Simultaneously, however, Central Asia shows the problems of this normative preference for desecuritization. If 'normal politics' is a Western-style, liberal democratic style of Western politics, characterized by the rule of law and open political deliberation, then this is not applicable to Central Asia where 'panic politics' is instead the norm. This makes securitization of an issue much easier to achieve than in a democratic polity – not simply because authoritarian leaders repress dissent over something becoming securitized but because the road to travel there is so much shorter.

While the state remains the primary referent for the Copenhagen School, which works with fairly stable or sedimented identities (Katzenstein 1996; Wendt 1999), critical constructivists focus on how certain narratives have become dominant over others. In his seminal article 'Security and Emancipation' Ken Booth (1991), 'called for a rethinking of security', defined it as 'emancipation' and coined the phrase 'critical security studies'. Unlike the Copenhagen School, emancipatory critical theorists say that solutions can be found through security, not outside it. Bilgin (2008: 98) writes: 'Whereas the Copenhagen School makes a case writes for 'desecuritization' (taking issues outside of the security agenda and addressing them through "normal" political processes), the Welsh School re-theorizes security as a "derivative concept" and calls for "politicizing security"'. Politicizing security also encourages us to look at alternative voices, not just those of the ruling elites.

A critical constructivist approach carries normative policy implications – if the world is constructed, then we are in a far better position to change it. The Welsh School does not see military solutions as necessarily a bad thing: it may be better than leaving the resolution of security issues in the hands of political elites who are ill-equipped or often unwilling to deal with them. Ultimately these enquiries show that a choice between 'desecuritization' and politicizing security 'must be answered empirically, historically, discursively' (Alker 2005: 198). As we recall in Chapter 4, Reeves shows how the construction of borders – traditional military solutions – has on the whole made societies and communities feel less secure. In the case of how Central Asian leaders have handled Islam, as we saw in

Chapters 4 and 5, the process of securitizing has heightened the sense of insecurity around this issue, in the same way that the representation of migration to Western Europe has often rendered 'constructive political and social engagement with the dangerous outsider(s) more difficult' (Huysmans 2006: 57).

Traditional theories: (neo)-realism and (neo)-liberalism

While constructivism has become an increasingly prominent theoretical approach to international relations since its emergence in the 1980s, two traditional approaches have dominated writing on Central Asian security since independence: realism and liberalism. As with constructivism, writers who fall under this umbrella do not necessarily accept that classification. Is a realist theorization central to our understanding of this region, namely its anarchy, the autonomy and sovereignty of states and the distribution of military power? Or is it, as liberalists would have it, the capacity for transactions/interactions among states and societies?

Liberalist accounts stress the state as the unit of analysis, the importance of domestic actors, power and the nature of political systems. State behaviour is considered a product of domestic circumstances, international relations are determined by the choices people make, and the approach overall is a more optimistic one, arguing that international politics has become more imbued with interdependence, co-operation, peace and security. In other words, the endogenous is seen as affecting the exogenous, 'in which civil liberties are protected and market relations prevail, can have an international analogue in the form of a peaceful global order' (Burchill in Burchill et al 1996: 61). The end of the Cold War seemed to confirm liberalism's triumph.

Realism, however, has shown enormous staying power. Colin Elman (2008: 16) distinguishes between six types of realism: classical realism, neorealism, and 'four flavours of contemporary realism: rise and fall,[2] neoclassical, offensive structural, and defensive structural realism'. Central Asian individual state behaviour speaks to classical realism in certain ways. For E.H. Carr (2001), the pursuit of power by individual states took the form of promoting 'national interests', a term later to be more broadly defined as the foreign policy goals of the nation but understood by realists to specifically mean strategic power. Its emphasis on flawed human nature that engages states in a constant struggle to increase state power and maximise national interest has been seen in certain foreign policy acts, such as the Uzbek government's unilateral demarcation of borders or its cutting off gas in an exercise of power and show of strength.

Despite hints of offensive realism by the Uzbek government (an approach explained in John Mearsheimer's (2001) *The Tragedy of Great Power Politics*), leaders of Central Asian states are closer to adopting the position of defensive realists where they look only for an 'appropriate amount of power' concordant with Stephen Walt's (2000) 'balance of threat' theory. A case in point is the reaction of neighbouring Central Asian states to the events of 2005 (and April 2010) in Kyrgyzstan: leaders were not responding to what was a real similar power balance change in their home countries but rather the perception that what happened there might happen to them and then busied themselves implementing policies of spill-over avoidance, for example, the closing of the Kazakh-Kyrgyz border.

Low-level tension rather than outright hostility, therefore, marks relations between Central Asian states and this is largely because their leaders are too busy state-building, and in so doing jealously guarding their autonomy, which is central to realist explanations of why states behave as they do. Even if Central Asian leaders acquired sovereignty by accident, once it had been granted they were not about to renounce it. Thus the suspicion and absence of communication surrounding anti-terrorism and water distribution policies discussed earlier in the chapter are direct consequences of leaders perceiving resolution of these issues as a direct infringement on their sovereignty. This is the classic security dilemma, a concept we encountered in Chapter 5 at the societal level between communities.

Walt's 'balance of threats' is developed differently by Randall Schweller (1998) in his 'balance of interests' argument. Also a neoclassical realist and in a departure from classical realism, Schweller (2006: 6) emphasizes how 'complex domestic political processes act as transmission belts that channel, mediate and (re)direct policy outputs in response to external forces (primarily changes in relative power). Hence states often react differently to similar systemic pressures and opportunities, and their responses may be less motivated by systemic level factors than domestic ones.' The more fragmented and diverse a state's various elite and societal groups, the less we can expect it to respond appropriately to external strategic pressures, and this goes some way to explaining the often erratic foreign policy outputs of Central Asian elites. So, for example, Turkmenistan's positive neutrality and its inglorious isolationism or Uzbekistan's policy of self-reliance would from this perspective be less a reaction to external strategic pressures than the outcome of these countries' specific mixes of bureaucratic politics, ideologies and leadership personalities. Or, again, the declared situating of their countries on the Silk Road (Kyrgyzstan and Tajikistan) or at the crossroads of Europe and Asia (Kazakhstan) has cultural, geographic and economic depth rather than existing as a mere device to bandwagon with the power that at any time best meets these countries' security needs.

Neorealism differs from realism in its emphasis on the international system. Exemplified by Kenneth Waltz's (1979) *Theory of International Politics*, it describes how an international system consists of three elements: an ordering principle (anarchic or hierarchical), the character of the units (functionally alike or differentiated), and the distribution of capabilities. The neo-realist perspective is the one most associated with the Great Game narrative. In the new Great Game, the three significant outside players are the regional powers, 'defined as those powers that have a significant impact on the region, including the United States' (Allison and Jonson 2001: 249). The other two are China and Russia. The EU, India, Pakistan, Iran and Turkey have declared strong interests in the region. Furthermore, the narrative holds that the motivating factor behind great power involvement is the drive to increase these external states' powers by acquiring resources, land or influence in the region. The interaction is competitive and the outcome zero-sum.

Few writers explicitly identify themselves as (neo-) realist when referring to the Great Game but many of their underlying assumptions are (neo-) realist. Writers vary on whether they view the ordering principle as anarchic or hierarchical, the latter assumed by those who argue that Russian preponderance in the region will remain. The region is characterized by units that have become functionally more alike with independence (for example Kyrgyzstan's slide to authoritarianism in line with the region more generally) even if simultaneously the countries have become (Chapter 5) culturally and linguistically more differentiated and from an identity perspective less cohesive. The distribution of capabilities has also changed in this short timespan: among the five, Kazakhstan has emerged as a competitor to Uzbekistan's regional hegemony and beyond the five India and China are emerging as great regional powers. Mearsheimer (2001: 140–55) argues that ultimate safety comes only from being the most powerful state in the system. However, the 'stopping power of water' makes such global hegemony all but impossible, except through attaining an implausible nuclear superiority. The second best, and much more likely, objective is to achieve regional hegemony.

The Central Asian region is unusual in having two great regional powers as great powers. Two principal factors increased this underlying competitiveness in the region: Russian 'involuntary disengagement' (Jonson 1998) in the early 1990s and Russian 'reassertion' (Allison 2004b) after the arrival of Putin and the stationing of US troops in Central Asia after September 11. Russia's 'involuntary disengagement' from Central Asia in the 1990s under Boris Yeltsin opened the space allowing for competition. Writing before 9/11 Jonson (2001: 120) notes how 'Russia's preoccupation with its domestic problems, above all in the North Caucasus, means that scarce resources have to be devoted to domestic problems that are more urgent than concerns in Central Asia'. By the time Russia began to re-engage under Vladimir Putin, China had begun a quiet interaction with the region in which it asked Central Asian governments to support its territorial integrity by not endorsing Xinjiang's calls for autonomy. China also began negotiations of some border land transfers to its advantage and stepped up trade and investment in the region. Iran only engaged when it saw Russia withdrawing as its priorities were relations with Russia, and then its interests were dictated by pragmatism not ideology (Herzig 2001: 187). Turkey's economic difficulties stalled its ambitions to become the regional leader it had hoped (Allison and Jonson 2001: 17; Winrow 2001), although it retains some influence, particularly in the construction sector, in Turkmenistan and Kazakhstan.

Co-operation marked the immediate period after September 11. Immediately after the attacks, great powers were prepared to co-operate in the region. So, for example, Putin initially agreed to Bush's request to station US troops in Central Asia – as a 'temporary' measure reflecting the 'Joint Declaration on a new US-Russia Relationship' – after the two presidents met in Moscow in May 2002. Central Asian governments had, however, in any case offered facilities regardless of what would be portrayed as Russian preferences. All Central Asian republics offered to share intelligence and grant US access to air space and permission for emergency landings while some offered more: Uzbekistan proffered use of a former Soviet air base at Karshi Khanabad (precluding, however, any involvement in positioning ground forces for an invasion of Afghanistan), Kyrgyzstan offered Manas near Bishkek; a more modest refuelling operation was also set up in Ashkhabad, Turkmenistan, as well as a small-scale presence in Dushanbe, Tajikistan; Kazakhstan also offered a base, which the US declined.

But the quantitative and qualitative increase of the US presence in Central Asia following September 11 ultimately intensified competition. The quantitative increment was in the amount of security co-operation and aid, the chief early beneficiary being Uzbekistan, which received nearly US$172m after 9/11, 'nearly ten times the amount budgeted for each of the other CARs in 2001–2003' (Dittmer 2007: 18). The stationing of US, and Western troops, also intensified the perception by Russia that it had to step up its activities. The qualitative increment was a shift to an almost exclusive focus on security co-operation and assistance, tacitly deprioritizing all human rights or democratic developmental concerns. This dropping of democratic concerns (Jones Luong and Weinthal 2002; Dave 2008) in favour of security co-operation paradoxically increased regional power competition. After reportedly intense negotiations, the US and Kyrgyzstan in June 2009 reached an agreement on maintaining US and NATO transit operations at Manas after the Kyrgyz government's February 2009 announcement that it was terminating the agreement. The renegotiation was a factor of Great Game competition – reported pressure by Russia having been one critical reason why the Kyrgyz reneged on their agreement.

This heightened competition notwithstanding, many question that there is a new Great Game (Chapter 1). Some express frustration with the narrative's oversimplification. Instead of being simply a game between outside actors, the template has been appropriated by local actors (Cooley 2011) and in turn transformed by them to their advantage. Others (e.g., Cummings 2004) argue that an overemphasis on the Great Game has obscured other sometimes more important and mainly domestically produced factors behind the content of the foreign policies of these states, a point already captured in the agency given to Central Asian states by constructivists and also by neoclassical realists.

Some suggest this is a 'not-so-great-game' (Sokov 2005), and others imply this qualification both in terms of the prize to be won and of the link between Central Asia and its perceived centrality to the national interests of the competing states. In the same 2002 Joint-Declaration the two presidents rejected 'the failed model of "Great Power" rivalry that can only increase the potential for conflict in those regions' (Allison 2004b). In this regard, 'the big question' for Buzan and Wæver (2003) is the degree of US interest. Anatol Lieven (1999: 71) writes that at hardly '2 percent of the world's proven oil reserves (around a thirtieth of the Gulf's reserves), it should be blindingly obvious that Caspian energy does not constitute a "vital U.S. interest"'. Buzan and Wæver (2003: 428) conclude that the 'main external actors have shown surprisingly low interest despite oil and pipelines'.

The US already achieved considerably much, in its foreign policy terms, with its nuclear diplomacy toward Kazakhstan. With US financial assistance by 1995 Kazakhstan's nuclear arsenal had been turned over to Russia (Lester 2010). A US withdrawal from Afghanistan and Iraq would further reduce their interest in Central Asia.

By contrast, China's interests involve both investment in Central Asian oil and gas (Chapter 6) and domestic security concerns. It is both borne, one writer contends, of common interests with a simultaneous fear by Central Asian countries of domination and external intervention (Swanström 2005: 569). China's energy interests, like Russia's and those of the US, predated September 11. Beijing had particularly warned against Central Asian governments supporting Xinjiang separatism, and 'Bejijing's fear that ethno-religious nationalism, which has emerged in Central Asia, will mobilize an ethno-religious war in Xinjiang, is, however, real' (Swanström 2005: 574), but Beijing realizes that it needs Central Asia's cooperation (Gladney in Swanström 2005). Sheives (2006: 206) finds fault with Swanström's assumptions of 'both a domineering Chinese foreign policy and continually conflicting US-China relations, neither of which are commonly accepted tenets of recent Chinese foreign policy scholarship' and he refers to the works particularly of Evan Medeiros and Taylor Fravel (2003) and Shambaugh (2003). Avery Goldstein (2005) argues that China uses multilateral fora such as the SCO to promote its own interests, not least to ensure its peaceful rise (*heping jueqi*), hence the pursuit of sovereign interests through multilateralism become compatible.

Questions remain about Russia's long-term role in the region. For Menon and Spruyt (1999: 102) 'there are really no viable means to balance Russia's potential threat to Central Asia' with Russia enjoying an asymmetric advantage over other powers. Soviet-trained personnel, indeed, still far outnumber an emerging Western or China-trained elite. English and Mandarin are spoken to nowhere near the extent that Russian is and Russian remains the lingua franca among the five. In the context of the CSTO, Russia is also the only foreign power to have provided a collective security guarantee. On soft power, Russia is again outdoing its competitors; Russian media still dominates the media landscape and, most critically, Russia is the primary destination of Central Asian migrants and seasonal workers (Hill 2004). Russia's dominance is for others primarily linked to the fate of its competitors. Swanström (2005:581) writes that '[n]either China nor America are concerned over Russian pressure over the long term, since they know Russia has severe economic and social problems of its own to deal with' with also 'no indications that the US will move out in the coming years but on the contrary it seems that the US is strengthening its position in Central Asia'. But if the US leaves, competitive dynamics still remain as Russia must still contend with China, India and to a lesser degree Turkey and Iran.

To sum up, so far. Central Asia thus offers an example of a region that generates limited co-operation but with lots of free riding. Realism has captured only some of these security dynamics. It fails to explain why: a) the five states do not exhibit strong competitive behaviour between each other; b) even if Russia was primus inter pares for most of the 1990s and arguably still enjoys primacy, there is no clear regional hegemon; and c) inconsistent but nevertheless limited co-operation exists. Parts of the answers are provided by liberalism and constructivism, and by the nature of Central Asia's regional security complex. First, liberalism, albeit constrained and often unintentionally so, may explain some of these features of peaceful coexistence and attempted co-operation. One indirect way has been through the means of 'protective integration' (Libman 2007; Allison 2008). Second, the absence of a discrete regional security complex goes some way toward explaining why Central Asian cooperation is awkward and why meaningful co-operation remains 'virtual'. The awkwardness of Central Asian regionalism has dictated that no single vision or player has been either willing or able to take the lead and in which interests and identities fail to bring together a coherent security architecture. To close this chapter, we explore each of these reasons in turn.

Neo-liberalism and multilateral institutionalism in Central Asia

Andrew Moravcsik (2001) has distinguished between ideational, commercial and republican liberalism following Michael Doyle (1998) who distinguished between international, commercial and ideological liberalism. According to Moravcsik, 'commercial liberalism' focuses on 'incentives created by opportunities for trans-border economic transactions' (2001: 14) and 'is generally a less costly means of accumulating wealth than war, sanctions or other coercive means' (2001: 50). This is echoed by writers who view Russia in Central Asia as increasingly exerting a benign economic influence in the region. In an article entitled 'The limits of neorealism' Spruyt (1999: 87) argues that such a transformation in Russia's role makes Russia's continued 'preponderance' in Central Asia an unlikely future source of conflict (as the neorealist argument would have it). Fiona Hill (2004) further characterizes Russia as a 'newly found "soft power"', concluding that while Russia 'may not be able to rival the United States in the nature and global extent of its "soft power"', in its immediate 'sphere of influence' it has nearly clawed back the level of influence it enjoyed in the Soviet period, not least by portraying itself as an economic magnet for migrants and remittances. Atkin (2011) argues that Tajikistan is 'a sovereign dependency', Buzan and Wæver (2003: 425) that it is 'de facto a Russian protectorate'. Russian (and to a lesser degree Chinese) leverage is one reason why Central Asia in security terms remains a sub-region rather than a regional security complex in its own right.

Neoliberalism, made famous in the 1970s by the writings of Keohane and Nye (1977), points to another way in which liberalists offer explanations behind Central Asia's limited co-operation, the emergence of regional security institutions. They point to the growth of multilateral institutions as a sign of how the international system is increasingly characterized by co-operation rather than anarchy. Alliances are sought to balance or bandwagon in a realist way against threats. By contrast, liberalism's account of multilateral security institutions emphasizes instead how such institutions exert a determinative effect on how states choose alliances with other states (Rubin and Snyder 1998).

The end of the Cold War and the replacement of bipolarity with multipolarity led to a surge in regional security institutions around the world. These institutions, conceptualized as 'regimes and formal organizations' (Fawcett 2008), continued to accept the state as gatekeeper of most global security activity (Russett and Oneal 2001). Since 1991 Central Asia's regional security institutions have been of two types: those that involve only the five Central Asian states and those that involve outside powers. The main examples of intra-five regional institutions are those in the economic realm but, as noted, these have remained largely dead-letter (Chapter 6); the main examples of regional institutions involving outside powers are the Commonwealth of Independent States, the Eurasian Union, the Partnership for Peace Programme under NATO and the Shanghai Cooperation Organization, the latter involving Russia and China.

These newly formed institutions (see Table 7.1) observed in Central Asia are responses to new balances of power in the international system with institutions designed to enhance and consolidate the position of both strong and new/weak states. Their growth in Central Asia, as elsewhere, can be interpreted in two different, though related ways. First, they may attempt to promote peaceful and predictable relations among its members, to build security and community through cooperation (Adler and Barnett 1998). Second, they may provide security guarantees to meet threats arising from inter- and intra-state conflicts, and increasingly from the sorts of threats outlined at this chapter's start. In Central Asia's case they have been partly successful at the former and unsuccessful at the latter.

With the important exception of Russia's CSTO declarations, none of Central Asia's current regional security institutions provide security guarantees. The absence of any such guarantees makes the second interpretation of why these regional institutions emerged – to provide security – difficult to support. The CIS has come closest to providing a form of collective security in this way, including the Collective Rapid Deployment Force (CRDF), formally launched on 25 May 2001 at the Yerevan summit of the CIS. Even at the height of the US presence immediately after September 11 the US stopped short of offering a security guarantee in the Declaration on Strategic Partnership and Cooperation Framework between the US and Uzbekistan (signed March 2002) – though it did agree to 'regard with grave concern any external threat'. The Russian-Uzbek treaty of 2005 went further, though any Russian response should still only be at the request of Tashkent.

Peaceful and predictable behaviour are more characteristic of regional organizations that involve additional outside powers. Dittmer (2007: 17) writes that by mid-1994, 'Kazakhstan, Kyrgyzstan, Turkmenistan and Uzbekistan had joined NATO's Partnership for Peace (PfP) program and military officers from these countries began participating in PfP exercises. In December 1995, Kazakhstan, Kyrgyzstan, and Uzbekistan formed a joint peacekeeping unit with the support of CENTCOM called Centrazbat, which held annual military exercises aimed at engaging these states into CENTCOM's collective engagement strategy'.

Table 7.1 Central Asian membership of security organizations (2010)

Organization	Kazakhstan	Kyrgyzstan	Tajikistan	Turkmenistan	Uzbekistan	Description
CICA	x	x	x		x	Promoting a multi-national forum for enhancing co-operation towards promoting peace, security and stability in Asia
CSTO	x	x	x		x	To co-ordinate military and political co-operation, to develop multilateral structures and mechanisms of co-operation for ensuring national security of the member states
EAPC	x	x	x	x	x	To discuss co-operation on mutual political and security issues
IAEA	x	x	x		x	To promote peaceful uses of atomic energy
ICAO	x	x	x	x	x	To promote international co-operation in civil aviation; a UN specialized agency
Interpol	x	x	x	x	x	To promote international co-operation among police authorities in fighting crime
NAM	observer	observer	observer	x	x	To establish political and military co-operation apart from the traditional East or West blocs
NSG	x					To establish guidelines for exports of nuclear materials, processing equipment for uranium enrichment, and technical information to countries of proliferation concern and regions of conflict and instability
OAS	observer					To promote regional peace and security as well as economic and social development

				Objectives
OPCW	x	x	x	To enforce the Convention on the Prohibition of the Development, Production, Stockpiling, and Use of Chemical Weapons and on Their Destruction; to provide a forum for consultation and co-operation among the signatories of the Convention
OSCE	x	x	x	To foster the implementation of human rights, fundamental freedoms, democracy and the rule of law; to act as an instrument of early warning, conflict prevention and crisis management; and to serve as a framework for conventional arms control and confidence-building measures
PFP	x	x	x	To expand and intensify political and military co-operation throughout Europe, increase stability, diminish threats to peace and build relationships by promoting the spirit of practical co-operation and commitment to democratic principles that underpin NATO; programme under the auspices of NATO
SCO	x	x	x	To combat terrorism, extremism and separatism; to safeguard regional security through mutual trust, disarmament and co-operative security; and to increase co-operation in political, trade, economic, scientific and technological, cultural and educational fields
WHO	x	x	x	To deal with health matters worldwide; a UN specialized agency
ZC	x			To establish guidelines for the export control provisions of the Nonproliferation of Nuclear Weapons Treaty (NPT)

For a comprehensive list of international organizations see Appendix A

This co-operation has in part sought to counter some of the threats outlined above. The CIS anti-terrorist centre in Moscow and intelligence co-operation also became increasingly useful as the Central Asian states prepared for anticipated attacks from the IMU and related groups. Buzan and Wæver (2003: 431):

> The SCO, originally formed to settle border questions, has now reorientated towards co-operation against terrorism, drugs trafficking, fundamentalism, and separatism. In practice, this is mainly about mutual support for repression of local revolts from Chechnya to Xinjiang. Islamic extremism is blamed for it all, and Afghanistan was singled out as a possible object for action.... This co-operation is enabled by China's recognition of Russian leadership in Central Asia ... which China so far sees as the best strategy to ensure stability and thus handle its main concern, Uighur rebels in Xinjiang.

But even in the context of all this co-operation, as in the economic sphere, the regional institutions formed do not seem to have furthered the practice of signing up to common rules and procedures or collaborative ventures (Deutsch 1957), and those broader regional institutions may well instead come closer to the Mearsheimerian (1994/5) view that describes how institutions are transient and reflect current power balances in the international system. For example: The Shanghai Five grouping, as the SCO was earlier named, arose out of a real functional need to address unresolved traditional security issues. Instead, the virtual regionalism that results, through 'protective integration' provides 'the benefits of political solidarity and a vicarious legitimacy to Central Asian political leaders who find difficulty in establishing this on the wider international stage. They seek to deflect appeals for good governance and substantive democracy in their domestic arrangements through a common front against the diffusion of "external" values in Central Asia' (Allison 2008: 198).

Writing on the dynamics of regional security institutions, Louise Fawcett (2008: 323), warns against 'attributing too much significance to concepts of regional identity. More important is the need for regions to project their power and influence, however limited, while attending to their own security concerns in a way that preserves regional autonomy and order'. Such projection of power and the attainment of regional order is greatly helped by the existence of a regional hegemon, but here again Central Asia is found wanting. While neither Kazakhstan nor Uzbekistan accept each other in this role, neither of these states is willing to unconditionally accept Russia as a broader regional hegemon either.

The balance needed to cement regional security institutions as suggested by Fawcett – regional projection, on the one hand, preservation of autonomy and order on the other – has not been achieved in Central Asia. This is partly a function of there being no hegemon, as described above. The imbalance also arises from weak states that are not interested in upsetting the status quo of boundary drawing and relative power balance. The region is easily penetrated for this reason and has also become quickly globalized and dependent. The outside powers who penetrate the region do not view Central Asian regional security as sufficiently bound with their national interest and thus for them Central Asia is often by itself not a national security interest. Threats are transnational rather than intrastate, again diminishing state-to-state rivalry among the five, and the usual way leaders have reacted is by defending their own statehood as regime security remains the primary goal of all five.

Conclusions

In many ways a case can be made that the newly created states of Central Asia present both 'traditional camps' with a new regional case study, with countries busy building states and asserting sovereignty at the same time as they try new partnerships and broader regional co-operation. At once a prize and a challenge, independence has rendered regime maintenance and the consolidation of sovereignty a priority over multilateral institution-building, in itself a costly operation for which Central Asian states have weak capacity. These pressures continue to make the traditional security challenges that accompany state sovereignty relevant for the region at the same time as the appearance of new transnational security threats. So, while the five states gained national independence in 1991, they face continuing challenges in securing that independence.

The challenge for writers on security in Central Asia is threefold: one, to acquire the information on sensitive issues in the first place; two, to aim for a reasonable and balanced representation of the hierarchy of issues confronting Central Asia; and three, to somehow overcome what is presented as the divide between discourse and evidence. The first is not germane to security studies nor to the region but begs questions about the need for good theoretical frameworks to write the correct questions. The second is about not allowing terrorism to swamp our analysis of other non-traditional threats nor of underlying causes (e.g., repression) for the rise of such issues. The third is striking a balance between available evidence – for example, of terrorist tactics of kidnapping and scaremongering – with using the fear of such terrorism to legitimate repressive acts. In other words, a careful evaluation of the level of threat cannot be discounted, and the recent rapid descent into violence in Osh has demonstrated this.

The case of human and environmental security offers a happy example of how two quite different types of security can work to mutually reinforce each other, but Central Asia has equally shown how they can be at odds with each other. Attempts to strengthen regime security, for example, by strengthening borders have often led to societal insecurity, as communities are cut off from each other or as they encounter hurdles to keep their cohesion and function. The opportunity to use border posts as instruments to block transit roads has in recent years often been grasped in order to push through political demands. Economic factors are rooted in the divergent national economic policies in the region. Uzbekistan, which tries to protect the domestic market, makes procedures at border posts particularly difficult. At the same time, the Central Asian region shows how these international organizations have rarely been implemented in practice, bedevilled by lack of capacity and lack of implementation mechanisms.

New threats and new referents have failed to generate a regional security complex (RSC) that would provide a propitious environment for the flourishing of regional security institutions. A security complex can exist whether or not states recognize the condition or not. Defined as 'a group of states whose primary security concerns link together sufficiently closely that their national securities cannot realistically be considered apart from one another' (Buzan 1991: 190). Buzan and Wæver (2003: 428–9) contend that 'Central Asia is a distinct subcomplex with the possibility of becoming an RSC. If the states in the region consolidate and gain an ability to threaten each other more directly, Russia is gradually weakened, and if no other external power steps decisively in, then RSC might become an RSC in its own right. If the USA hangs on with a few small bases becoming semi-permanent, this is likely actually to stimulate the formation of an independent RSC because it weakens Russian hegemony while being insufficient to constitute an alternative source of external domination (see Starr 2001)'.

Allison, by contrast, questions whether Central Asia has sufficient commonalities to form a regional security complex in and of itself, to the exclusion of surrounding states. Complexes may not encourage regional institutionalization at all – they could simply represent negative and hostile security interdependencies. For example, is there enough to bind Kyrgyzstan and Turkmenistan in a common security complex, given the former's continued reliance on Russia and the latter's widening of relations to states like Iran. For example, northern Afghanistan, the northern and eastern parts of Xinjiang, parts of the Russian-Kazakh border region, and even the Caspian Caucasus Muslim state of Azerbaijan might form as convincing a unit as one limited to Central Asia proper. He proposes instead, and convincingly, the case for several smaller sub-regional security complexes within Central Asia such as the Ferghana Valley and the Caspian Sea.

Given the absence for now of a broader complex, has the attraction of outside powers to this region made it more or less secure? Lutz Kleveman's (2003: 269) 'central argument' is that 'the sudden Caspian oil boom has been more a curse than a blessing for the local people'. In part this is a reference to how oil and the fear of Islamic terrorism are coupled. The coupling of such phenomena can lead to inappropriate policy responses as the sources of radicalism are incorrectly analysed. Moreover, the international discourse of a war on terror, as we saw, is conveniently adopted by regimes as national discourse and as legitimation for blanket repression. In practical terms, external power involvement has still in general fallen short of security guarantees and they are generally involved to secure other regions of the world rather than Central Asia. Furthermore, the fact that two regional powers are contiguous – Russia and China – creates greater possibilities for bilateral rather than multilateral approaches, almost letting these powers off the hook of institution-building.

That said, so far the Central Asian region is probably better off as a result of regional power involvement than it would be without such involvement, which has generated global economic and cultural interest. It has helped dilute tensions between the five states and sought to assist in areas vital to Central Asian leaders, such as border controls and scarce resources, where Central Asian leaders themselves have been unable to co-operate. They are also better equipped to handle non-traditional security challenges, for Swanström (2010: 36) these soft security threats in Central Asia are particularly 'damning ... because [they are] interlinked with traditional security threats and trans-national implications'. Central Asian leaders and their policy think-tanks seem above all to favour the SCO – probably because they view this institution as itself diluting the preponderance of either Russia or China but at the same time locking them into competitive relationships with Central Asia.

Is this particular juncture in the region's history calling for a specific type of approach to security over another? At the time of writing it is probably fair to say that attempts to understand Central Asian security have not yet generated new theoretical approaches but they have underscored the importance of a broad understanding of security. The experience of Central Asia seems to support earlier research that regionalism is not a promising way to mitigate conflict (Allison 2004a; Swanström 2005). The region has, however, brought to our attention again some of the limitations of the application of any single theoretical explanation to understanding it, as well as the sometimes Western-generated understandings that defy application to a region with its own set of historical, cultural and political dynamics. If anything, our brief overview of Central Asia has made a strong case for 'thick' theorizing and for broadening the referents of security, mindful of how this broadening must not lead to misleading coupling of origins of threats.

Notes

1 It is important to stress here that these authors often do not openly classify themselves as such, but their underlying epistemological approach and assumptions see identity and norms as the determinant factors behind certain sectors or policies.
2 Rise and fall realism, represented by writers like Robert Gilpin's (1981) *War and Change in World Politics*, portrays how the rise to domination or the fall to marginalized positions by states is cyclical.

8   Conclusion

State of the state in Central Asia

As Anatoly Khazanov (1983: 162) writes in relation to the evolution of nomadism on the Eurasian steppe, he knows 'of no examples of a state emerging as a result of the internal development of a nomadic society'. The importance of external players to the domestic politics of these five Central Asian states remains as critical today and, by way of conclusion, this chapter offers some closing remarks on the interface between regime security and state-building, on the one hand, and the jockeying by outside powers for influence and access to resources, on the other.

Domestic statehood, we have seen, is much broader than the act of governing; it is the sum of discourses, practices and relationships that tie individuals together as groups to feel a collective responsibility to a defined territory. Over time, societies develop expectations of what such statehood should provide. Central Asian populations in the Soviet era have developed expectations of state intervention to continue into the Soviet era, particularly in welfare provision. Instead, state provision of basic services has often fallen away by default or intent and where the state was previously not involved, such as in the (then black) market, it now is. In the words of an entrepreneur from Karaganda, Kazakhstan: 'The state is doing business; our job. We do the state's job by acting as social providers. This should be reversed' (quoted in Özcan 2010: 59).

Politically, the independence experience has provoked searching questions about what states are, how they are experienced and what should be expected of them in a period of flux. Transition theorists dominated political analysis of post-communist societies in the 1990s but largely ignored the role of the state. Political theorists make a distinction between the regime, the way power is organized, and the state, and the channels and institutions that enforce that power (by regulation, coercion or extraction). According to Joel S. Migdal (1988: 56), the relative strength of a state must be considered in light of its capacity to 'penetrate society, regulate social relationships, extract resources and appropriate or use resources in determined ways'. The shift in emphasis from regime to state came about largely through a disillusionment, which after just ten years might be considered premature, with the few successes in regime change. Thomas Carothers summarizes the shift in his two articles of 2002 and 2006. Anna Gryzmale-Busse and Pauline Jones Luong (2002: 2) refer to the mistaken assumption that 'these states were over-endowed with state structures'. They argue instead for a dialogue between people working on the state and those working on post-communist transformation, and thus 'to shift the analytical focus of the study of post-communism from "transitology" to state formation'.

This shift in emphasis has had practical implications for the international donor community. In the first ten years of independence, partly influenced by the thrust of democratization activity, funders viewed society rather than the state as the better channel through which to transform a polity. Funding was channelled to the non-governmental organizations, not the state. When those countries (notably Kazakhstan and Kyrgyzstan) failed to change in the direction those funders had hoped, the international community suggested a shift to state-building as opposed to society-building as a funding operative. This in turn led to all sorts of views about whether channelling money in this way could lead to state strengthening, and to what exactly is being strengthened when we talk about the state.

The absence of statehood shaped the way the region developed in the early modern era and also how Great Powers historically interacted with the region. Geopolitical and cultural understandings of what constitutes the Central Asian region have been partly affected by and have affected the emergence of statehood in the region. Chapter 2 mentioned how the existence or disappearances of entities with discrete borders has affected the region's centrality or otherwise, the notion of a 'black hole'. At the same time late state formation and permeable statehoods increased the ease of great power penetration into the region. Russia's expansion southward would have been considerably harder were it facing established states, or were it not a contiguous landmass (even acknowledging the huge distances involved). Similarly, the fluidity of boundaries up to Soviet rule increased the propensity of the region to be absorbed by regional powers. Landlocked statehood intensified cultural interchange and the difficulties of establishing a discrete regional identity. Some continue to view the region as isolated instead of central and even go so far as to link this marginality to the likelihood of state failure.

As Chapter 3 further illustrated, this has been a region of late-modern state formation. State formation and Sovietisation thus occurred simultaneously in Central Asia. Russian imperial rule territorialized power in this region for the first time while its Soviet successor created units that came closest to creating a form of modern statehood. This in part explains the reluctance to declare independence, in that independence might be paradoxically associated with the loss of statehood. Dudoignon (1997a: 58) describes 'the intellectual mediocrity prevalent in Dushanbe, as in all the Soviet provincial capitals, precluded any hope of the intelligentsia's survival outside the national Socialism of which it had made itself the official custodian'.

Late state formation means that many of the processes that elsewhere took centuries to achieve have been accelerated. In some senses latecomers benefit from avoiding the mistakes of their predecessors but in other ways they are forced to come to terms simultaneously with a number of transformative, contradictory processes, the simultaneity sometimes making problems intractable and violence often the result. Snyder's (2000) *From Voting to Violence*, for example, is about the dangers of early liberalization and its tendency to lead to violent nationalism. According to Rubin and Snyder (1998), three challenges followed Soviet collapse: first, the security of the individual was under threat; second, the political participation which allowed for large-scale mobilization without clear channels of organization and mediation was widened; and, third, the Soviet economy collapsed.

Some 20 years on from 1991, however, most scholars writing on Central Asian statehood agree that concepts like 'state failure' and 'weak state' do not adequately capture the complexities and peculiarities of state transformation. Heathershaw (2011: 154, 150), for example, takes issue with several international donor or agency reports that 'remain wedded to a moribund, exogenous and self-referential concept of the state', for example, depicting Tajikistan as a 'failed state', and he criticizes authors who predict collapse. He also cites Fiona Hill's (2002) assessment of a potential 'Afghanization' of post-Soviet Central Asia given these states' 'extreme domestic fragility'. By contrast, Anna Matveeva (2006, 2009) refers to the 'resilient' nature of the Tajik state and argues that 'state-building' should replace 'peace-building'. The result, aptly coined by McMann (2004), is a 'strong-weak' state.

Traditional labels of weakness and strength are indeed misplaced if we consider the peculiar nature of the statehood bequeathed by the Soviets, and therefore the difficulty and perhaps inappropriateness of applying a Western concept to a process that displayed quite different properties to the European experience. Far from a Weberian ideal-type, the post-Soviet Central Asian state has not displayed the rationality, coherence and co-ordination of the means of violence over a specific territory associated with that term. Nor is the state a unitary actor (a point contested by many generally in analyses of the state, making the application of state as person very difficult). Given the fusion of bureaucracy and politics in the Soviet era – the Communist party was the state and the state was the Communist party – the state emerged strongly politicized and not 'rational'. References here to 'the state', used as shorthand, should also be understood as reflective of the people in the state or institutions of the state, rather than denoting some single entity with free-floating properties existing external to the actors who constitute it or the subjects who are affected by it.

Nor is the post-Soviet state a traditional post-colonial state, even if reference to post-colonial literature can be useful. Although resembling a post-colonial state previously deprived of external sovereignty, the post-Soviet state had developed stronger pockets of domestic capacity and autonomy. This was partly because by the late Soviet era republican leaders had acquired considerable freedom in personnel policy. Also, unlike colonial states, the Soviet state's ideology demanded a tight suppression of any form of civil society, which offered another explanation for the absence of mobilization and dissent. The 'bureaucratic sovereignty' (Lewis 2011) that resulted explains why and partly how Soviet leaders were able to become post-Soviet leaders. The suppression of civil society led to a particular fusion already in the Communist period that made a neat separation of state and society analytically and practically impossible. The transformative nature of Soviet ideology, coupled with its dual assimilation policy, has resulted in a semi-colonial structure.

The policy of dual assimilation is critical to our understanding of the Soviet period. Society, or social cohesion, was given its identity by communist authorities not only as an international community of people marching to socialism but also as a group of nations organized according to ethnicity and coexisting with each other. In reality, ethnicity alone did not determine the border drawing of republican states. Realpolitik, economic considerations, divide-and-rule premises and geography were also factors. But the attempt to give the largest ethnic groups their own republic was certainly a defining criterion. Lenin saw this approach primarily as a tactic of winning support for the Bolshevik programme, envisioning the eventual 'withering away of the state' in a world community of communists. Stalin, appointed Commissar of Nationalities Policy in 1917, turned tactics to strategy with theoretical content, and under him an ethnographic approach to nation-building and nationhood was elaborately developed. Between 1917 and 1991 there were not one but several nationalities policies. They emphasized either the *sblizhenie* (coming together) or the *sliyanie* (merger) of different peoples, the latter being characteristic of the more ideological eras when attempts were made to hasten the withering away of the state and create a homo sovieticus. The Soviet period has left dual legacies of Soviet internationalism and nationalism.

With the opening of Soviet archives, also discussed in Chapter 3, the picture we have of border drawing is less one of an arbitrary process than one that also involved Soviet ethnographers, local cultural and political elites and wider populations. The biggest losers were the Tajiks: despite having their status upgraded from ASSR in 1924 to Tajik SSR in 1929, some 60 per cent of Tajikistan's citizens ended up resident outside their newly designated Tajik SSR state, losing also the historic centres of Bukhara and Samarkand to the Uzbek SSR. Land, and claims of land, became a premium in this exercise. Osh, originally part of Uzbekistan, was transferred to the Kyrgyz SSR on its later formation in 1936. The settlement of a large number of Slav colonizers in the northern regions of Kazakhstan transformed it into a republic with a Russian-dominated North and Kazakh-dominated South with non-Kazakhs outnumbering Kazakhs by the time independence was reached, creating existential challenges for the state in the early independence years. To date, however, irredentism has remained almost exclusively at the level of rhetoric, post-independence leaders showing strong support for the status quo of existing borders.

Elites at the helm of their newly independent countries have sought various legitimating strategies to justify their power, and all have involved, as Chapter 5 elaborated, titular nationalism, even if 'by stealth' (Bohr 1998a). Writing on Tajikistan, Atkin (2010: 2) points out that 'the Samanid dynasty, which ruled most of the eastern Iranian world in the ninth and tenth centuries from its capital in Bukhara, is extolled as a Tajik state. Yet the Samanids would not have agreed with their Soviet characterization as Tajiks distinct from the broader population of Persian-speakers'. In the aftermath of the civil war, which elites have used as 'a strange kind of foundation myth' (Atkin 2010: 1), a new Aryan myth has been propagated. In multi-ethnic Kazakhstan and Kyrgyzstan, elites in the early independence years sought to try to portray both civic and national nation-building policies. Bhavna Dave (2004) argues that the success of language policy and implementation in Kazakhstan relative to Kyrgyzstan can best be explained by the greater degree of consensus among cultural elites. Central Asian states are endowed with different ideas of the state.

In this legitimation process, performance and symbolism matter (Cummings 2010). Symbolic legitimation is critical to power maintenance and to imbuing a sense of belonging into citizens of newly independent states. The picture in Central Asia encourages us to look at the complementarity rather than competitiveness of these layers of identity. Clans compose state, titular identities feed state national identities and state rhetoric feeds on multi-ethnicity to further encourage civic identities. While staunchly defending their states as secular and suppressing Islam when it was perceived as threatening their rule, elites have nonetheless carefully used Islam in their legitimating strategies. Judith Beyer et al (forthcoming) write on the performance of the state and encourage ways 'to explore how the scope for the political, the categories through which political action proceeds, the possibilities for how the political is constituted, are located within Central Asian lifeworlds'.

The picture emerging is of a set of institutions that is neither a static nor a separately existing entity. Rather like the use of the verb 'legitimate' in place of the noun 'legitimacy' (Chapter 5), the verb 'become' helpfully describes a notion of feeling part of a state. The state and sovereignty are a process rather than an outcome. The idea of states and state-building as process, rather than states being stable and consolidated, is captured by Gryzmala-Busse and Jones Luong (2002: 3) thus as:

> *a competitive process of establishing authority over a given territory.* This process consists of individual or institutional actors who face different modes of competition (self-contained or representative) and employ different mechanisms to win this competition (formal or informal structures and practices). The various combinations of these modes and mechanisms produce different degrees of elite constraint and popular compliance, which, in turn, comprise distinct state-building trajectories – hegemonic, personalistic, democratic, and fractured.

In this competitive process perception is a critical element in that how leaders have perceived their strength relative to other elites and society influenced how they bargained or negotiated pacts and how successful they were at doing so.

The state becomes a domain of unfinished identity construction where narratives and imaginaries compete. Chapters 4 and 6 suggested that political and economic elites, who in Central Asia continue to be unified, compete often intensively over access to resources. The state, moreover, is endowed with varying capacities. On the one hand, these may be mapped sectorally. Jones Luong (2004: 276) refers to how 'the state tends to struggle against itself' and of our need to 'disaggregate the state'. In all five, state capacity in the sectors of welfare and infrastructure has been enormously neglected. ICG (2011: i) states that 'Barring a turnaround in policies they face a future of decaying roads, schools and medical institutions staffed by pensioners, or a new generation of teachers, doctors or engineers whose qualifications were purchased rather than earned'. Furthermore (2011: 36):

> Kyrgyzstan and Tajikistan are in the worst shape. Infrastructure is at the edge of collapse and has been deprived of investment. Turkmenistan and Uzbekistan are experiencing slow, but consistent decline. Their situation in the near future may be no less disastrous than in Kyrgyzstan and Tajikistan, as the scope of decline becomes harder to hide. There is little hope that the downward spiral in these four countries can be stopped. Kazakhstan has made patchy progress in some sectors and conserved Soviet endowments in others.

Even when, as in Uzbekistan and Turkmenistan, a gradual economic reform process was chosen over shock therapy, the state, while cushioning reform, was forced to withdraw from huge sectors. The Uzbekistani government has substantially slowed the development of the cotton sector by instituting a policy designed to make farmers pay for only partial reform (in particular the maintenance of high input prices along with the refusal to pay farmers world prices for cotton). To different degrees, the state has retreated from its obligation to provide basic services to its society. Those services, as the businessman from Karaganda noted, have sometimes been provided by private entrepreneurs, in other cases by criminal groups or social organizations. By contrast, in its state banking and pensions sectors, Kazakhstan, for example, already by the end of the 1990s built up considerable state capacity to extract, coerce and regulate. Kyrgyzstan and Kazakhstan's state capacity in relation to civil society has displayed significant disparities (Cummings and Nørgaard 2004).

On the other hand, state capacities vary geographically. In Kazakhstan's regions with heavy international investment regional elites become tied to global capital and institutions beyond the borders of their nation-states (Cummings 2000). The degree to which the centre is able to preserve its regional links depends on the degree to which it has a hold over the region, and the ability of an authoritarian regime to keep that centralized state control. Pavlodar's aluminium factory, one of several industrial plants negotiated to foreign management in the 1994–7 mass privatization period under Kazakhstan's first prime minister Akezhan Kazhegeldin, shows how the centre was directly involved with the region's contacts with the outside world and similarly Rahmonov's attempts since 2004 to take dominant control over the Tajik State Aluminium Company, TALCO brought him into a web of global economic and political contacts. Some state sectors have become more globalized, others more localized and the state

has experienced globalization and de-industrialization, consolidation and fragmentation simultaneously.

Again, we pause to reflect on what this says about the nature of the state,
particularly about the confluence of domestic and international forces in state
creation. Central Asia appears to confirm the now increasingly accepted view
that globalization transforms the state rather than sounding its deathknell,
incorporating outside influences into new statehood forms and functions rather
like the Soviets did. The internal/external becomes difficult to disaggregate.
Politically – including after the coloured revolutions – some authors express
disquietude about aggressive international efforts to promote democracy.
Heathershaw (2011: 154) for example, warns that in Tajikistan for instance, order
and authority 'would be shattered if there were, by some means, the imposition
of a depersonalized and highly competitive system against both elite and societal
demands'. Internal state-building through foreign intervention may be less a
contradiction in terms than an affirmation of today's world in which boundaries
between domestic and the external are blurred.

Fuzzy boundaries also characterize Central Asia's state-society relations. This
is a direct result of the state's thorough penetration of society in the Soviet era
but has been actively nurtured by post-Soviet elites. The most obvious way in
which the state has sought to keep lines blurred is through its use of informal
networks. These, as Chapters 4 and 5 detailed, are primarily patron–client
relationships that explain how appointments are made, how policies become
enacted and how mobilization is controlled or suppressed. These informal
networks do not make the concept of a modern state meaningless; they simply
make its content and practices different.

The relationship between the formal and the informal remains contested:

> Informal structures were a pervasive feature of communism. Yet, they var-
> ied in form and scope across the post-communist states: from the social and
> economic networks based on barter between enterprises and individuals
> in East Central Europe and Russia to more traditional patronage networks
> in Central Asia and the Caucasus. In the former, they served primarily as a
> means of surviving both the political excesses and economic shortages of
> communism, and thus were more useful tools for resisting than establish-
> ing authority. In the latter, however, they came to define the political and
> economic system itself.
>
> (Gryzmale-Busse and Jones Luong 2002: 26)

We saw how these may be viewed, for example, in regional (Jones Luong 2002)
or in clan (Collins 2006) terms.

For others the informal in Central Asia is more akin to the social and economic
networks apparent in East Central Europe and Russia and has very little
tradition about it. It is an instrumentalist patrimonialism that can use all sorts of
identities – social, traditional, economic – to further the aim particular elites set
for it. This is the argument promoted by Tunçer-Kilavuz (2011) in her network

analysis of the mobilization of Tajikistan. But it is also the argument made by those who feel we must avoid the trap of putting all politics in Central Asia down to sub-national clan identities when the legacies of Soviet modernization and contemporary globalization ensure the continuation of modern institutional forms and functions. The point is that there is still a state that even legitimates itself and manipulates through informal means (Schatz 2004). 'The crucial starting point in determining whether formal or informal mechanisms dominate is the extent to which a centralized state apparatus exists prior to the inception of the state formation process (Gryzmale-Busse and Jones Luong 2002: 15).

State elites have managed to keep boundaries blurred because of their continued monopoly over economic resources which affords them also a significant degree of control. Kelly McMann (2004: 226–7) argues that activist attitudes have been less influenced by Central Asian traditions and foreign influences than Soviet economic legacies: 'the state in Kyrgyzstan has a de-facto monopoly on certain goods. The limited sources of goods leads even those civic groups that see themselves as state adversaries and those groups that fear dependence on the state to seek government assistance'.

Expectations play a large part in this narrative. On the one hand, elites' 'de-facto monopoly' over economic resources make societal actors continue to expect considerable provision of public goods (positive sovereignty), partly because the Soviet era did, and partly because the free market has failed to step into the Soviet state's place. Citizens emerged from Soviet rule with strong expectations of what the state should provide. Marianne Kamp (2006) shows how Soviet rule's elevation of the status of women has led women to want a more equal role again in society. On the other hand, McMann (2004: 214) notes that '[a]lthough most post-Soviet governments do not manage public life to the extent that the Communist regime did, states continue to shape the expectations of civic activists because governments possess a relative wealth of resources'. Swanström (2010: 46) concludes that '[m]uch of the radicalization we see today has its roots in the failure of the regional governments to act and provide security for an individual's economic and social development'. When the overarching state as neutral arbiter is perceived to be absent, the security dilemma can result, often rapidly, at societal level. Societal security is a direct function of state security: the more secure a society perceives its state to be, the less it feels threatened.

Central Asian states have come to resist international, mainly Western, pressures for domestic reform, de-monopolization of their power, and a rebalancing of these expectations. Kazakhstan, the Kyrgyz Republic and Tajikistan were open to these influences largely in the early 1990s. Jones Luong (2004: 280, 279) comments that '[a]lthough this regional convergence toward authoritarian regimes and closed economies began in the mid-1990s, it has accelerated since the incursion of armed Islamic militants into the region beginning in 1999'. Also, external rents can allow 'Kazakhstan, Turkmenistan, and Uzbekistan [to be] more insulated from the international community as well as from their own populations'.

Deniz Kandiyoti (2002: 282) argues that in order to fully understand the post-Soviet trajectories of the Central Asian republics, students of the region should not only take into account 'the historical specificities of their colonial encounters but also very different modalities and temporalities of their insertion into world capitalist markets'. It is argued here that the initial policies and choices of the post-Soviet regime firmly linked the future of the country to the volatile commodity prices on the international markets. This argument is supported by the fact that despite the collapse of cotton prices towards the end of the 1990s, in the beginning of the 2000s the primary commodities, together with cotton fibre, still accounted for 75 per cent of merchandise exports, with cotton alone accounting for about 40 per cent (Gleason 2003: 119). In the second decade of independence, the Uzbek government attempted to cushion the fall in cotton prices with a partial liberalization of its economy. Yet, the cotton industry remained subject to state orders and state control.

Referring to the concept of 'suspended state' (Schlichte 2005), Elmira Satybaldieva (2010: 235) describes the Kyrgyzstani state as '"suspended" between local and international expectations', and finds both politics and state-society relations as structured by neo-liberal development programmes which, overall, have weakened rather than strengthened both formal and informal state institutions. Focusing also on rural Kyrgyzstan, Judith Beyer (2007: 2) shows how these discourses can lead to unexpected appropriations since, while state officials try and state-build and 'think of strengthening what they consider to be customary law, the courts of elders "imagine the state" and apply procedures and norms they trace to state law'.

Part of the state's hybridity stems from the rentier nature of the state, covered in Chapter 6. While more recent research (Jones Luong and Weinthal 2010) shows that the extent of rentierism can depend on the particular structure of domestic institutions, corruption and patrimonial regimes, also in the semi-rentier states of Kyrgyzstan and Tajikistan, dependencies have prevailed. Ostrowski (2011: 299), writes that 'both [rentier and semi-rentier states'] foreign policies are entangled and shaped by various types of dependencies: dependencies which inevitably pose vital questions concerning state survival, state security and ultimately the sovereignty of rentier and semi-rentier states'. China and Russia, in contrast to the west, have actively endorsed Central Asian authoritarianism.

In the international pecking order, Central Asian states remain largely consumers rather than producers of international relations (Chapter 7). They are all small states in the international system. At the same time, however, their states have branded new international images of themselves that have, on the whole, been successful. Thus, for example, the initial self-branding of Kyrgyzstan as the Switzerland of Central Asia and as a liberalizer open for business played a huge part in attracting foreign aid. Kazakhstan's self-branding as a modern, Eurasian nation was pivotal in its obtaining Chairmanship of the OSCE in 2010. Identity and construction have thus to a degree overcome some of the geopolitical disadvantages of being small, landlocked states.

As small states with some success at independent ideologies and branding, they have also managed to carve out some independence in foreign policy creation. The Great Game captures therefore only part of the dynamic. The part it successfully captures is the element of competition between Great Powers in the region. Less successfully captured is how local powers have been known to use, exploit or ignore this competition.

Part of the reason why the Central Asian state defies clear-cut categorization is its unfinished nature. It is 'unstructured', and therefore dynamics form at other levels and the region is relatively open to penetration by external powers (Buzan and Wæver 2003: 426). This penetration can be as far as the de facto dependency, puppet state of Russia that some say Kyrgyzstan is becoming or the penetration can occur by two powers. Some writers say that the Kyrgyz Republic is carved up between China and Russia and these zones of influence will eventually lead to the country's separation. Even in apparently more autonomous and structured states like Uzbekistan and Turkmenistan, penetration by outside powers is higher than for many other countries of the world.

The nature of the state has also helped to explain regime type, and in turn, systems which are largely authoritarian have affected the nature of state-building. Late-formed statehood and imperfect units, coupled with the absence of civil society, dissident culture and mobilizational features, have ensured the survival of elites into the post-communist period. Turkmenistan's first president, accessing power at the same as Gorbachev in 1985, managed to maintain his republic's isolation from the events of perestroika and glasnost. The creation of independent statehood by default has also explained a number of subsequent developments: it explained why the intelligentsia was ultimately unable, even in Tajikistan, to consolidate its hold over independent political movements and it explains why presidents were quickly able to monopolize power or at least be in a better perceived bargaining position to monopolize power.

On the whole, elites have preferred to work at preserving their power (regime maintenance) as opposed to building capacities of states (state-building). The aim of regime maintenance has also played a large role in shaping these fledgling states' partners in security and economics. The international community ignored or sought to dismantle the state in the first decade of its interest in the region in the name of economic and political liberalization. Disempowering state institutions, while at the same time allowing individual elites to enrich themselves, ensured not only rampant corruption but also a growing dysfunctionality and delegitimizing of the state. Regime preservation has encouraged the pursuit of state interests but has primarily discouraged the pooling of sovereignty out of fear that an outside power will encroach upon their policy-making. Regime preservation has also been the primary reason why regional co-operation has assumed only a 'virtual' (Allison 2008) dimension. The sorts of shared purposes and common institutions necessary for the development of an international (here regional society in English School or rationalism's terms) does not therefore exist, and the Central Asian space remains at the level only of an international (here regional) system, in which states interact with one another and calculate each other's economic and military capacities and political institutions. The state, therefore, is a hybrid of Soviet construction, temporality and templates, mixed with independent, globalized protectorate status. The elites in Central Asia have often resorted to similar state-building techniques and have often used communist templates. It is not entirely as yet post-Soviet, with traces of this past era remaining infused in patterns of governing and state imaginations. At the same time the state has changed. It has been forced to loosen its grip on society even in the most authoritarian of regimes. Its future trajectories remain uncertain.

Appendix A (Further tables)

Elections

Date	Country	Election type	Results (if parliamentary, majority winner only)
24-Mar-1990	Uzbek SSR	Presidential	Karimov elected President of Uzbek SSR by the Supreme Soviet
24-Apr-1990	Kazakh SSR	Presidential	Nazarbaev elected President of Kazakh SSR by the Supreme Soviet
27-Oct-1990	Kyrgyz SSR	Presidential	Akaev elected President of Kyrgyz SSR by the Supreme Soviet
27-Oct-1990	Turkmen SSR	Presidential	Niyazov elected President of Turkmen SSR by the Supreme Soviet
30-Nov-1990	Tajik SSR	Presidential	Kahar Mahkamov elected President of Tajik SSR by the Supreme Soviet
1-Dec-1991	Kazakhstan	Presidential	Nazarbaev runs unopposed
29-Dec-1991	Uzbekistan	Presidential	Karimov (86%)
21-Jun-1992	Turkmenistan	Presidential	Niyazov (99.5%)
6-Nov-1994	Tajikistan	Presidential	Rahmonov (58%)
11-Dec-1994	Turkmenistan	Parliamentary – Majilis	Democratic Party (45 seats)
25-Dec-1994	Uzbekistan	Parliamentary	People's Democratic Party (69 seats)
12-Mar-1995	Tajikistan	Parliamentary	Communist Party and affiliates (100 seats)
5-Nov-1995	Kyrgyzstan	Parliamentary	Unavailable
5-Dec-1995	Kazakhstan	Senate (indirect)	Independent state officials (25 seats)

Continued

Elections   (Continued)

Date	Country	Election type	Results (if parliamentary, majority winner only)
9-Dec-1995	Kazakhstan	Parliamentary	People's Unity Party (24 seats)
24-Dec-1995	Kyrgyzstan	Presidential	Akaev (75%)
10-Jan-1999	Kazakhstan	Presidential	Nazarbaev (81.7%)
10-Oct-1999	Kazakhstan	Parliamentary	Otan (23 seats)
6-Nov-1999	Tajikistan	Presidential	Rahmonov (97%)
12-Dec-1999	Turkmenistan	Parliamentary – Majilis	Democractic Party wins majority (all seats preapproved by Niyazov)
17-Dec-1999	Kazakhstan	Senate (indirect)	Unavailable
19-Dec-1999	Uzbekistan	Parliamentary	People's Democratic Party (48 seats)
9-Jan-2000	Uzbekistan	Presidential	Karimov (91.9%)
27-Feb-2000	Tajikistan	Parliamentary	Assembly of Representatives (percentage of vote by party): People's Democratic Party of Tajikistan 65%
12-Mar-2000	Kyrgyzstan	Parliamentary	Union of Democratic Forces (12 seats)
29-Oct-2000	Kyrgyzstan	Presidential	Akaev (74%)
6-Apr-2003	Turkmenistan	Parliamentary – People's Council (Halk Maslahaty)	Unavailable
19-Sep-2004	Kazakhstan	Parliamentary	Otan (42 seats)
19-Dec-2004	Turkmenistan	Parliamentary – Majilis	Democratic Party (50 seats)
9-Jan-2005	Uzbekistan	Parliamentary	Liberal Democratic Party of Uzbekistan (41 seats)
27-Feb-2005	Kyrgyzstan	Parliamentary	See Timeline – 'The Tulip "Revolution"'
27-Feb-2005	Tajikistan	Parliamentary	People's Democratic Party of Tajikistan (51 seats)
10-Jul-2005	Kyrgyzstan	Presidential	Bakiev (88.6%)
4-Dec-2005	Kazakhstan	Presidential	Nazarbaev (91.9%)
6-Nov-2006	Tajikistan	Presidential	Rahmonov (79.3%)
11-Feb-2007	Turkmenistan	Presidential	Berdymukhamedov (89.2%)
18-Aug-2007	Kazakhstan	Parliamentary	Nur Otan (98 seats)
16-Dec-2007	Kyrgyzstan	Parliamentary	Ak Jol (71 seats)
23-Dec-2007	Uzbekistan	Presidential	Karimov (88.1%)

Elections   (Continued)

Date	Country	Election type	Results (if parliamentary, majority winner only)
14-Dec-2008	Turkmenistan	Parliamentary	Democratic Party and the Revival Movement, both preapproved by president, gain all seats
23-Jul-2009	Kyrgyzstan	Presidential	Bakiev (76.1%)
27-Dec-2009	Uzbekistan	Parliamentary	Liberal Democratic Party of Uzbekistan (53 seats)
28-Feb-2010	Tajikistan	Parliamentary	People's Democratic Party of Tajikistan (55 seats)
10-Oct-2010	Kyrgyzstan	Parliamentary	Ata-Jurt (28 seats)
3-Apr-2011	Kazakhstan	Presidential	Nazarbaev (95.5%)

Elections results compiled from the following sources:

(1995)   'News in brief', *Sydney Morning Herald*, 1 Sep., retrieved through Nexis.

(1996)   *The World Factbook*, Washington, DC: Central Intelligence Agency; retrieved through Project Gutenberg.

(1998)   'Kyrgyzstan: Country Profile', *Asia & Pacific Review of World Information*, Nov., retrieved through Nexis.

(1998)   'UPDATE ON THE KYRGYZ REFERENDUM ON ALTERATION OF THE CONSTITUTION', 'Vesti' Radio Program from *What the papers say*, 28 Oct, retrieved through Nexis.

(1999)   'Niyazov Elected President for Life', *World News Digest*, 31 Dec., retrieved through Nexis.

(1999)   'TAJIK REFERENDUM RESULTS ANNOUNCED', Tajik Radio First Programme, *BBC Monitoring Central Asia Unit*, 4 Oct., retrieved through Nexis.

(2000)   'Kyrgyz Republic Parliamentary Elections: Final Report', *OSCE*, Apr.

(2001)   *The World Factbook*, Washington, DC: Central Intelligence Agency.

(2003)   'Controversial changes to Kyrgyzstan constitution become law', *Agence France Presse*, 18 Feb., retrieved through Nexis.

(2003)   'Tajik President Wins Mandate for Two Additional Terms', *Defense & Foreign Affairs Daily*, 21(98), 24 Jun., retrieved through Nexis.

(2005)   *The World Factbook*, Washington, DC: Central Intelligence Agency.

(2008)   *The World Factbook*, Washington, DC: Central Intelligence Agency.

(2011)   *ElectionGuide*, International Foundation for Electoral Systems, available at: http://www.electionguide.org/

(2011)   *The World Factbook*, Washington, DC: Central Intelligence Agency.

Isamova, L. (1999) 'Final results confirm constitutional changes, allowing Islamic parties', *Associated Press*, 2 Oct., retrieved through Nexis.

International organizations and their aims

Acronym	Full name	Mission
ADB	Asian Development Bank	To promote regional economic co-operation
CICA	Conference of Interaction and Confidence-Building Measures in Asia	Promoting a multi-national forum for enhancing co-operation towards promoting peace, security, and stability in Asia
CIS	Commonwealth of Independent States	To co-ordinate intercommonwealth relations and to provide a mechanism for the orderly dissolution of the USSR
CSTO	Collective Security Treaty Organization	To co-ordinate military and political co-operation, to develop multilateral structures and mechanisms of co-operation for ensuring national security of the member states
EAEC	Eurasian Economic Community	To create a common economic and energy policy
EAPC	Euro-Atlantic Partnership Council	To discuss co-operation on mutual political and security issues
EBRD	European Bank for Reconstruction and Development	To facilitate the transition of seven centrally planned economies in Europe (Bulgaria, former Czechoslovakia, Hungary, Poland, Romania, former USSR and former Yugoslavia) to market economies by committing 60% of its loans to privatization
ECO	Economic Cooperation Organization	To promote regional co-operation in trade, transportation, communications, tourism, cultural affairs and economic development
FAO	Food and Agriculture Organization	To raise living standards and increase availability of agricultural products; a UN specialized agency
GCTU	General Confederation of Trade Unions	To consolidate trade union actions to protect citizens' social and labor rights and interests, to help secure trade unions' rights and guarantees, and to strengthen international trade union solidarity
G-77	Group of 77	To promote economic co-operation among developing countries; name persists in spite of increased membership
IAEA	International Atomic Energy Agency	To promote peaceful uses of atomic energy

IBRD	International Bank for Reconstruction and Development (World Bank)	To provide economic development loans; a UN specialized agency
ICAO	International Civil Aviation Organization	To promote international co-operation in civil aviation; a UN specialized agency
ICRM	International Red Cross and Red Crescent Movement	To promote worldwide humanitarian aid through the International Committee of the Red Cross (ICRC) in wartime, and International Federation of Red Cross and Red Crescent Societies (IFRCS; formerly League of Red Cross and Red Crescent Societies or LORCS) in peacetime
IDA	International Development Association	To provide economic loans for low-income countries; UN specialized agency and IBRD affiliate
IDB	Islamic Development Bank	To promote Islamic economic aid and social development
IFAD	International Fund for Agricultural Development	To promote agricultural development; a UN specialized agency
IFC	International Finance Corporation	To support private enterprise in international economic development; a UN specialized agency and IBRD affiliate
IFRCS	International Federation of Red Cross and Red Crescent Societies	To organize, co-ordinate and direct international relief actions; to promote humanitarian activities; to represent and encourage the development of National Societies; to bring help to victims of armed conflicts, refugees and displaced people; to reduce the vulnerability of people through development programmes
ILO	International Labor Organization	To deal with world labour issues; a UN specialized agency
IMF	International Monetary Fund	To promote world monetary stability and economic development; a UN specialized agency
IMO	International Maritime Organization	To deal with international maritime affairs; a UN specialized agency
Interpol	International Criminal Police Organization	To promote international co-operation among police authorities in fighting crime
IOC	International Olympic Committee	To promote the Olympic ideals and administer the Olympic games
IOM	International Organization for Migration	To facilitate orderly international emigration and immigration

Continued

International organizations and their aims (Continued)

Acronym	Full name	Mission
IPU	Inter-Parliamentary Union	Fosters contacts among parliamentarians, considers and expresses views of international interest and concern with the purpose of bringing about action by parliaments and parliamentarians, contributes to the defense and promotion of human rights, contributes to better knowledge of representative institutions
ISO	International Organization for Standardization	To promote the development of international standards with a view to facilitating international exchange of goods and services and to developing co-operation in the sphere of intellectual, scientific, technological and economic activity
ITSO	International Telecommunications Satellites Organization	To act as a watchdog over Intelsat, Ltd., a private company, to make sure it provides on a global and non-discriminatory basis public telecommunication services
ITU	International Telecommunication Union	To deal with world telecommunications issues; a UN specialized agency
MIGA	Multilateral Investment Guarantee Agency	Encourages flow of foreign direct investment among member countries by offering investment insurance, consultation and negotiation on conditions for foreign investment and technical assistance; a UN specialized agency
NAM	Nonaligned Movement	To establish political and military cooperation apart from the traditional East or West blocs
NSG	Nuclear Suppliers Group	To establish guidelines for exports of nuclear materials, processing equipment for uranium enrichment and technical information to countries of proliferation concern and regions of conflict and instability
OAS	Organization of American States	To promote regional peace and security as well as economic and social development
OIC	Organization of the Islamic Conference	To promote Islamic solidarity in economic, social, cultural, and political affairs

OPCW	Organization for the Prohibition of Chemical Weapons	To enforce the Convention on the Prohibition of the Development, Production, Stockpiling and Use of Chemical Weapons and on Their Destruction; to provide a forum for consultation and co-operation among the signatories of the Convention
OSCE	Organization for Security and Cooperation in Europe	To foster the implementation of human rights, fundamental freedoms, democracy and the rule of law; to act as an instrument of early warning, conflict prevention and crisis management; and to serve as a framework for conventional arms control and confidence-building measures
PFP	Partnership for Peace	To expand and intensify political and military co-operation throughout Europe, increase stability, diminish threats to peace and build relationships by promoting the spirit of practical co-operation and commitment to democratic principles that underpin NATO; programme under the auspices of NATO
SCO	Shanghai Cooperation Organization	To combat terrorism, extremism and separatism; to safeguard regional security through mutual trust, disarmament and co-operative security; and to increase co-operation in political, trade, economic, scientific and technological, cultural, and educational fields
UN	United Nations	To maintain international peace and security and to promote co-operation involving economic, social, cultural and humanitarian problems
UNCTAD	United Nations Conference on Trade and Development	To promote international trade
UNESCO	United Nations Educational, Scientific, and Cultural Organization	To promote co-operation in education, science and culture
UNIDO	United Nations Industrial Development Organization	UN specialized agency that promotes industrial development especially among the members
UNMIL	United Nations Mission in Liberia	To support the cease-fire agreement and peace process, protect UN facilities and people, support humanitarian activities and assist in national security reform

Continued

International organizations and their aims (Continued)

Acronym	Full name	Mission
UNMIS	United Nations Mission in the Sudan	To support implementation of the comprehensive Peace Agreement by monitoring and verifying the implementation of the Cease Fire Agreement, by observing and monitoring movements of armed groups, and by helping disarm, demobilize and reintegrate armed bands
UNWTO	World Tourism Organization	To promote tourism as a means of contributing to economic development, international understanding and peace
UPU	Universal Postal Union	To promote international postal co-operation; a UN specialized agency
WCO	World Customs Organization	To promote international co-operation in customs matters
WFTU	World Federation of Trade Unions	To promote the trade union movement
WHO	World Health Organization	To deal with health matters worldwide; a UN specialized agency
WIPO	World Intellectual Property Organization	To furnish protection for literary, artistic and scientific works; a UN specialized agency
WMO	World Meteorological Organization	To sponsor meteorological co-operation; a UN specialized agency
WTO	World Trade Organization	To provide a forum to resolve trade conflicts between members and to carry on negotiations with the goal of further lowering and/or eliminating tariffs and other trade barriers
ZC	Zangger Committee	To establish guidelines for the export control provisions of the Nonproliferation of Nuclear Weapons Treaty (NPT)

Source: (2011) *The World Factbook*, Washington, DC: Central Intelligence Agency

Appendix B (Maps)

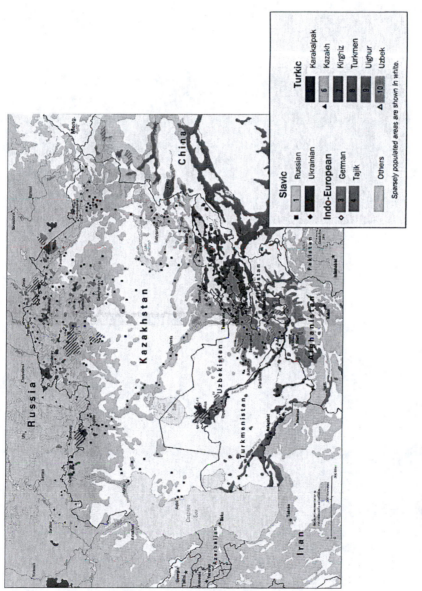

Map 3 Major ethnic groups in Central Asia in 1993. Map produced by the US Central Intelligence Agency and retrieved from the Perry-Castañeda Library's Map Collection at University of Texas at Austin. Available in colour at: www.lib. utexas.edu/maps/middle_east_and_asia/casia_ethnic_93.jpg

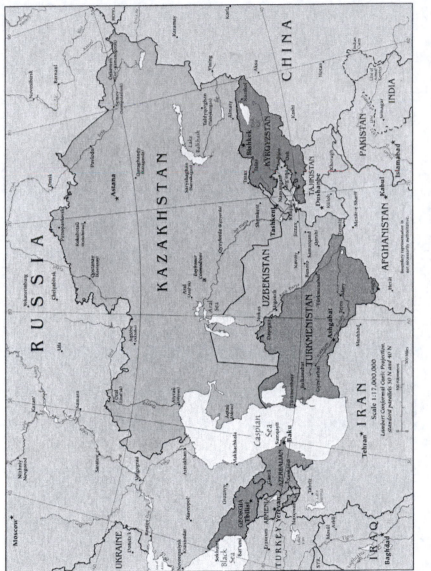

Map 4 Central Asia in 2009. Map produced by the US Central Intelligence Agency and retrieved from the Perry-Castañeda Library's Map Collection at University of Texas at Austin. Available in colour at: www.lib.utexas. edu/maps/middle_east_and_asia/caucasus_central_asia_pol_2009.jpg

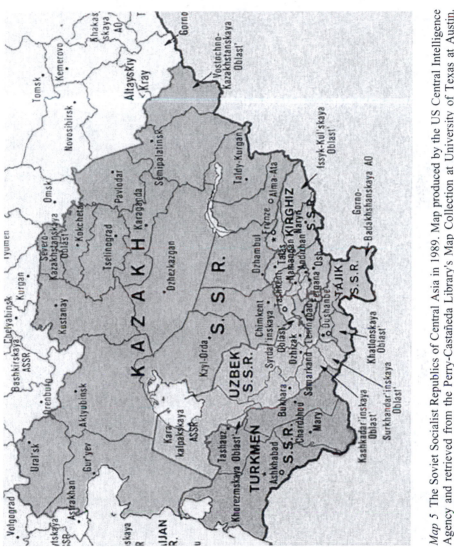

Map 5 The Soviet Socialist Republics of Central Asia in 1989. Map produced by the US Central Intelligence Agency and retrieved from the Perry-Castañeda Library's Map Collection at University of Texas at Austin. Available at: www.lib.utexas.edu/maps/commonwealth/soviet_union_admin_1989.jpg

Map 6 The Central Asia region in 1892. From (1892) 'Asia', *Americanized Encyclopaedia Britannica*, 1, Chicago and retrieved from the Perry-Castañeda Library's Map Collection at University of Texas at Austin. Available at: www.lib.utexas.edu/maps/historical/asia_1892_amer_ency_brit.jpg

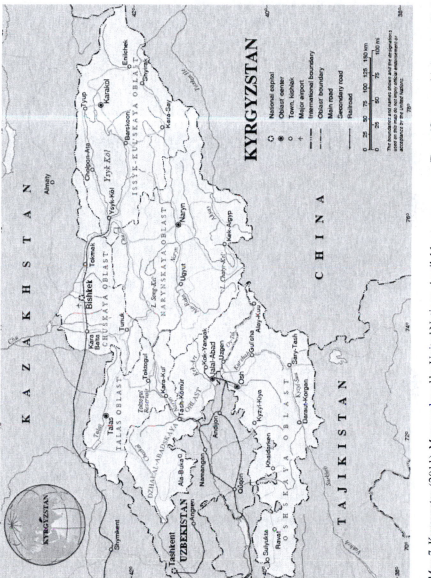

Map 7 Kyrgyzstan (2011). Map produced by United Nations. Available at: www.un.org/Depts/Cartographic/map/profile/ kyrgysta.pdf

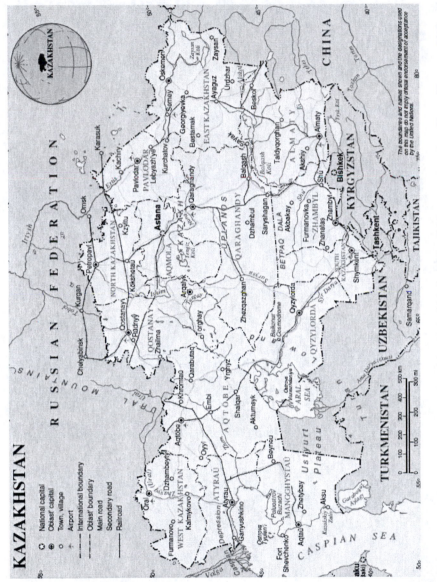

Map 8 Kazakhstan (2004). Map produced by United Nations. Available at: www.un.org/Depts/Cartographic/map/profile/kazakhst.pdf

Map 9 Tajikistan (2009). Map produced by United Nations. Available at: www.un.org/Depts/Cartographic/map/profile/tajikist.pdf

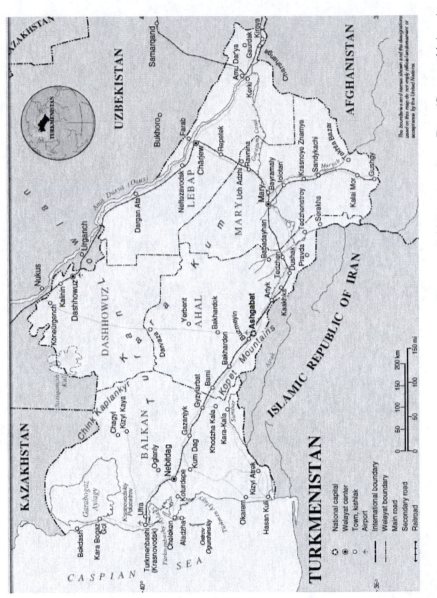

Map 10 Turkmenistan (2004). Map produced by United Nations. Available at: www.un.org/Depts/Cartographic/map/profile/turkmeni.pdf

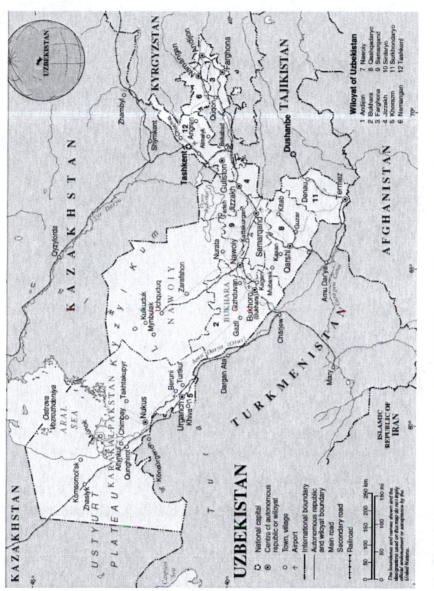

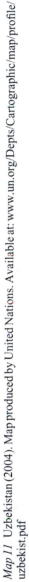

Map 11 Uzbekistan (2004). Map produced by United Nations. Available at: www.un.org/Depts/Cartographic/map/profile/uzbekist.pdf

Map 12 Ferghana Valley with ethnic enclaves (2005). From: Rekacewicz, P. (2005) 'Ferghana Valley: Population Groups', *UN Environmental Programme*. Available at: http://reliefweb.int/sites/reliefweb.int/files/resources/12973315352EEE3185257014005A 0B8C-unep_POP2_fer300405.jpg

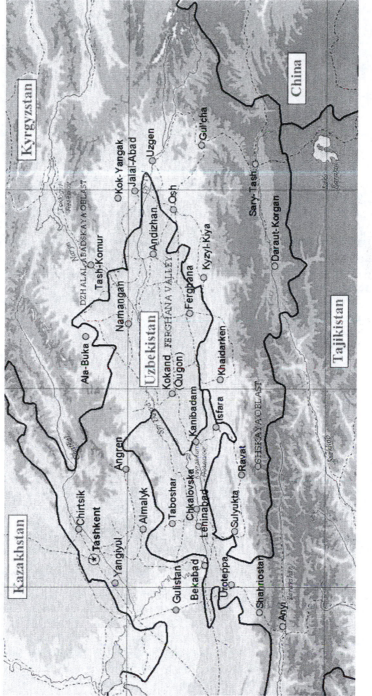

Map 13 Ferghana Valley. (2001) 'Ferghana Valley Elevation Map', *Relief Web.* Available at: http://reliefweb.int/node/2066

Bibliography and further reading

Abazov, Rafis (1999) *The Formation of Post-Soviet International Politics in Kazakhstan, Kyrgyzstan, and Uzbekistan*, Donald Treadgold paper No. 21, Seattle: The Henry M. Jackson School of International Studies, The University of Washington.

Abbas, Najam (2010) 'Author-critic Forum: The Politics of Peace-building in Tajikistan Review and Commentary 2', *Central Asian Survey*, 29(2), pp. 221–23.

Abdullaev, Kamoludin (2010) *Integrating Political Islam in Central Asia: The Tajik Experience*. Available at http://kamolkhon.com (accessed 8 November 2011).

Abramson, David M. and Karimov, Elyor E. (2007) in Jeff Sahadeo and Russell Zanca (eds) *Everyday Life in Central Asia*, Bloomington, IN: Indiana University Press, pp. 319–38.

Abykeev, A.K. et al (2006) *Eldik revolyoutsiya, 24 mart 2005 – Narodnaya revolyoutsiya*, Bishkek: Uchkun.

Abylkhozhin, Zhuldyzbek B., Manash Kozybaev and Makash Tatimov (1989) 'Kazakstanskaia Tragediia', *Voprosy Istorii*, 7, pp. 53–71.

Adams, Laura L. (2008) 'Can we Apply Postcolonial Theory to Eurasia?' *Central Eurasian Studies Review*, 7(1), pp. 2–7.

Adams, Laura L. (2010) *The Spectacular State: Culture and National Identity in Uzbekistan*, Durham: Duke University Press.

Adler, Emanuel, and Barnett, Michael N. (eds) (1998) *Security Communities*, Cambridge, UK: Cambridge University Press.

Adshead, Samuel Adrian (1993) *Central Asia in World History*, New York: St Martin's Press.

Agnew, John (1999) *Geopolitics: Re-visioning World Politics*, London and New York: Routledge.

Agzamkhodzhaev, Saidakbar (2006) *Istoriya Turkestanskoi Avtonomii*, Tashkent: Toshkent Islom Universiteti.

Aitmatov, Chingiz (1983) *The Day Lasts More than a Hundred Years*, Bloomington, IN: Indiana University Press.

Akaev, Askar (1994) 'Kyrgyzstan v Tsentralnoi Azii i SNG: Problemy i Perspektivy', in *God Planety*, Moscow: Respublika, pp. 29–30.

Akbarzadeh, Shahram (1996) 'Why Did Nationalism Fail in Tajikistan?' *Europe-Asia Studies*, 48(7), pp. 1105–30.

Akbarzadeh, Shahram (1999) 'National Identity and Political Legitimacy in Turkmenistan', *Nationalities Papers*, 27(2), pp. 271–90.

Akbarzadeh, Shahram (2000) 'The Plague of Regionalism and Patronage in Tajikistan', *Central Asia and Caucasus Analyst*, Washington, DC: Central Asia and Caucasus

Institute, Johns Hopkins University. Available at www.cacianalyst.org (accessed 6 December 2005).

Akçali, Pinar (1998) 'Islam as a "Common Bond" in Central Asia: Islamic Renaissance Party and the Afghan Mujahidin', *Central Asian Survey*, 17(2), pp. 267–84.

Akhmedzhanov, G.A. (1989) *Sovetskaya Istoriografiya Prisoedineniya Srednei Azii k Rossii*, Tashkent: FAN.

Akiner, Shirin (ed.) (1991) *Cultural Change and Continuity in Central Asia*, London: Kegan Paul International in association with the Central Asia Research Forum School of Oriental and African Studies.

Akiner, Shirin (ed.) (1994) *Political and Economic Trends in Central Asia*, London: British Academic Press.

Akiner, Shirin (1995) *The Formation of Kazakh Identity: From Tribe to Nation-state*, London: Royal Institute of International Affairs.

Akiner, Shirin (1997) 'Between Tradition and Modernity: The Dilemma Facing Contemporary Central Asian Women', in Mary Buckley (ed.) *Post-Soviet Women: From the Baltic to Central Asia*, Cambridge: Cambridge University Press, pp. 261–304.

Akiner, Shirin (1998) 'Conceptual Geographies of Central Asia', in Akiner (ed.) *Sustainable Development in Central Asia*, Richmond: Curzon Press, pp. 3–6.

Akiner, Shirin (2001) *Tajikistan: Consolidation or Disintegration?* London: Royal Institute of International Affairs.

Akiner, Shirin (2003a) 'Political Processes in Post-Soviet Central Asia', *Perspectives on Global Development and Technology*, 2(3–4), pp. 431–58.

Akiner, Shirin (2003b) 'The Politicization of Islam in Post-Soviet Central Asia', *Religion, State and Society*, 31(2), pp. 97–122.

Akiner, Shirin (ed.) (2004) *The Caspian: Politics, Energy and Security*, London: Routledge Curzon.

Akiner, Shirin (2005) *Violence in Andijan, 13 May 2005: An Independent Assessment*, Washington, DC: Central Asia-Caucasus Institute, Silk Road Studies Program, Silk Road Paper.

Akiner, Shirin, Tideman, Sander and Hay, Jon (eds) (1998) *Sustainable Development in Central Asia*, London: Curzon Press.

Alker, Hayward (2005) 'Emancipation in the Critical Security Studies Project', in Ken Booth (ed.) *Critical Security Studies and World Politics*, Boulder, CO: Lynne Rienner, pp. 189–213.

Allison, Roy (2004a) 'Regionalism, Regional Structures and Security Management in Central Asia', *International Affairs*, 80(3), pp. 463–83.

Allison, Roy (2004b) 'Strategic Reassertion in Russia's Central Asia Policy', *International Affairs*, 80(2), pp. 277–93.

Allison, Roy (2008) 'Virtual Regionalism, Regional Structures and Regime Security in Central Asia', *Central Asian Survey*, 27(2), pp. 185–202.

Allison, Roy and Jonson, Lena (eds) (2001) *Central Asian Security: The New International Context*, Washington, DC: Brookings Institution.

Allworth, Edward (1990) *The Modern Uzbeks: From the 14th Century to the Present: A Cultural History*, Stanford, CA: Hoover Institution Press.

Ambrosio, Thomas (2008) 'Catching the "Shanghai Spirit": How the Shanghai Cooperation Organization Promotes Authoritarian Norms in Central Asia', *Europe-Asia Studies*, 60(8), pp. 1321–44.

Anceschi, Luca (2008) *Turkmenistan's Foreign Policy Positive Neutrality and the Consolidation of the Turkmen Regime*, London: Routledge.

Anderson, John (1997a) *The International Politics of Central Asia*, Manchester: Manchester University Press.

Anderson, John (1997b) 'Elections and Political Development in Central Asia', *Journal of Communist and Transition Politics*, 13(4), pp. 28–53.

Arabov, Oumar (2004) 'A Note on Sufism in Tajikistan: What Does it Look Like?' *Central Asian Survey*, 23(3), pp. 345–47.

Aslund, Anders (2003) 'Sizing Up the Central Asian Economies', *Journal of International Affairs* 56(2), pp. 75–87.

Atkin, Muriel (1989) *The Subtlest Battle: Islam in Soviet Tajikistan*, Philadelphia, PA: Foreign Policy Research Institute, The Philadelphia Papers.

Atkin, Muriel (1992) 'Religious, National, and Other Identities in Central Asia' in Jo-Ann Gross (ed.), *Muslims in Central Asia: Expressions of Identity and Change*, Durham and London: Duke University Press, pp. 46–72.

Atkin, Muriel (1993) 'Tajik National Identity', *Iranian Studies*, 26(1), pp. 151–8.

Atkin, Muriel (1994a) 'Tajikistan's Relation with Afghanistan', in Ali Banuazizi and Myron Weiner (eds) *The New Geopolitics of Central Asia*, London: I.B. Tauris, pp. 91–117.

Atkin, Muriel (1994b) 'The Politics of Polarization in Tajikistan', in Hafeez Malik (ed.) *Central Asia: Its Strategic Importance and Future Prospects*, Basingstoke, UK: Palgrave, pp. 211–31.

Atkin, Muriel (1994c) 'Tajiks and the Persian World', in Beatrice, Manz (ed.) *Central Asia in Historical Perspective*, Oxford: Westview Press, pp. 127–43.

Atkin, Muriel (1997) 'Tajikistan: Reform, Reaction, and Civil War', in Ian Bremmer and Ray Taras (eds) *Nations and Politics in the Soviet Successor States*, Cambridge: Cambridge University Press, pp. 603–34.

Atkin, Muriel (2002) 'Tajikistan: A President and His Rivals', in Sally N. Cummings (ed.) *Power and Change in Central Asia*, London: Routledge, pp. 97–114.

Atkin, Muriel (2010) 'Author-critic Forum: The Politics of Peace-building in Tajikistan "Review and Commentary 1"', *Central Asian Survey*, pp. 219–21.

Atkin, Muriel (2011) 'From De Facto Colony to Sovereign Dependency', in Sally N. Cummings and Raymond Hinnebusch (eds) *Sovereignty After Empire: Comparing the Middle East and Central Asia*, Edinburgh: Edinburgh University Press, pp. 304–25.

Auty, R.M. (1997) *Sustainable Mineral-driven Development in Turkmenistan,* Environment Discussion Paper No. 36, Harvard Institute for International Development.

Azarolli, Augusto (1985) *An Early History of Horsemanship*, Leiden: Brill.

Babajanov, Bakhtiar (2008) 'Secularism and the Inter-Confessional Rift (Central Asia's Experience)', *Central Asia and the Caucasus: Journal of Social and Political Studies*, 2(50). Available at: www.ca-c.org/journal/2008-02-eng/00.shtml (accessed 25 May 2010).

Baldauf, Ingeborg (1995) 'Identitätsmodelle, Nationenbildung und Regionale Kooperation in Mittelasien', in Brunhild Staiger (ed.) *Nationalismus und Regionale Kooperation in Asien*, Hamburg: Institut für Asienkunde, pp. 119–40.

Banuazizi, Ali and Weiner, Myron (eds) (1994) *The New Geopolitics of Central Asia and Its Borderlands*, London: I.B. Tauris.

Barfield, Thomas J. (1989) *The Perilous Frontier: Nomadic Empires and China*, Cambridge, MA: Blackwell.

Barkey, Karen and Von Hagen, Mark (eds) (1997) *After Empire. Multiethnic Societies and Nation-Building: The Soviet Union and the Russian, Ottoman and Habsburg Empires,* Boulder, CO: Westview Press.

Barnett, Michael and Finnemore, Matha (eds) (2004) *Rules for the World: International Organizations in Global Politics*, Ithaca, NY: Cornell University Press.

Bartol'd, Vasilij V. (1958) Volume 2 *Four Studies on the History of Central Asia*, Leiden: Brill.

Bartol'd, Vasilij V. (1968) Volume 4 *Four Studies on the History of Central Asia*, Leiden: Brill.

Bartol'd, Vasilij V. (1997) 'Sart', in *The Encyclopaedia of Islam*, Leiden: Brill.

Bates, Robert H. (1981) *Markets and States in Tropical Africa*, Berkeley: University of California Press.

BBC News (2005) 'Kyrgyz Protestors Take Over Town', *BBC News*, 21 March. Available at: http://news.bbc.co.uk/2/hi/asia-pacific/4365945.stm (accessed 10 January 2011).

BBC News (2005) 'How the Andijan Killings Unfolded', *BBC News*, 17 May. Available at: http://news.bbc.co.uk/2/hi/4550845.stm. (accessed 10 February 2010)

BBC News (2010) 'Final Kyrgyzstan Election Results Announced', *BBC News*, 1 November. Available at: www.bbc.co.uk/news/world-asia-pacific-11664990 (accessed 10 December 2010).

BBC News (2011a) 'Kyrgyzstan Timeline', *BBC News*, 31 March. Available at: http://news.bbc.co.uk/2/hi/asia-pacific/1296570.stm (accessed 15 July 2011).

BBC News (2011b) 'Timeline: Tajikistan', *BBC News*, 17 May.

Beblawi, Hazem (1987) 'The Rentier State in the Arab World', in Hazam Beblawi and Giancomo Luciani (eds), *The Rentier State: Vol. II*, London: Croom Helm, pp. 49–62.

Beckwith, Christopher (1993) *The Tibetan Empire in Central Asia*, Princeton, NJ: Princeton University Press.

Beetham, David (1991) *The Legitimation of Power*, London: Macmillan.

Beissinger, Mark R. (2002) *Nationalist Mobilization and the Collapse of the Soviet State*, Cambridge: Cambridge University Press.

Beissinger, Mark R. (2005) 'Rethinking Empire in the Wake of Soviet Collapse', in Zoltan Barany and Robert G. Moser (eds) *Ethnic Politics after Communism*, Ithaca, NY: Cornell University Press, pp. 14–45.

Beissinger, Mark R. and Young, Crawford (eds) (2002) *Beyond State Crisis? Postcolonial Africa and Post-Soviet Eurasia in Comparative Perspective*, Baltimore, MD: Woodrow Wilson Center Press.

Bennigsen, Alexandre and Lemercier-Quelquejay, Chantal (1961) *The Evolution of the Muslim Nationalities of the U.S.S.R. and their Linguistic Problems*, London: Central Asian Research Centre.

Bennigsen, Alexandre and Lemercier-Quelquejay, Chantal (1967) *Islam in the Soviet Union*, London: Praeger.

Bennigsen, Alexandre and Wimbush, S. Enders (1985) *Muslims of the Soviet Empire*, London: C. Hurst.

Bergne, Paul (2007) *The Birth of Tajikistan: National Identity and the Origins of the Republic*, London: I.B. Tauris.

Beyer, Judith (2007) *Imagining the State in Rural Kyrgyzstan: How Perceptions of the State Create Customary Law in the Kyrygz Aksakal Courts*, Halle/Saale: Max Planck Institute for Social Anthropology Working Papers.

Beyer, Judith, Rasanayagam, Johan and Reeves, Madeleine (forthcoming) 'Introduction: Performances, Possibilities and Practices of the Political in Central Asia', in *Performing Politics: Anthropological Perspectives from Central Asia*.

Biard, Aurelie (2010) 'The Religious Factor in the Reification of Neo-ethnic Identities in Kyrgyzstan', *Nationalities Papers: The Journal of Nationalism and Ethnicity*, 38(3), pp. 323–35.

Bichsel, Christine (2009) *Conflict Transformation in Central Asia. Irrigation Disputes in the Ferghana Valley*, London: Routledge.

Bilgin, Pinar (2008) 'Critical Theory', in Paul D. Williams (ed.) *Security Studies: An Introduction,* London: Routledge, pp. 89–102.

Black, Cyril E., Dupree, Louis, Endicott-West, Elizabeth, Matuszewski, Daniel, Naby, Eden, and Waldron, Arthur (1991) *The Modernization of Inner Asia*, Armonk, NY: M. E. Sharpe.

Blackmon, Pamela (2005) 'Back to the USSR: Why the Past Does Matter in Explaining Differences in the Economic Reform Processes of Kazakhstan and Uzbekistan', *Central Asian Survey*, 24(4), pp. 391–404.

Blackmon, Pamela (2007) 'Divergent Paths, Divergent Outcomes: Linking Differences in Economic Reform to Levels of US Foreign Direct Investment and Business in Kazakhstan and Uzbekistan', *Central Asian Survey*, 26(3), pp. 355–72.

Blank, Stephen J. (1994) *Energy and Security in Transcaucasia*, Carlisle, PA: United States Army War College Strategic Studies Institute.

Blank, Stephen J. (2010) *Russia's Prospects in Asia*, Carlisle, PA: United States Army War College Strategic Studies Institute.

Blyth, Mark (2002) *Great Transformations: Economic Ideas and Institutional Change in the Twentieth Century*, Cambridge: Cambridge University Press.

Bogatyrev, Valentin (2009) 'Tsentral'naya Aziya. Vmesto Sotrudnichestva – Geopoliticheskii Razlom' 15 May. Available at www.ipp.kg (accessed 12 May 2010).

Bohr, Annette (1996) 'Turkmenistan and the Turkmen', in Graham Smith (ed.) *The Nationalities Question in the Post-Soviet States*, 2nd edn, London and New York: Longman, pp. 122–39.

Bohr, Annette (1998a) 'The Central Asian States as Nationalizing Regimes', in Smith, Graham, Law, Vivien, Wilson, Andrew, Bohr, Annette and Allworth, Edward, *Nation-building in the Post-Soviet Borderlands: The Politics of National Identities*, Cambridge: Cambridge University Press, pp. 139–62.

Bohr, Annette (1998b) *Uzbekistan: Domestic and Regional Policy*, London: Royal Institute of International Affairs.

Bohr, Annette (2003) 'Independent Turkmenistan', in Sally N. Cummings (ed.) *Oil, Transition and Security in Central Asia*, London: Routledge, pp. 9–24.

Bohr, Annette (2004) 'Regionalism in Central Asia: New Geopolitics, Old Regional Order', *International Affairs*, 80(3), pp. 485–502.

Booth, Ken (1991) 'Security and Emancipation', *Review of International Studies*, 17(4), pp. 313–26.

Brach-von Gumppenberg, Markus (2006) 'Sowjetische Hinterlassenschaft und Russische Sicherheitspolitik in Zentralasien', *Österreichische Militärische Zeitschrift*, 5(44), pp. 555–62. Available at www.bmlv.gv.at/omz/ausgaben/artikel.php?id=424 (accessed 27 January 2010).

Brauer, Birgit (2004) 'Kasachstans Weg zum Petro-Staat', *Internationale Politik Deutsche Gesellschaft für Auswärtige Politik*, 59(8), pp. 58–60.

Bregel, Yuri (1995) *Biography of Islamic Central Asia Volume 1*, Research Institute for Inner Asian Studies, Indiana University.

Bregel, Yuri (1996) *Notes on the Study of Central Asia, Papers on Inner Asia no. 28*, Bloomington, IN: Indiana University Publications.

Bremmer, Ian and Welt, Cory (1995) 'Kazakhstan's Quandary', *Journal of Democracy*, 6(3), pp. 139–54.

Bremmer, Ian and Welt, Cory (1996) 'The Trouble with Democracy in Kazakhstan', *Central Asian Survey*, 15(2), pp. 179–99.

Brenninkmeijer, Olivier A.J. (1997) 'International Concern for Tajikistan: UN and OSCE Efforts to Promote Peace-building and Democratization', in Djalili Mohammad-Reza, Frédéric Grare and Shirin Akiner (eds) *Tajikistan: The Trials of Independence*, New York: St. Martin's Press, pp. 180–215.

Brown, Bess A. (1998) 'The Civil War in Tajikistan, 1992–3', in Djalili, Mohammad-Reza, Frédéric, Grare and Shirin, Akiner (eds) *Tajikistan: The Trials of Independence*, New York: St. Martin's Press, pp. 86–96

Brubaker, Rogers (1996a) *Nationalism Reframed*, Cambridge: Cambridge University Press.

Brubaker, Rogers (1996b) *Nationalism Reframed: Nationhood and the National Question in the New Europe*, Cambridge: Cambridge University Press.

Bunce, Valerie (1995) 'Should Transitologists Be Grounded?' 54(1), pp. 111–27.

Burchill, Scott (1996) 'Introduction', in Scott Burchill and Andrew Linklater with Richard Devetak, Matthew Patterson and Jacqui True, *Theories of International Relations*, London: Macmillan, pp. 1–27.

Burgis, Michelle (2011) 'Mandated Sovereignty: The Role of International Law in the Construction of Arab Statehood During and After Empire', in Sally N. Cummings and Raymond Hinnebusch (eds) *Sovereignty after Empire*, Edinburgh: Edinburgh University Press, pp. 104–26.

Burnashev, Rustam and Chernykh, Irina (2003) 'Vooryzhennye Sily i Voenno-politicheskii kurs Respubliki Uzbekistan'. Available at www.centrasia.ru

Bush, G.W. (2005) 'Transcript: Bush's News Conference', republished in *The New York Times*, 31 May.

Buzan, Barry (1991) *People, States and Fear*, 2nd edn, New York and London: Harvester Wheatsheaf.

Buzan, Barry and Ole Wæver (2003) *Regions and Powers: The Structure of International Security*, Cambridge: Cambridge University Press.

Caballero-Anthony, Mely, Emmers, Ralf and Acharya, Amitav (eds) (2006) *Non-traditional Security in Asia: Dilemmas in Securitization*, Aldershot: Ashgate.

Canfield, Robert (ed.) (1991) *Turko-Persia in Historical Perspective*, Cambridge: Cambridge University Press.

Canfield, Robert and Rauly-Paleczek, Gabriele (2010) (eds) *Ethnicity, Authority, and Power in Central Asia: New Games Great and Small*, London: Routledge.

Carlisle, Donald (1994) 'Soviet Uzbekistan: State and Nation in Historical Perspective', in Manz, Beatrice (ed.) *Central Asia in Historical Perspective*, Oxford: Westview Press, pp. 103–26.

Carothers, Thomas (2002) 'The End of the Transition Paradigm', *Journal of Democracy*, 13(January), pp. 5–21.

Carothers, Thomas (2006) 'The Backlash against Democracy Promotion', *Foreign Affairs*, 85(2), pp. 55–68.

Carr, Edward Hallett (2001) *The Twenty Years' Crisis 1919–1939*, new edn., Basingstoke: Palgrave Macmillan.

Carrère d'Encausse, Hélène (1992) *The Great Nationalities and the Bolshevik State 1917–1930* [1987]; translation from French, New York: Holmes and Meier.

Childress, Malcolm D. (2003) 'Agricultural Restructuring in Kyrgyzstan: The Next Phase', in Sally N. Cummings (ed.), *Oil, Transition and Security in Central Asia*, London: Routledge, pp. 131–40.

Chotaeva, Cholpon (2003) 'Islam in the Social-Political Context of Kyrgyzstan', *Central Asia and the Caucasus: Journal of Social and Political Studies*, 6(24). Available at: www.ca-c.org.ezproxy.st-andrews.ac.uk/online/2003/journal_eng/cac-06/07.choten. shtml (accessed 24 March 2009).

Chotaeva, Cholpon (2004a) 'Language as a Nation-building Factor in Kyrgyzstan', *Central Asia and the Caucasus: Journal of Social and Political Studies*, 2(26), pp. 177–84.

Chotaeva, Cholpon (2004b) *Ethnicity, Language and Religion in Kyrgyzstan*, Tohoku University.

Clement, Victoria (2007) 'Alphabet Changes in Turkmenistan, 1904-2004', in Jeff Sahadeo and Russell Zanca (eds) *Everyday Life in Central Asia*, Bloomington, IN: Indiana University Press, pp. 266–80.

Cohen, Saul B. (1999) *Geography and Politics in a World Divided*, New York: Free Press.

Collins, Kathleen (2002) 'Clans, Pacts, and Politics in Central Asia', *Journal of Democracy*, 13(3), pp. 137–52.

Collins, Kathleen (2006) *Clan Politics and Regime Transition in Central Asia*, New York: Cambridge University Press.

Collins, Kathleen (2009) 'Economic and Security Regionalism among Patrimonial Authoritarian Regimes: The Case of Central Asia', *Europe-Asia Studies*, 61(2), pp. 249–81.

Commission on Human Security (2003) available at www.humansecurity-chs.org/finalreport/index.html (accessed 12 January 2007).

Connor, Walker (1984) *The National Question in Marxist-Leninist Theory and Strategy*, Princeton: Princeton University Press.

Cooley, Alexander (2011) 'Geopolitical Competition and Political Stability: The Case of Kyrgyzstan', draft chapter 8 of *Great Games, Local Rules: The US-Russia-China Struggle for Central Asia*, Oxford: Oxford University Press, forthcoming.

Cornell, Svante E. (2005) 'Narcotics, radicalism, and Armed Conflict in Central Asia: The Islamic Movement of Uzbekistan', *Terrorism and Political Violence*, 17(4), pp. 619–39.

Cornell, Svante E. (2006) 'The Narcotics Threat in Greater Central Asia: From Crime-Terror Nexus to State Infiltration?' *China and Eurasia Forum Quarterly*, 4(1), pp. 37–67.

Cornell, Svante E. and Swanström, Niklas (2005) 'Kyrgyzstan's "Revolution": Poppies or Tulips', Central Asia Caucasus Institute Analyst, 18 May.

Cox, Robert W. (1981) 'Social Forces, States and World Orders: Beyond International Relations Theory', *Millennium: Journal of International Studies*, 10(2), pp. 126–55.

Craumer, Peter (1995) *Rural and Agricultural Development in Uzbekistan*, London: Royal Institute of International Affairs.

Crawford, Neta C. (2003) *Argument and Change in World Politics*, Cambridge: Cambridge University Press.

Critchlow, James (1990) 'Islam in Soviet Central Asia: Renaissance or Revolution?' *Religion in Communist Lands*, 18(3), pp. 196–211.

Critchlow, James (1991) *Nationalism in Uzbekistan: A Soviet Republic's Road to Sovereignty*, Boulder, CL: Westview Press.

Cummings, Sally N. (2000) *Kazakhstan: Centre-Periphery Relations*, Washington, DC: Brookings Institution and London: Royal Institute of International Affairs.

Cummings, Sally N. (ed.) (2003) *Oil, Transition and Stability in Central Asia*, London: Routledge.

Cummings, Sally N. (2004) 'Eurasian Bridge or Murky Waters between East and West? Ideas, Identity and Output in Kazakhstan's Foreign Policy', in Rick Fawn (ed.) *Ideology and National Identity in Post-communist Foreign Policies*, London: Frank Cass, pp. 139–55.

Cummings, Sally N. (2005) *Kazakhstan: Power and the Elite*, London and New York: I.B. Tauris.

Cummings, Sally N. (ed.) (2008) *Domestic and International Perspectives on the Tulip Revolution: Motives, Mobilization and Meaning*, London: Routledge.

Cummings, Sally N. (2009) 'Co-optation and Control: Managing Heterogeneity in Kazakhstan', in Lars Johannsen and Karin Hilmer Pedersen (eds) *Pathways: A Study of Six Post-Communist Countries*, Aarhus: Aarhus University Press, pp. 30–51.

Cummings, Sally N. (ed.) (2010) *Symbolism and Power in Central Asia: Politics of the Spectacular*, London: Routledge.

Cummings, Sally N. and Hinnebusch, Raymond (eds) (2011) *Sovereignty after Empire: Comparing the Middle East and Central Asia*, New York: Columbia University Press and Edinburgh: Edinburgh University Press.

Cummings, Sally N. and Norgaard, Ole (2004) 'Conceptualising State Capacity: Comparing Kazakhstan and Kyrgyzstan', *Political Studies*, 52(4), pp. 685–708.

Cummings, Sally N. and Ochs, Michael (2002) 'Turkmenistan: Saparmurat Niyazov's Inglorious Isolation', in Sally N. Cummings (ed.) *Power and Change in Central Asia*, London: Routledge, pp. 115–29.

Dadabaeva, Gulnara and Adibayeva, Aigul (2010) 'Post-Soviet Kazakhstan: Nationalism and Language Issues', *The Soviet and Post-Soviet Review*, 37(2), pp. 125–41.

Dalby, Simon (2002) *Environmental Security*, Minneapolis, MN: University of Minnesota Press.

Dani, A.H. and Masson, V.M. (eds) (1992) *History of Civilizations of Central Asia Volume 1*, Paris: UNESCO Publishing.

Dave, Bhavna (2004) 'A Shrinking Reach of the State? Language Policy and Implementation in Kazakhstan', in Pauline Jones Luong (ed.) *The Transformation of Central Asia: States and Societies from Soviet Rule to Independence*, Ithaca, NY: Cornell University Press, pp. 120–58.

Dave, Bhavna (2007) *Kazakhstan: Ethnicity, Language and Power*, New York: Routledge.

Dave, Bhavna (2008) 'The EU and Kazakhstan: Is the Pursuit of Energy and Security Cooperation Compatible with the Promotion of Human Rights and Democratic Reforms?' in Neil J. Melvin (ed.) *Engaging Central Asia: The European Union's Strategy in the Heart of Eurasia*, Brussels: Centre for European Policy Studies, pp. 43–67.

Dawisha, Karen and Parrot, Bruce (eds) (1997) *The End of Empire? The Transformation of the USSR in Comparative Perspective*, Armonk, NY: M.E. Sharpe.

Demko, George (1969) *The Russian Colonization of Kazakhstan, 1896–1916*, Bloomington, IN: Indiana University Press.

Denison, Michael (2006) *Why Do Sultanistic Regimes Arise and Persist? A Study of Government in the Republic of Turkmenistan, 1992–2006*, Ph.D. Dissertation in Politics, University of Leeds.

Deudney, Daniel (1999) 'Environmental Security: A Critique', in Daniel Deudney and Richard Matthew (eds) *Contested Grounds: Security and Conflict in the New Environmental Politics*, Albany, NY: State University of New York Press, pp. 187–219.

Deutsch, Karl W. (1957) *Political Continuity in the North Atlantic Area*, Princeton, NJ: Princeton University Press.

DeWeese, Devin (ed.) (2001) *Studies on Central Asian History in Honor of Yuri Bregel*, Bloomington, IN: Indiana University Research Institute for Inner Asian Studies.

DeWeese, Devin (2002) 'Islam and the Legacy of Sovietology: A Review Essay on Yaacov Roi's "Islam in the Soviet Union"', *Journal of Islamic Studies*, 13(3), pp. 298–330.

Diener, Alexander C. (2009) *One Homeland or Two? The Nationalization and Transnationalization of Mongolia's Kazakhs*, Stanford: Stanford University Press.

Dittmer, Lowell (2007) 'Central Asia and the Regional Powers', *China and Eurasia Forum Quarterly*, 5(4), pp. 7–22.

Doty, Roxanne Lynn (1993) 'Foreign Policy as Social Construction', *International Studies Quarterly*, 37(3), pp. 297–320.

Doyle, Michael W. (1998) *Ways of War and Peace*, New York: Norton.

Dudoignon, Stephane A. (1997a) 'Political Parties and Forces in Tajikistan, 1989–1993', in Djalili, Grare and Akiner. pp. 52–85.

Dudoignon, Stephane A. (1997b) 'Political Forces and their Structures in Tajikistan', *Central Asian Survey*, 16/4(December), pp. 611–22.

Dudoignon, Stephane A. (2011) 'From Revival to Mutation: the religious personnel of Islam in Tajikistan, from de-Stalinization to Independence (1955–91)', *Central Asian Survey*, 30(1), pp. 53–80.

Dudoignon, Stephane A. and Hisao, Komatsu (eds) (2003) *Research Trends in Modern Central Eurasian Studies (18th–20th Centuries): A Selective and Critical Bibliography of Works Published between 1985 and 2000, in Cooperation with Abstracta Iranica*, Tokyo: The Toyo Bunko.

Dukhovny, V.A. et al. (2005) *Integrated Water Resource Management*. Tashkent. Dzhunushaliev.

Dzhunushaliev, Dzhenish and Ploskikh, Vladimir (2000) 'Tribalism and Nation Building in Kyrgyzstan', *Central Asia and the Caucasus: Journal of Social and Political Studies*, 3. Available at: www.ca-c.org.ezproxy.st-andrews.ac.uk/online/2000/journal_eng/eng03_2000/eng03_2000.shtml (accessed 25 March 2011).

Dzyubenko, O. (2010) 'Otunbayeva Sworn In as Kyrgyz Interim President', Reuters, 3 July. Available at: http://uk.reuters.com/article/2010/07/03/uk-kyrgyzstan-president-idUKTRE6620OL20100703 (accessed 17 August 2010).

Economakis, Evel (1991) 'Soviet Interpretations of Collectivization', *The Slavonic and East European Review*, 69(2), pp. 257–81.

Edgar, Adrienne Lynn (2001) 'Genealogy, Class and Tribal Policy in Soviet Turkmenistan, 1924-1934', *Slavic Review*, 60(2), pp. 266–88.

Edgar, Adrienne Lynn (2004) *Tribal Nation: The Creation of Soviet Turkmenistan*, Princeton, NJ: Princeton University Press.

Edgar, Adrienne Lynn (2007) 'Everyday Life Among the Turkmen Nomads', in Jeff Sahadeo and Russell Zanca (eds) *Everyday Life in Central Asia*, Bloomington, IN: Indiana University Press, pp. 37–44.

Edmunds, Timothy (1998) 'Power and Powerlessness in Kazakhstani Society', *Central Asian Survey*, 17(3), pp. 463–70.

Edwards, Matthew (2003) 'The New Great Game and the New Great Gamers: Disciples of Kipling and Mackinder', *Central Asian Survey*, 22(1), pp. 83–102.

EIU, *Tajikistan Country Report*, December 2010.

EIU, *Kyrgyzstan Country Report*, January 2011.

EIU, *Turkmenistan Country Report*, January 2011.

EIU, *Kazakhstan Country Report*, January 2011.

EIU, *Uzbekistan Country Report*, March 2011.

Elman, Colin (2008) 'Realism', in Paul D. Williams (ed.) *Security Studies: An Introduction*, London: Routledge, pp. 15–28.

Epkenhans, Tim (2011) 'Defining Normative Islam: Some Remarks on Contemporary Islamic Thought in Tajikistan – Hoji Akbar Turajonzoda's *Sharia and Society'*, *Central Asian Survey*, 30(1), pp. 81–96.

Esenova, Saulesh (1998) '"Tribalism" and Identity in Contemporary Circumstances: The Case of Kazakstan', *Central Asian Survey*, 17(3), pp. 443–62.

EurasiaNet (2006) 'Kyrgyzstan: Revolution Revisited', *EurasiaNet*. Available at: www. eurasianet.org/kyrgyzstan/timeline/index.html (accessed 15 January 2011).

EurasiaNet (2010) 'Kyrgyzstan: Bakiyev confronts political crisis', *EurasiaNet*, 6 April. Available at: www.eurasianet.org/departments/insight/articles/eav040610.shtml (accessed 10 December 2010).

Fairbanks, Douglas (2007) 'Revolution Reconsidered', *Journal of Democracy*, 18(1), pp. 42–57.

Fathi, Habiba (1997) 'Otines: The Unknown Women Clerics of Central Asian Islam', *Central Asian Survey*, 16(1), pp. 27–44.

Fathi, Habiba (2006) 'Gender, Islam, and Social Change in Uzbekistan', *Central Asian Survey*, 25(3), pp. 303–17.

Fawcett, Louise (2008) 'Regional Institutions', in Paul D. Williams (ed.) *Security Studies: An Introduction*, London: Routledge, pp. 307–24.

Fawn, Rick (2009) '"Regions" and Their Study: Where From, What For and Where To', in Rick Fawn (ed.) *Globalising the Regional, Regionalising the Global*, Cambridge: Cambridge University Press, pp. 5–34.

Fearon, James D. and Laitin, David D. (2003) 'Ethnicity, Insurgency, and Civil War', *American Political Science Review*, 97(1), pp. 75–90.

Feldman, Stacy (2003) 'Promoting Democracy: An Interview with Stephen Sestanovich, (Foreign Policies Toward the Region)', *Journal of International Affairs*, 56(2).

Fierke, K.M. (1998) *Changing Games, Changing Strategies: Critical Investigations in Security*, Manchester: Manchester University Press.

Fierman, William (1991) *Language Planning and National Development: The Uzbek Experience*, Berlin: Mouton de Gruyter.

Fierman, William (1997) 'Political Development in Uzbekistan: Democratization?', in Karen Dawisha and Bruce Parrot (eds) *Conflict, Cleavage and Change in Central Asia and Caucasus*, Cambridge: Cambridge University Press.

Fierman, William (2009) 'Identity, Symbolism, and the Politics of Language in Central Asia', *Europe-Asia Studies*, 61(7), pp. 1207–28.

Finnemore, Martha (1996) *National Interests in International Security*, Ithaca, NY: Cornell University Press.

Foroughi, Payam (2002) 'Tajikistan: Nationalism, Ethnicity, Conflict, and Socio-economic Disparities Sources and Solutions', *Journal of Muslim Minority Affairs*, 22(1), pp. 39–61.

Forsythe, Rosemary (1996) *The Politics of Oil in the Caucasus and Central Asia: Problems, Prospects and Policy*, Adelphi Papers 300, London: International Institute for Strategic Studies.

Freedom House (2011) *Nations in Transit 2011*, Available at: www.freedomhouse.org/ images/File/nit/2011/NIT-2011-Release_Booklet.pdf

Fumagalli, Matteo (2007) 'Framing Ethnic Minority Mobilisation in Central Asia: The Cases of Uzbeks in Kyrgyzstan and Tajikistan', *Europe-Asia Studies*, 59(4), pp. 567–90.

Geiss, Paul G. (2003) *Pre-Tsarist and Tsarist Central Asia: Communal Commitment and Political Order in Change*, London: Routledge.

Gellner, Ernest (1983) *Nations and Nationalism*, Ithaca, NY: Cornell University Press.

Gilpin, Robert (1981) *War and Change in World Politics*, Cambridge: Cambridge University Press.

Gladney, Dru C. (1990) 'The Ethnogenesis of the Uighur', *Central Asian Survey*, 9(1), pp. 1–28.

Gladney, Dru C. (1996) *Muslim Chinese: Ethnic Nationalism in the People's Republic*, Cambridge, MA: Council of East Asian Studies, Harvard University.

Gladney, Dru C. (2003) 'Islam in China: Accommodation or Separatism', *The China Quarterly*, 174, pp. 451–67.

Gleason, Gregory (1997) *The Central Asian States: Discovering Independence*, Oxford: Westview Press.

Gleason, Gregory (2001a) 'Mixing Oil and Water' posted *Eurasianet*, September 6.

Gleason, Gregory (2001b) 'Foreign Policy and Domestic Reform in Central Asia', *Central Asian Survey*, 20(2), pp. 167–82.

Gleason, Gregory (2001c) 'Inter-State Cooperation in Central Asia from the CIS to the Shanghai Forum', *Europe-Asia Studies*, 53(7), pp. 1077–95.

Gleason, Gregory (2003) *Markets and Politics in Central Asia (Economies in Transition to the Market)*, Abingdon, Oxon; New York: Routledge.

Glenn, John (1999) *The Soviet Legacy in Central Asia*, Basingstoke: Palgrave Macmillan.

Glenn, John (2003) 'The Economic Transition in Central Asia: Implications for Democracy', *Democratization*, 10(3), pp. 124–47.

Gokominvest/UNDP Development Report (1999).

Golden, Peter B. (2011) *Central Asia in World History*, New York: Oxford University Press.

Goldstein, Avery (2005) *Rising to the Challenge: China's Grand Strategy and International Security*, Stanford: Stanford University Press.

Golovnina, M. (2010) 'Kyrgyz President Formally Resigns after Turmoil', Reuters, 16 April. Available at: www.reuters.com/article/2010/04/16/us-kyrgyzstan-unrest-id USTRE6363CR20100416 (accessed 17 August 2010).

Golunov, Sergei (2001) 'The Post-Soviet Borders of Central Asia: Security and Cooperation', *Central Asia and the Caucasus: Journal of Social and Political Studies*, 5(11). Available at: www.ca-c.org.ezproxy.st-andrews.ac.uk/online/2001/journal_eng/cac-05/17.golen.shtml (accessed 13 March 2010).

Green, David J. (2001) 'Regional Co-operation Policies in Central Asia', *Journal of International Development*, 13, pp. 1157–9.

Gretsky, Sergey (1995) 'Civil War in Tajikistan: Causes, Development and Prospects for Peace', in Roald Sagdeev and Susan Eisenhower (eds), *Central Asia: Conflict, Revolution, and Change* (Washington: CSPS), pp. 228–45.

Gross, Jo-Ann (ed.) (1992) *Muslims in Central Asia: Expressions of Identity and Change*, Durham: Duke University Press.

Grotz, F. (2001) 'Tajikistan', in D. Nohlen, F. Grotz, and C. Hartmann (eds) *Elections in Asia and the Pacific: A Data Handbook, Volume 1*, Oxford: Oxford University Press.

Grousset, René (2005) *The Empire of the Steppes: A History of Central Asia*, New Brunswick, New Jersey, and London.

Gryzmala-Busse, Anna and Jones Luong, Pauline (2002) 'The Ignored Transition: Post-Communist State Development', Weatherhead Center for International Affairs Working Paper Series #02-02.

The Guardian (2005) 'In Pictures: Protests in Kyrgyzstan', *The Guardian*. Available at: www.guardian.co.uk/gall/0,1444067,00.html (accessed 12 January 2011).

Gullette, David (2007) 'Theories of Central Asian Factionalism: The Debate in Political Science and its Wider Implications', *Central Asian Survey*, 26(3), pp. 373–87.

Gunder Frank, André (1992) *The Centrality of Central Asia Studies History*, 8(1), pp. 43–97.

Gurr, Ted Robert and Harff, Barbara (1994) *Ethnic Conflict in World Politics*, Boulder, CO: Westview Press.

Halbach, Uwe (1997) *Zentralasien als Auswanderungsregion*, Cologne: Bundesinstitut für Ostwissenschaftliche und Internationale Studien. Available at www.ssoar.info/ssoar/files/swp/berichte/BER97_44.pdf (accessed 28 January 2010).

Hambly, Gavin (1969) *Central Asia*, London: Weidenfeld & Nicolson.

Hampson, Fen Osler (2008) 'Human Security', in Paul D. Williams (ed.) *Security Studies: An Introduction,* London: Routledge, pp. 229–43.

Hanks, Reuel (2009) 'Multi-vector Politics and Kazakhstan's Emerging Role as a Geo-strategic Player in Central Eurasia', *Journal of Balkan and Near Eastern Studies*, 11(3), pp. 257–67.

Hann, Chris and Pelkmans, Mathijs (2009) 'Realigning Religion and Power in Central Asia: Islam, Nation-state and (post) Socialism', *Europe-Asia Studies*, 61(9), pp. 1517–41.

Harding, L. (2010) 'Uzbeks in Desperate Plea for Aid as Full Horror of Ethnic Slaughter Emerges', *The Guardian*, 20 June. Available at: www.guardian.co.uk/world/2010/jun/20/kyrgyzstan-uzbekistan-ethnic-civil-war (accessed 17 August 2010).

Harding, L. and Gabbatt, A. (2010) 'Kyrgyzstan's Interim Government Claims Referendum Victory', *The Guardian*, 28 June. Available at: www.guardian.co.uk/world/2010/jun/28/kyrgyzstan-interim-government-referendum-victory (accessed 17 August 2010).

Haugen, Arne (2003) *The Establishment of National Republics in Soviet Central Asia*, Basingstoke: Palgrave Macmillan.

Heathershaw, John (2005) 'The Paradox of Peacebuilding: Peril, Promise, and Small Arms in Tajikistan', *Central Asian Survey*, 24(1), pp. 21–38.

Heathershaw, John (2009) *Post-Conflict Tajikistan: The Politics of Peacebuilding and the Emergence of Legitimate Order*, New York: Routledge.

Heathershaw, John (2010a) 'Author-critic Forum: The Politics of Peace-building in Tajikistan "Review and Commentary 1"', *Central Asian Survey*, 29(2), pp. 219–21.

Heathershaw, John (2010b) 'Kyrgyzstan, Fractured But Not Broken'. Available at: www.opendemocracy.net/od-russia/john-heathershaw/kyrgystan-fractured-but-not-broken (accessed 12 January 2011).

Heathershaw, John (2010c) 'Book Review: Conflict Transformation in Central Asia: Irrigation Disputes in the Ferghana Valley', *Central Asian Survey*, 29(1), pp. 133–5.

Heathershaw, John (2011) 'Tajikistan Amidst Globalization: State Failure or State Trans-formation?' *Central Asian Survey*, 30(1), pp. 147–68.

Heathershaw, John and Megoran, Nick (2011) 'Contesting Danger: A New Agenda for Policy and Scholarship on Central Asia', *International Affairs* (Royal Institute of International Affairs), 87(3), pp. 589–612.

Helmke, Gretchen and Levitsky, Steven (2004) 'Informal Institutions and Comparative Politics: A Research Agenda', *Perspectives on Politics*, 2(4), pp. 725–40.

Herzig, Edmund (1995) *Iran and the Former Soviet South*, London: Royal Institute of International Affairs.

Herzig, Edmund (2001) 'Iran in Central Asia', in Roy Allison and Lena Jonson (eds) *Central Asian Security: The New International Context*, London: Royal Institute of International Affairs, pp. 171–98.

Hill, Fiona (2002) 'The United States and Russia in Central Asia: Uzbekistan, Tajikistan, Afghanistan, Pakistan and Iran', *The Aspen Institute Congressional Program*. Available at www.brookings.edu/speeches/2002/0815russia_hill.aspx (accessed 25 February 2010).

Hill, Fiona (2004) 'Russia's Newly Found Soft Power', *The Globalist*, 26 August.

Hill, Fiona (2005a) 'The Eurasian Security Environment' (Testimony of Fiona Hill), Washington, DC: House of Representatives Armed Services Committee, Defense Review Threat Panel.

Hill, Fiona (2005b) 'Uzbek Fury', *The Wall Street Journal*, 20 May.

Hiro, Dilip (2009) *Inside Central Asia: A Political and Cultural History of Uzbekistan, Turkmenistan, Kazakhstan, Kyrgyzstan, Tajikistan, Turkey, and Iran*, New York and London: Overlook Duckworth.

Hirsch, Francine (2005) *Empire of Nations: Ethnographic Knowledge and the Making of the Soviet Union*, Cornell, NY: Cornell University Press.

Hopf, Ted (1998) 'The Promise of Constructivism in International Relations Theory', *International Security*, 23(1), pp. 171–200.

Hopkirk, Kathleen (1993) *Central Asia: A Traveller's Companion*, London: John Murray.

Horsman, Stuart (1999) 'Uzbekistan's Involvement in the Tajik Civil War 1992–97: Domestic Considerations', *Central Asian Survey*, 18(1), pp. 37–48.

Horsman, Stuart (2001) 'Water in Central Asia: Regional Cooperation or Conflict?' in Roy Allison and Lena Jonson (eds) *Central Asian Security: The New International Context*, London: The Royal Institute of International Affairs, pp. 69–94.

Horsman, Stuart (2003) 'The Caspian Sea: The Management and Politicisation of the Maritime Ecosystem in a Period of Transition', in Sally N. Cummings (ed.) *Oil, Transition and Stability in Central Asia*, London: Routledge, pp. 192–202.

Howell, Jude (1995) 'Household Coping Strategies in Kyrgyzstan', *Development in Practice*, 5(4), pp. 361–4.

Human Rights Watch (ND) 'Andijan Massacre: Timeline of Events, 2005-2006', *Human Rights Watch*. Available at: www.hrw.org/legacy/campaigns/andijan/timeline.htm (accessed 17 August 2010).

Human Rights Watch (1999) 'Presidential Elections in Tajikistan a Farce', *Human Rights Watch*, 28 Oct.

Humphrey, Caroline and Mandel, Ruth (2002) *Markets and Moralities*, London: Berg Publishers.

Humphrey, Caroline and Sneath, David (1999) *The End of Nomadism? Society, State and the Environment*, Durham, NC: Duke University Press.

Hunter, Shireen T. (1996) *Central Asia Since Independence*, Washington, DC: Praeger for the Center for Strategic and International Studies.

Huntington, Samuel P. (1968) *Political Order in Changing Societies*, London: Yale University Press.

Huntington, Samuel P. (1998) *Clash of Civilisations and the Remaking of the World Order*, New York: Simon & Schuster.

Huskey, Eugene (1997) 'Kyrgyzstan: The Politics of Demographic and Economic Frustration', in Ian Bremmer and Ray Taras (eds) *New States New Politics: Building the Post-Soviet Nations*, Cambridge: Cambridge University Press, pp. 655–84.

Huskey, Eugene (2002) 'An Economy of Authoritarianism? Askar Akaev and presidential leadership in Kyrgyzstan', in Sally N. Cummings (ed.) *Power and Change in Central Asia*, pp. 74–96.

Huskey, Eugene (2004) 'National Identity from Scratch: Defining Kyrgyzstan's Role in World Affairs', in Rick Fawn (ed.) *Ideology and National Identity in Post-Communist Foreign Policies*, London: Frank Cass, pp. 111–38.

Huskey, Eugene and Iskakova, Gulnara (2010) 'Narrowing the Sites and Moving the Targets Institutional Instability and the Development of a Political Opposition in Kyrgyzstan', *Problems of Post-Communism*, 58(3), pp. 3–10.

Huysmans, Jef (2006) *The Politics of Insecurity: Fear, Migration and Asylum in the EU*, London: Routledge.

Ilkhamov, Alisher (2001) 'Impoverishment of the Masses in the Transition Period: Signs of an Emerging "New Poor" Identity in Uzbekistan', *Central Asian Survey*, 20(1), pp. 33–54.

Ilkhamov, Alisher (2004) 'Archaeology of Uzbek Identity', *Central Asian Survey*, 23(3), pp. 289–326.

Ilkhamov, Alisher (2007) 'Neopatrimonialism, Interest Groups and Patronage Networks: the Impasses of the Governance System in Uzbekistan', *Central Asian Survey*, 26(1), 65–84.

Imanaliev, Muratbek (2008) 'Sbornik Statei o Tsentral'noi Azii', Available at www.ipp.kg/ uploads/publications_/Imanaliev_About_Central_Asia.pdf (accessed 24 April 2009).

Imanaliev, Muratbek (2010) *Foreign Policy of Kyrgyzstan: Contemporary Status and Future Perspectives*. Available at www.ipp.kg/uploads/publications_/NED_book_ final_ru.pdf (23 March 2011).

Imomov, A., Saunders, H. and Chufrin, G. (ND) 'The Inter-Tajik Dialogue Within the Framework of the Dartmouth Conference', *CA & CC Press AB*. Available at: www. ca-c.org/dataeng/st_07_imomov.shtml (accessed 17 August 2010).

Inoue, Koichi (ND) 'In memorium – Dr. Yutaka Akino (1950-1998)'. Available at: http:// src-h.slav.hokudai.ac.jp/akino/akino-e.html (accessed 17 August 2010).

International Crisis Group (ICG) (2002) *The IMU and the Hizb-ut-Tahrir: Implications of the Afghanistan Campaign*, Asia Briefing N°11, 30 Jan 2002.

International Crisis Group (2003a) *Central Asia: Islam and the State*, Asia Report, No. 59, 10 July.

International Crisis Group (2003b) *Is Radical Islam Inevitable in Central Asia? Priorities for Engagement*', Asia Report, No. 72, 22 December.

International Crisis Group (2004) *The Curse of Cotton: Central Asia's Destructive Monoculture*, Asia Report No. 93.

International Crisis Group (2005a) *Kyrgyzstan: A Faltering State*, Asia Report No. 109, 16 December.

International Crisis Group (2005b) *Uzbekistan: The Andijon Uprising*, Asia Briefing No. 38, 25 May.

International Crisis Group (2005c) *Kyrgyzstan: After the Revolution*, Asia Report No. 97, 4 May.

International Crisis Group (2010a) *The Pogroms in Kyrgyzstan*, Asia Report No. 193, 23 August.

International Crisis Group (2010b) *Kyrgyzstan: A Hollow Regime Collapses*, Asia Briefing No. 102, 27 April.

International Crisis Group (2011) Central Asia: Decay and Decline, Asia Report No. 201, 3 February 2011.

Isaacs, Rico (2011) *Party System Formation in Kazakhstan*, London: Routledge.

Ishiyama, John (2002) 'Neopatrimonialism and the Prospects for Democratization in the Central Asian Republics', in Sally N. Cummings (ed.) *Power and Change in Central Asia*, pp. 42–58.

Jackson, Nicole J. (2005) 'The Trafficking of Narcotics, Arms and Humans in Post-Soviet Central Asia: (Mis)perceptions, Policies and Realities', *Central Asian Survey*, 24(1), pp. 39–52.

Jawad, Nassim and Tadjbaksh, Shahranou (1995) *Tajikistan: A Forgotten Civil War*, London: Minority Rights Group.

Job, Brian (2004) 'The UN, Regional Organizations, and Regional Conflict', in Richard Price and Mark Zacher (eds) *The United Nations and Global Security*, New York: Palgrave, pp. 227–43.

Jones Luong, Pauline (2002) *Institutional Change and Political Continuity in Post-Soviet Central Asia: Power, Perceptions, and Pacts*, Cambridge: Cambridge University Press.

Jones Luong, Pauline (ed.) (2004) *The Transformation of Central Asia: States and Societies from Soviet Rule to Independence*, Ithaca, NY: Cornell University Press.

Jones Luong, Pauline and Weinthal, Erika (1999) 'The NGO Paradox: Democratic Goals and Non-democratic Outcomes in Kazakhstan', *Europe-Asia Studies*, 51(7), pp. 1267–84.

Jones Luong, Pauline and Weinthal, Erika (2003) 'New Friends, New Fears in Central Asia', *Foreign Affairs*, 81(2), pp. 61–70.

Jones Luong, Pauline and Weinthal, Erika (2010) *Oil is Not a Curse: Ownership Structure and Institutions in Soviet Successor States*, New York: Cambridge University Press.

Jonson, Lena (1998) *Russia and Central Asia: A New Web of Relations*, London: Royal Institute of International Affairs.

Jonson, Lena (2006) *Tajikistan in the New Central Asia*, London and New York: IB Tauris.

Jowitt, Ken (1992) *The New World Disorder: The Leninist Extinction*, Berkeley, CA: University of California Press.

Kadyrov, Shokhrat (2001) *Rossiisko-Turkmenskii Istoricheskii Slovar Volume 1*, Bergen, Norway.

Kadyrov, Shokhrat (2003) 'Turkmenistan: The Political Elite in an Ethnic Society', in Sally N. Cummings (ed.) *Oil, Transition and Security in Central Asia*, London: Routledge, pp. 108–18.

Kamp, Marianne (2006) *The New Woman in Uzbekistan: Islam, Modernity, and Unveiling Under Communism*, Seattle, WA: University of Washington Press.

Kamp, Marianne (2007) 'The Wedding Feast: Living the New Uzbek Life in the 1930s', in Jeff Sahadeo and Russell Zanca (eds) *Everyday Life in Central Asia*, Bloomington, IN: Indiana University Press, pp. 103–114.

Kandiyoti, Deniz (1998) 'Rural Livelihoods and Social Networks in Uzbekistan: Perspectives from Andijan', *Central Asian Survey*, 17(4), pp. 561–78.

Kandiyoti, Deniz (2002) 'Post-Colonialism Compared: Potentials and Limitations in the Middle East and Central Asia', *International Journal of Middle East Studies*, 34: 279–97.

Kandiyoti, Deniz (2005) 'Andijan: Prelude to a Massacre' (20 May). Available http: www.opendemocracy.net/globalization-institutions_government/Andijan_2527.jsp (20 December 2005).

Kandiyoti, Deniz (ed.) (2007) *The Cotton Sector in Central Asia: Economic Policy and Development Challenges: Proceedings of a Conference held at SOAS, University of London*, London: School of Oriental and African Studies.

Kandiyoti, Deniz and Azimova, Nadira (2004) 'The Communal and the Sacred: Women's Worlds of Ritual in Uzbekistan', *The Journal of the Royal Anthropological Institute*, 10(2), pp. 327–49.

Kandiyoti, Rafael (2008) 'What Price Access to Open Seas? The Geopolitics of Oil and Gas Transmission from the Transcaspian Republics', *Central Asian Survey*, 27(1), pp. 75–93.

Kangas, Roger (1996) 'Taking the Lead in Central Asian Security', *Transitions*, 2(9). Available at: www.tol.org/client/archives/ (accessed 23 May 2010).

Kangas, Roger (2002) 'Uzbekistan: The Karimov Presidency – Amir Timur Revisited', in Sally N. Cummings (ed.) *Power and Change in Central Asia*, London: Routledge, pp. 130–49.

Kaplan, Robert D. (1994) 'The Coming Anarchy', *Atlantic Monthly*, 273(2), pp. 44–76.

Kappeler, Andreas (2001) *The Russian Empire: A Multiethnic History*, London: Longman.

Karl, Terry (1997) *The Paradox of Plenty: Oil Booms and Petro-States*, Berkeley: University of California Press.

Kaser, Michael and Mehrotra, Santosh K. (1992) *The Central Asian Economies after Independence*, London: Royal Institute of International Affairs.

Kaser, Michael (1997) *The Economies of Kazakhstan and Uzbekistan*, London: Royal Institute of International Affairs.

Kassymbekova, Botakoz (2011) 'Helpless Imperialists: European State Workers in Soviet Central Asia in the 1920s and 1930s', *Central Asian Survey*, 30(1), pp. 21–37.

Katzenstein, Peter J. (ed.) (1996) *The Culture of National Security*, New York: Columbia University Press.

Kehl-Bodrogi, Krisztina (2006) 'Who Owns the Shrine? Competing Meanings and Authorities at a Pilgrimage Site in Khorezm', *Central Asian Survey*, 25(3), pp. 235–50.

Kendirbaeva, Gulnar (1999) "We Are Children of Alash" The Kazakh Intelligentsia at the Beginning of the 20th Century in Search of National Identity and Prospects of the Cultural Survival of the Kazakh People', *Central Asian Survey*, 18(1), pp. 5–36.

Keohane, Robert O. and Nye, Jr., Joseph S. (1977) *Power and Interdependence: World Politics in Transition*, New York: Little Brown and Co.

Khakim, Abdullo (2005) 'Religious Thought in Central Asia: It Needs a Major Overhaul', *Central Asia and the Caucasus: Journal of Social and Political Studies*, 1(31).

Khalid, Adeeb (1998) *The Politics of Muslim Cultural Reform: Jadidism in Central Asia*, Berkeley: University of California Press.

Khalid, Adeeb (2003) 'A Secular Islam: Nation, State, and Religion in Uzbekistan', *International Journal of Middle East Studies*, 35(4), pp. 573–98.

Khalid, Adeeb (2006) 'Backwardness and the Quest for Civilization: Early Soviet Central Asia in Comparative Perspective', *Slavic Review*, 65(2), pp. 231–51.

Khalid, Adeeb (2007b) 'Locating the (post-)Colonial in Soviet history', *Central Asian Survey*, 26(4), pp. 465–73.

Khalid, Adeeb (2007c) *Islam After Communism: Religion and Politics in Central Asia*, Berkeley: University of California Press.

Khazanov, Anatoly (1983) *Nomads and the Outside World*, Cambridge: Cambridge University Press.

Khazanov, Anatoly (1984) *Nomads and the Outside World*, Cambridge: Cambridge University Press.

Khong, Yuen Foong (2001) 'Human Security: A Shotgun Approach to Alleviating Human Misery?' *Global Governance*, 7(3), pp. 231–36.

Khudonazarov, Davlat (1995) 'The Conflict in Tajikistan: Questions of Regionalism', in Roald Z. Sagdeev and Susan Eisenhower (eds) *Islam and Central Asia*, Washington, DC: CPSS Press, pp. 249–63.

Kipling, Rudyard (1901) *Kim*, London: Macmillan.

Klare, Michael T. (2004) *Blood and Oil: The Dangers and Consequences of America's Growing Dependency on Imported Petroleum*, New York: Metropolitan Books/Henry Holt.

Kleinbach, Russ and Salimjanova, Lilly (2007) '*Kyz ala kachuu* and *adat*: Non-consensual Bride Kidnapping and Tradition in Kyrgyzstan', *Central Asian Survey*, 26(2), pp. 217–33.

Kleveman, Lutz (2004) *The New Great Game: Blood and Oil in Central Asia*, London: Atlantic Books.

Koenig, Matthias (1999) 'Social Conditions for the Implementation of Linguistic Human Rights through Multicultural Policies: The Case of the Kyrgyz Republic', *Current Issues in Language & Society*, 6(1), pp. 57–84.

Kolstø, Pål. (1999) 'Territorialising Diasporas: The Case of the Russians in the Former Soviet Republics', *Millennium: Journal of International Studies*, 28(3): 607–31.

Kondaurova, Viktoria (2008) 'Looking for a Way to Resolve the Legal Status of the Caspian Sea: International Law Provides No Answer', *Central Asia and the Caucasus: Journal of Social and Political Studies*, 6(54). Available at: www.ca-c.org.ezproxy.st-andrews.ac.uk/online/2008/journal_eng/cac-06/07.shtml (accessed 15 January 2011).

Kornai, János (1992), *The Socialist System: The Political Economy of Communism*, Princeton, NJ: Princeton University Press.

Koroteyeva, Victoria and Makarova, Ekaterina (1998) 'Money and Social Connections in the Soviet and post-Soviet Uzbek city', *Central Asian Survey*, 17(4), pp. 579–96.

Krasner, Stephen D. (1999) *Sovereignty: Organised Hypocrisy*, Princeton, NJ: Princeton University Press.

Krasner, Stephen D. (ed.) (2001) *Problematic Sovereignty*, New York: Columbia University Press.

Kubicek, Paul (1997) 'Regionalism, Nationalism and Realpolitik in Central Asia', *Europe-Asia Studies*, 49(4), pp. 637–55.

Kubicek, Paul (1998) 'Authoritarianism in Central Asia: Curse or Cure?' *Third World Quarterly*, 19(1), pp. 29–43.

Kuchkin, A.P. (1962) *Sovetizatsiya Kazakhskogo Aula: 1926–1929*, Moscow: USSR Academy of Sciences.

Kudabaev, Z.I. (2009a) 'Economic Reform Strategy in the Kyrgyz Republic'. Available at: http://hdl.handle.net/123456789/588 (accessed 23 February 2011).

Kudabaev, Z.I. (2009b) 'Economic Growth and Well-being – Statistical Perspective'. Available at: http://hdl.handle.net/123456789/481 (accessed 24 February 2011).

Kudabaev, Z.I. (2009) 'Ekonomicheskii rost Kyrgyzstana: Rol' Sektorov Ekonomiki', *The Review of Central Asian Studies*, 2 (30 November).

Kuehnast, Kathleen and Dudwick, Nora (2004) 'Better a Hundred Friends than a Hundred Rubels? Social Networks in Transition – the Kyrgyz Republic, *World Bank Working Paper*, No. 39, Washington, DC: World Bank.

Kushkumbaev. S. (2002) *Tsentral'naia Azia na Putiah Integratsii: Geopolitika, Etnichnost, Bezopasnost*, Almaty: Kazakhstan Publishers.

Kutan, Ali M. and Wyzan, Michael L. (2005) 'Explaining the Real Exchange Rate in Kazakhstan, 1996–2003: Is Kazakhstan Vulnerable to the Dutch disease? Original Research Article', *Economic Systems*, 29(2), pp. 242–55.

Lal, B.B. (1992) 'The Painted Grey Ware Culture of the Iron Age', in A.H. Dani and V.M. Masson (eds) *History of Civilizations of Central Asia Volume 1*, Paris: UNESCO Publishing, pp. 421–40.

Landau, Jacob M. (1995) *Pan-Turkism: From Irredentism to Cooperation*, London: Hurst & Company.

Landau, Jacob M. and Kellner-Heinkele, Barbara (2001) *Politics of Language in the ex-Soviet Muslim States: Azerbayjan, Uzbekistan, Kazakhstan, Kyrgyzstan, Turkmenistan, and Tajikistan*, Ann Arbor, MI: University of Michigan Press.

Laruelle, Marlene (2007) 'Religious Revival, Nationalism and the "Invention of Tradition": Political Tengrism in Central Asia and Tatarstan', *Central Asian Survey*, 26(2), pp. 203–16.

Laumulin, Murat T. (2005) Tom 1 *Tsentral'naya Aziya v Zarubezhnoi Politologii I Mirovoi Geopolitike*, Almaty: KISI.

Laumulin, Murat T. (2006) Tom 2 *Tsentral'naya Aziya v Zarubezhnoi Politologii I Mirovoi Geopolitike*, Almaty: KISI.

Lester, Anne E. (ed.) (2010) *Central Asia: Background, Issues and U.S. Interests (Countries, Regional Studies, Trading Blocks, Unions, World Organizations)*, Hauppauge, NY: Nova Science Pub. Inc.

Levgold, Robert (2003) *Thinking Strategically: The Major Powers, Kazakhstan and the Central Asian Nexus*, Cambridge: The MIT Press.

Levi, Scott (ed.) (2007a) *India and Central Asia: Commerce and Culture, 1500–1800*, New Delhi: Oxford University Press.

Levi, Scott (2007b) 'Turks and Tajiks in Central Asian History', in Jeff Sahadeo and Russell Zanca (eds) *Everyday Life in Central Asia*, Bloomington, IN: Indiana University Press, pp. 15–31.

Levi, Scott and Sela, Ron (eds) (2010) *Islamic Central Asia: An Anthology of Historical Sources*, Bloomington, IN: Indiana University Press.

Levy, Marc A. (1995) 'Is the Environment a National Security Issue?' *International Security*, 20(2), pp. 35–62.

Levy, C. (2010a) 'Upheaval in Kyrgyzstan Could Imperil Key U.S. Base', *The New York Times*, 7 April. Accessed 10 December 2010.

Levy, C. (2010b) 'Kyrgyzstan President Says He Will Not Step Down', *The New York Times*, 8 April. Accessed 17 August 2010.

Lewis, Robert (1992) *Geographic Perspectives on Soviet Central Asia*, London: Routledge.

Lewis, David (2011) in Sally N. Cummings and Raymond Hinnebusch (eds) *Sovereignty After Empire: Comparing the Middle East and Central Asia*, Edinburgh: Edinburgh University Press, pp. 178–95.

Lewis, Martin W. and Wigen, Karen E. (1997) *The Myth of Continents: A Critique of Metageography*, Berkeley: University of California Press.

Lewis, Robert A. (1986) *Geographic Perspectives on Central Asia*, London and New York: Routledge.

Libiszewiski Stephan (1992) *What is an Environmental Conflict?* Center for Security Studies and Conflict Research, Swiss Federal Institute of Technology.

Libman, Alexander (2007) 'Regionalisation and Regionalism in the Post-Soviet Space: Current Status and Implications for Institutional Development', *Europe-Asia Studies*, 59(3), pp. 401–30.

Lieven, Anatol (1999/2000) 'The (Not So) Great Game', *The National Interest*, pp. 69–80.

Lieven, Dominic (2002) *The Russian Empire and Its Rivals*, New Haven, CT: Yale University Press.

Lillis, J. (2010a) 'Kyrgyzstan: Ousted President's Comeback Bid Ends in Retreat', *EurasiaNet*, 15 April. Available at: www.eurasianet.org/departments/insightb/articles/eav041510a.shtml (accessed 17 August 2010).

Lillis, J. (2010b) 'Ousted Kyrgyz President's Stronghold Calm', *EurasiaNet*, 16 April. Available at: www.eurasianet.org/departments/insight/articles/eav041610.shtml (accessed 17 August 2010).

Lipset, Martin Seymour (1960) *Political Man: The Social Bases of Politics*, Garden City, NY: Doubleday.

Louw, Maria (2006) 'Pursuing "Muslimness": Shrines as Sites for Moralities in the Making in Post-Soviet Bukhara', *Central Asian Survey*, 25(3), pp. 319–39.

Luciani, Giancomo (1990) 'Allocation vs Production States: A Theoretical Framework', in Giacomo Luciani (ed.) *The Arab State*, London: Routledge, pp. 63–82.

Lynch, Dov (2001) 'The Tajik Civil War and Peace Process', *Civil Wars*, 4(4), pp. 49–72.

MacFarlane, S. Neil and Yuen Foong Khong (2006) *Human Security and the UN: A Critical History* , Bloomington, IN: Indiana University Press.

MacFarlane, S. Neil and Torjesen, Stina (2007) *Small Arms in Kyrgyzstan: Post-Revolutionary Proliferation*, Small Arms Survey, Geneva: Graduate Institute of International Studies.

Mack, Andrew (2001) 'Notes on the Creation of a Human Security Report'. Paper presented to the Kennedy School of Government, Harvard University, 1–2 December.

Mack, Andrew (2005) *Human Security Report 2005: War and Peace in the 21st Century*, New York: Oxford University Press.

Mackinder, Halford J. (1942) *Democratic Ideals and Reality*, New York: HJ Holt & Co.

Madi, Maral (2004) 'Drug Trade in Kyrgyzstan: Structure, Implications and Counter-measures', *Central Asian Survey*, 23(3), pp. 249–73.

Makarenko, Tamara (2002) 'Crime, Terror and the Central Asian Drug Trade', *Harvard Asia Quarterly*, 6(3). Available at www.fas.harvard.edu/~asiactr./haq/200203/0203a004.htm (accessed 23 February 2011).

Makarenko, Tamara (2004) 'The Crime-terror Continuum: Tracing the Interplay Between Transnational Organized Crime and Terrorism', *Global Crime*, 6(1), pp. 129–45.

Malashenko, Aleksei (1994) 'Islam and Politics in the Southern Zone of the Former USSR', in Vitaly V. Naumkin (ed.) *Central Asia and Transcaucasia: Ethnicity and Conflict*, Westport, CT: Greenwood Press.

Mandel, Ruth (1998) 'Structural Adjustment and Soap Opera: A Case Study of a Development Project in Central Asia', *Central Asian Survey*, 17(4), pp. 629–38.

Mandel, Ruth and Humphrey, Caroline (eds) (2002) *Markets and Moralities: Ethnographies of Postsocialism*, Oxford; New York: Berg.

Manning, Robert A. and Jaffe, Amy M. (1998) 'The Myth of the Caspian Great Game: Real Geopolitics of Energy', *Survival*, 40(4), pp. 112–9.

Marat, Erica (2008) 'March and After: What Has Changed? What Has Stayed the Same?' *Central Asian Survey*, 27(3), pp. 229–40.

Marat, Erica (2009a) *Labor Migration in Central Asia: Implications of the Global Economic Crisis*, Washington, DC: Central Asia-Caucasus Institute, Silk Road Studies Program, Silk Road Paper.

Marat, Erica (2009b) 'Nation Branding in Central Asia: A New Campaign to Present Ideas about the State and the Nation', *Europe-Asia Studies*, 61(7), pp. 1123–36.

Marat, Erica (2009c) *The Military and the State in Central Asia: From Red Army to Independence*, London and New York: Routledge.

Marat, Erica (2010) 'Kyrgyz Parliament Forms New Coalition', Eurasia Daily Monitor, 7(225). Available at: www.jamestown.org/programs/edm/single/?tx_ttnews%5Btt_news%5D= 37287&cHash=04c50f4d44 (accessed 17 August 2010).

March, Andrew F. (2002) 'The Use and Abuse of History: "National Ideology" as Transcendental Object in Islam Karimov's "Ideology of National Independence"', *Central Asian Survey*, 21(4), pp. 371–84.

March, Andrew F. (2003) 'State Ideology and the Legitimation of Authoritarianism: the Case of post-Soviet Uzbekistan', *Journal of Political Ideologies*, 8(2), pp. 209–32.

Martin, Terry (2001) *The Affirmative Action Empire: Nations and Nationalism in the Soviet Union 1923–1939*, Ithaca, NY: Cornell University Press.

Masson, V.M. (1992) 'The Environment', in A.H. Dani and V.M. Masson (eds) *History of Civilizations of Central Asia Volume 1*, Paris: UNESCO Publishing.

Matthews, Jessica Tuchman (1989) 'Redefining Security', *Foreign Affairs*, 68, pp. 162–77.

Matveeva, Anna (2006) *Central Asia: A Strategic Framework for Peacebuilding*, London: International Alert.

Matveeva, Anna (2009a) 'Legitimising Central Asian Authoritarianism: Political Manipulation and Symbolic Power', *Europe-Asia Studies*, 61(7), pp. 1095–121.

Matveeva, Anna (2009b) 'Tajikistan: "Revolutionary Situation" or a Resilient State?' EUCAM Policy Brief [online]. December. Available at www.ceps.eu/book/tajikistan-revolutionary-situation-or-resilient-state (accessed 20 March 2011).

McAllister, Brad and Khersonsky, Julia (2007) 'Trade, Development, and Nonproliferation: Multilevel Counterterrorism in Central Asia Studies', *Conflict & Terrorism*, 30(5), pp. 445–58.

McBrien, Julie (2006) 'Listening to the Wedding Speaker: Discussing Religion and Culture in Southern Kyrgyzstan', *Central Asian Survey*, 25(3), pp. 341–57.

McChesney, R.D. (1996) *Central Asia: Foundations of Change*, Princeton, NJ: The Darwin Press.

McFaul, Michael (2001) *Russia's Unfinished Revolution: Political Change from Gorbachev to Putin*, Ithaca, NY: Cornell University Press.

McGlinchey, Eric (2007) 'Divided Faith: Trapped between State and Islam in Uzbekistan', in Jeff Sahadeo and Russell Zanca (eds) *Everyday Life in Central Asia*, Bloomington, IN: Indiana University Press.

McMann, Kelly (2004) 'The Civil Realm in Kyrgyzstan: Soviet Economic Legacies and Activists' Expectations', in Pauline Jones Luong (ed.) *The Transformation of Central Asia: States and Societies from Soviet Rule to Independence*, Ithaca, NY: Cornell University Press, pp. 213–45.

McMann, Kelly (2007) 'The Shrinking of the Welfare State: Central Asians' Assessments of Soviet and Post-Soviet Governance', in Jeff Sahadeo and Russell Zanca (eds) *Everyday Life in Central Asia*, Bloomington, IN: Indiana University Press, pp. 198–222.

Mearsheimer, John J. (2001) *The Tragedy of Great Power Politics*, New York: W.W. Norton.

Medeiros, Evan S. and Fravel, M. Taylor (2003) 'China's New Diplomacy', *Foreign Affairs*, 82(6), pp. 74–90.

Megoran, Nick (2004) 'Revisiting the Pivot: The Influence of Halford Mackinder on Analysis of Uzbekistans International Relations', *The Geographical Journal*, 170(4), pp. 347–58.

Megoran, Nick (2005) 'The Critical Geopolitics of Danger in Uzbekistan and Kyrgyzstan', *Environment and Planning D: Society and Space*, 23(4), pp. 555–80.

Megoran, Nick (2008) 'Framing Andijon, Narrating the Nation: Islam Karimov's Account of the Events of 13 May 2005', *Central Asian Survey*, 27(1), pp. 15–31.

Melvin, Neil J. (2004) 'Authoritarian Pathways in Central Asia: A Comparison of Kazakhstan, the Kyrgyz Republic and Uzbekistan', in Yaacov Ro'i (ed.) *Democracy and Pluralism in Muslim Eurasia*, London: Frank Cass, pp. 119–42.

Melvin, Neil J. (2008) *Engaging Central Asia: The European Union's Strategy in the Heart of Eurasia*, Brussels: Centre for European Policy Studies.

Menon, Rajan (1995) 'In the Shadow of the Bear: Security in Post-Soviet Central Asia', *International Security*, 20(1), pp. 149–81.

Menon, Rajan (2003) 'The New Great Game in Central Asia', *Survival*, 45(2), pp. 187–204.

Menon, Rajan and Spruyt, Hendrik (1998) 'Possibilities for Conflict and Conflict Resolution in post-Soviet Central Asia', in Barnett Rubin and Jack Snyder (eds) *Post-Soviet Political Order: Conflict and State-Building*, London: Routledge, pp. 104–27.

Menon, Rajan and Spruyt, Hendrik (1999) 'The Limits of Neorealism: Understanding Security in Central Asia', *Review of International Studies*, 25(1), pp. 87–105.

Michaels, Paula A. (2000) 'Medical Propaganda and Cultural Revolution in Soviet Kazakhstan, 1928–41', *Russian Review*, 59(2), pp. 159–78.

Michaels, Paula A. (2003) *Curative Powers: Medicine and Empire in Stalin's Central Asia*, Pittsburgh, PA: University of Pittsburgh Press.

Micklin, Philip P. (1987) 'The Fate of Sibaral: Soviet Water Politics in the Gorbachev Era', *Central Asian Survey*, 6(2), pp. 67–88.

Micklin, Philip P. (2000) *Managing Water in Central Asia*, London: Royal Institute of International Affairs.

Migdal, Joel S. (1988) *Strong Societies and Weak States: State-Society Relations and State Capacities in the Third World*, Princeton, NJ: Princeton University Press.

Minogue, Kenneth and Williams, Beryl (1992) 'Ethnic Conflict in the Soviet Union: The Revenge of Particularism', in Alexander J. Motyl (ed.) *Thinking Theoretically about Soviet Nationalities*, New York: Columbia University Press, pp. 225–42.

Miroshnikov, L.I. (1992) 'A Note on the Meaning of the Term "Central Asia" As Used in the Book', in A.H. Dani and V.M. Masson (eds) *History of Civilizations of Central Asia Volume 1*, Paris: UNESCO Publishing, pp. 477–80.

Moravcsik, Andrew (2001) *Liberal International Relations Theory: A Social Scientific Assessment,* Cambridge, MA: Harvard University Press.

Morgan, David (1990) *The Mongols*, Cambridge, MA and Oxford: Blackwell.

Morgenthau, Hans (2005) *Politics Among Nations: The Struggle for Power and Peace*, Maidenhead, Berkshire: McGraw-Hill Higher Education.

Morrison, Alexander (2008) *Russian Rule in Samarkand, 1868–1910: A Comparison with British India*, Oxford: Oxford University Press.

Motyl, Alexander J. (2001) *Imperial Ends: The Decay, Collapse, and Revival of Empires*, New York: Columbia University Press.

Mukhamedzhanov, A. (2006) *Istoriya Uzbekistana*, Tashkent: Izdatel'stvo Narodnogo Naslediya Imeni Abdully Kadyri.

Murzakhalilov, Kanatbek, Mamataliev, Kanybek and Mamaiusupov, Omurzak (2005) 'Islam in the Democratic Context of Kyrgyzstan: Comparative Analysis', *Central Asia and the Caucasus: Journal of Social and Political Studies*, 3(33). Available at: www.ca-c.org.ezproxy.st-andrews.ac.uk/online/2005/journal_eng/cac-03/06.mureng.shtml (accessed 24 May 2011).

Murzakulova, Asel and Schoeberlein, John (2010) 'The Invention of Legitimacy: Struggles in Kyrgyzstan to Craft an Effective Nation-state Ideology', in Sally N. Cummings (ed.) *Symbolism and Power in Central Asia: Politics of the Spectacular*, London: Routledge, pp. 144–63.

Mutschke, Ralf (2000) 'The Threat Posed by the Convergence of Organized Crime, Drugs Trafficking and Terrorism', Testimony to the Subcommittee on Crime of the Judiciary Committee, U.S. House of Representatives, 13 December.

Myers, S. L. (2005) 'Uprising Erupts in Uzbek City', *The New York Times*, 14 May.

NA (1997) 'The Civil War in Tajikistan', *Strategic Comments*, 3(6), 1–2.

Najibullah, F. (2010a) 'At Least 49 Dead as State of Emergency Declared in Southern Kyrgyzstan', *RFE/RL*, 6 June.

Najibullah, F. (2010b) 'Kyrgyzstan Mobilizes Troops as Violence Spreads in Southern Cities', *RFE/RL*, 12 June.

Najibullah, F. (2010c) 'Aid Arrives to Help Kyrgyzstan Refugees as Stories of Rape, Torture Emerge', *RFE/RL*, 17 June.

Najibullah, F. (2010d) 'Kyrgyzstan Ends Curfew Amid UN Warning of Risk of Violence', *RFE/RL*, 25 June.

Najibullah, F. and Abdraimov, R. (2010) 'OSCE Calls for Restraint After Deadly Kyrgyz Unrest', *RFE/RL*, 20 May.

Najibullah, F. (2011) 'Ethnic Uzbeks Suffered "Disproportionately" in Kyrgyz Violence, Report Concludes', *RFE/RL*, 3 May.

Nakaya, Sumie (2009) 'Aid and Transition from a War Economy to an Oligarchy in Post-war Tajikistan', *Central Asian Survey*, 28(3), pp. 259–73.

National Statistical Committee of the Kyrgyz Republic (2009) *Perepis' Naseleniya I Zhilishchnogo Fonda Kyrgyzskoi Respubliki 2009 Goda*, vol. 1.

Naumkin, Vitaly (2003) *Russian Oriental Studies: Current Research on Past and Present Asian and African Societies*, Leiden: Brill Academic Publishers.

Nazarbaev, Nursultan (1997) *Kazakhstan-2030: Poslanie Prezidenta Strany Narodu Kazakhstana*, Almaty: Bilim.

Nazarbaev, Nursultan (1997) *Evraziiskii Soiuz: Idei, Praktika, Perspektivy*, Moscow: Fond sodeistvya razvitiyu sotsial'nykh i politicheskikh nauk.

Nazarbaev, Nursultan (2008) *The Kazakhstan Way*, London: Stacey International.

Nazarbaeva, D. (2003) 'Spetsifika i Perspektivy Politicheskogo Razvitia Kazakhstana,' Biulleten No. 3, 2003, Mezhdunarodniy institut sovremennoy politiki, 17 February 2006.

Nazpary, Joma (2002) *Post-Soviet Chaos: Violence and Dispossession in Kazakhstan*, London: Pluto Press.

The New York Times (2005) 'Gunfire Continues in Uzbekistan', *The New York Times*, 16 May.

The New York Times (2005) 'Suspects in Uzbek Unrest Seized as Leader Rejects an Inquiry', *The New York Times*, 21 May.

Nichol, James P. (1995) *Diplomacy in the Former Soviet Republics*, Westport, CT: Praeger.

Niklasson, Charlotte and Hedenskog, Jakob (2008) *Russian Leverage in Central Asia*, Stockholm: Swedish Defence Research Agency.

Northrop, Douglas (2004) *Veiled Empire: Gender and Power in Stalinist Central Asia*, Ithaca, NY: Cornell University Press.

Nove, Alec and Newth, J.A. (1966) *The Soviet Middle East: A Communist Model for Development*, Westport, CT: Praeger.

Ochs, Michael (1997) 'Turkmenistan: The Quest for Stability and Control', in Karen Dawisha and Bruce Parrott (eds) *Conflict, Cleavage, and Change in Central Asia and the Caucasus*, Cambridge: Cambridge University Press.

O'Hara, Sara (1998) 'Managing Central Asia's Water Resources: Prospects for the 21st Century', ICREES Seminar on Environmental Issues in Central Asia, University of Nottingham, 9 December 1998.

Olcott, Martha Brill (1992) 'Catapult to Independence', *Foreign Affairs*, 71(3), pp. 108–13.

Olcott, Martha Brill (1987, 1995) *The Kazakhs,* 1st and 2nd edns, Stanford, CA: Stanford University Press.

Olcott, Martha Brill and Babajanov, Bakhtiyar (2003) 'The Terrorist Notebooks', *Foreign Policy*, March–April, pp. 30–40.

Olcott, Martha Brill and Udalova, Natalia (2000) *Drug Trafficking on the Great Silk Road*, Number 11, Washington DC: Carnegie Endowment for International Peace.

Olimova, Saodat (2000) 'Islam and the Tajik Conflict', in Roald Sagdeev and Susan Eisenhower (eds.) *Islam in Central Asia: An Enduring Legacy or an Evolving Threat?*, Washington, DC: Center for Political and Strategic Studies, pp. 42–60.

Omarov, Nur (2004) 'Samoidentifikatsiya Kak Strategicheskii Vybor Gosudarstv Tsentralnoi Azii v Nachale 3-go Tysyacheletiya' (accessed at http://omarov-nur.narod.ru/).

Omelicheva, Mariya (2007) 'Combating Terrorism in Central Asia: Explaining Differences in States' Responses to Terror', *Terrorism and Political Violence*, 19(3), pp. 369–93.

Omelicheva, Mariya (2009) 'Convergence of Counterterrorism Policies: A Case Study of Kyrgyzstan and Central Asia Studies', *Conflict and Terrorism*, 32(10), pp. 893–908.

Omelicheva, Mariya (2010) *Counterterrorism Policies in Central Asia (Central Asian Studies)*, Abingdon, Oxon, New York: Routledge.

Omelicheva, Mariya (2011) 'Islam in Kazakhstan: A Survey of Contemporary Trends and Sources of Securitization', *Central Asian Survey*, 30(2), pp. 243–56.

Oneal, John R. and Russett, Bruce M. (1999) 'The Kantian Peace: The Pacific Benefits of Democracy, Interdependence, and International Organizations, 1884–1992', *World Politics*, 52(1), pp. 1–37.

Onuf, Nicholas (1989) *World of Our Making*, Columbia, SC: University of South Carolina Press.

O'Prey, K.P. (1996) 'Keeping the Peace in the Borderlands of Russia', in W. Durch (ed.) *United Nations Peacekeeping, American Politics, and the Uncivil Wars of the 1990s*, Palgrave Macmillan.

Ortmann, Stephanie (2008) 'Diffusion as Discourse of Danger: Russian Self-representations and the Framing of the Tulip Revolution', *Central Asian Survey*, 27(3–4), pp. 363–78.

Osmanaliev, Kairat (2003) *Organizovannaia Prestupnast v Kirgizskoi Respublike*, published in the framework of the UN Evaluation Project of Organized Crime in Central Asia, Bishkek.

Osmonaliev, Kairat (2005) 'Developing Counter-Narcotics Policy in the Central Asia: Legal and Political Dimensions', *Silk Road Paper*, Washington DC and Uppsala: Central Asia Caucasus Institute and Silk Road Studies Program, January.

Osmonov, O. Dzh (2005) *Istoriya Kyrgyzstana*, Bishkek Publishers.

Ostrowski, Wojciech (2011) 'Rentierism, Dependency and Sovereignty in Central Asia', in Sally N. Cummings and Raymond Hinnebusch (eds) *Sovereignty After Empire: Comparing the Middle East and Central Asia*, Edinburgh: Edinburgh University Press, pp. 282–303.

Özcan, Gül B. (2010) *Building States and Markets: Enterprise Development in Central Asia*, Basingstoke: Palgrave Macmillan.

Paris, Roland (2001) 'Human Security: Paradigm Shift or Hot Air?' *International Security*, 26(2), pp. 87–102.

Park, Andrus (1997) 'Theories of Post-communist Nationalism', in David Carlton and Paul Ingram (eds) *The Search for Stability in Russia and the Former Soviet Bloc*, Aldershot: Ashgate, pp. 119–39.

Peimani, Hooman (1998) *Regional Security and the Future of Central Asia: The Competition of Iran, Turkey, and Russia*, Westport, CT: Praeger.

Peters, J. (1964) 'Stalin's Nationality Policy: An Interpretation', Unpublished Ph.D. thesis, University of Pennsylvania.

Pétric, Boris-Mathieu (2002) *Pouvoir, Don et Réseaux en Ouzbékistan Post-Soviétique*, with an introduction by Olivier Roy, Paris: Presses Universitaires de France.

Pétric, Boris-Mathieu (2005) 'Post-Soviet Kyrgyzstan or the Birth of a Globalized Protectorate', *Central Asian Survey*, 24(3), pp. 319–32.

Pétric, Boris-Mathieu (2010) 'Political Games in Post-Soviet Uzbekistan: Factions, Protection, and New Resistances', in Robert Canfield and Gabriele Rauly-Paleczek (eds) *Ethnicity, Authority, and Power in Central Asia: New Games Great and Small*, London: Routledge, pp. 165–73.

Peyrouse, Sébastien (2003) *Des Chrétiens Entre Athéisme et Islam. Regards sur la Question Religieuse en Asie Centrale Soviétique et Post-Soviétique*, with an introduction by Patrick Michel, Paris: Maisonneuve & Larose.

Peyrouse, Sébastien (2007a) 'Nationhood and the Minority Question in Central Asia: The Russians in Kazakhstan', *Europe-Asia Studies*, 59(3), pp. 481–501.

Peyrouse, Sébastien (2007b) 'Christians as the Main Religious Minority in Central Asia', in Jeff Sahadeo and Russell Zanca (eds) *Everyday Life in Central Asia*, Bloomington, IN: Indiana University Press, pp. 371–83.

Peyrouse, Sébastien (2008a) 'The Partnership between Islam and Orthodox Christianity in Central Asia', *Religion, State and Society*, 36(4), pp. 393–405.

Peyrouse, Sébastien (2008b) 'The Russian Minority in Central Asia: Migration, Politics and Language', *Occasional Paper no. 297*, Kennan Institute 2008.

Pianciola, Niccolò (2008) 'Décoloniser l'Asie Centrale? Bolcheviks et Colons au Semireč'e (1920–1922)', *Cahiers du Monde Russe*, 49(1), pp. 101–43.

Pipes, Richard (1997) *The Formation of the Soviet Union: Communism and Nationalism 1917–1923*, Harvard: Harvard University Press.

Pohl, Otto (2007) 'A Caste of Helot Labourers: Special Settlers and the Cultivation of Cotton in Soviet Central Asia: 1944-1956', in Deniz Kandiyoti (ed.) *The Cotton Sector in Central Asia: Economic Policy and Development Challenges*, London: SOAS, pp. 12–28.

Poliakov, Sergei P. (1992) *Everyday Islam: Religion and Tradition in Rural Central Asia*, London: M.E. Sharpe.

Pomfret, Richard (2000) 'The Uzbek Model of Economic Development, 1991–1999', *Economics of Transition*, 8(3), pp. 733–48.

Pomfret, Richard (2006) *The Central Asian Economies Since Independence*, Princeton, NJ: Princeton University Press.

Poujol, Catherine (1997) 'Some Reflections on Russian Involvement in the Tajik Conflict, 1992-1993', in Djalili Mohammad-Reza, Frédéric Grare and Shirin Akiner (eds) *Tajikistan: The Trials of Independence*, New York: St. Martin's Press, pp. 99–118.

Privratsky, Bruce G. (2001) *Muslim Turkistan: Kazak Religion and Collective Memory*, Richmond, Surrey: Curzon.

Radnitz, Scott (2005) 'Networks, Localism and Mobilization in Aksy, Kyrgyzstan', *Central Asian Survey*, 24(4), pp. 405–24.

Radnitz, Scott (2006) 'What Really Happened in Kyrgyzstan', *Journal of Democracy*, 17(2), pp. 132–146.

Radnitz, Scott (2010) *Weapons of the Wealthy: Predatory Regimes and Elite-led Protests in Central Asia*, Ithaca, NY: Cornell University Press.

Ragigh-Aghsan, Ali (2000) *The Dynamics and Inertia of the Northern Tier Cooperation: The Growing Role of Turkey and Iran and the Formation of a Cooperative Regional Hegemonic System in the Context of the ECO*, Copenhagen: Institute of Political Science, PhD dissertation series 2000/05.

Rakowska-Harmstone, Teresa (1994) 'Soviet Legacies' *Central Asia Monitor*, 3, pp. 23–34.

Rasanayagam, Johan (2006a) 'Healing with Spirits and the Formation of Muslim Selfhood in Post-Soviet Uzbekistan', *The Journal of the Royal Anthropological Institute*, 12(2), pp. 377–93.

Rasanayagam, Johan (2006b) 'Introduction', in *Central Asian Survey*, 25(3), pp. 219–33.

Rasanayagam, Johan (2007) 'Book review of *Islam after Communism: Religion and Politics in Central Asia*', *Central Asian Survey*, 26(1), pp. 157–9.

Rasanayagam, Johan (2011) *Islam in Post-Soviet Uzbekistan: The Morality of Experience*, Cambridge, UK: Cambridge University Press.

Rashid, Ahmed (2001) *Taliban: Islam, Oil and the New Great Game in Central Asia*, London: I.B. Tauris.

Rashid, Ahmed (2002) *Jihad: The Rise of Militant Islam in Central Asia*, New Haven, CT: Yale University Press.

Reeves, Madeleine (2005) 'Locating Danger: Konfliktologiia and the Search for Fixity in the Ferghana Valley Borderlands', *Central Asian Survey*, 24(1), pp. 67–81.

Reeves, Madeleine (2007) 'Travels in the Margins of the State: Everyday Geography in the Ferghana Valley Borderlands', in Jeff Sahadeo and Russell Zanca (eds) *Everyday Life in Central Asia*, Bloomington, IN: Indiana University Press, pp. 281–300.

Reeves, Madeleine (2009) 'Materialising State Space: "Creeping Migration" and Territorial Integrity in Southern Kyrgyzstan', *Europe-Asia Studies*, 61(7), pp. 1277–313.

Reeves, Madeleine (2011) '"We're With the People"? Political Crisis and the Ethnicization of Violence in Southern Kyrgyzstan', talk given at the University of St Andrews, 8 March.

Report on Tajikistan (1998) New York: The Open Society Institute.

RFE/RL (1992) 'Belorussian Film Director Shot in Tajikistan', *RFE/RL*, No. 185, September 25. Retrieved using the internet archive service *Wayback Machine*.

RFE/RL (1998) 'Tajikistan: Government Condemns Opposition Leader's Murder', *RFE/RL*, September 22. Available at: www.rferl.org/content/article/1089544.html (accessed 17 August 2010).

RFE/RL (2005) 'Factbox – Andijon Timeline', RFE/RL, Sep. 20. Available at: www.rferl.org/content/article/1061536.html (accessed 17 August 2010).

RFE/RL (2010a) 'More than Half of Osh Citizens Have Left the City', *RFE/RL*, 17 June.

RFE/RL (2010b) 'Thousands of Ethnic Uzbeks Returning to Kyrgyzstan', RFE/RL, 22 June.

RFE/RL (2010c) 'Kyrgyz Protest Electricity Price Hike', RFE/RL, 25 February. Available at: www.rferl.org/content/Kyrgyz_Protest_Electricity_Price_Hike_/1968192.html. Accessed 10 December 2010.

Robbins, Richard (2007) *Global Problems and the Culture of Capitalism*, 4th edn, Harlow, England: Pearson/Allyn & Bacon.

Roberts, John (2003) 'Caspian Oil and Gas: How Far Have We Come and Where Are We Going?' in Sally N. Cummings (ed.) *Oil, Transition and Security in Central Asia*, London: Routledge, pp. 143–60.

Roberts, Sean (2007) 'Everyday Negotiations of Islam in Central Asia: Practicing Religion in the Uyghur Neighborhood of *Zarya Vostoka* in Almaty, Kazakhstan', in Jeff Sahadeo and Russell Zanca (eds) *Everyday Life in Central Asia*, Bloomington, IN: Indiana University Press, pp. 339–54.

Rogers, Paul (2008) *Global Security and the War on Terror: Elite Power and the Illusion of Control*, London: Routledge.

Ro'i, Yaacov (2000) *Islam in the Soviet Union: From World War II to Perestroika*, London: Hurst.

Ro'i, Yaacov and Wainer, Alon (2009) 'Muslim Identity and Islamic Practice in Post-Soviet Central Asia', *Central Asian Survey*, 28(3), pp. 303–22.

Roy, Olivier (1997) 'Is the Conflict in Tajikistan a Model for Conflicts throughout Central Asia?' in Djalili Mohammad-Reza, Frédéric Grare and Shirin Akiner (eds) *Tajikistan: The Trials of Independence*, New York: St. Martin's Press, pp. 132–48.

Roy, Olivier (2000, 2007) *The New Central Asia: Geopolitics and the Birth of Nations*, New York: New York University Press.

Rubin, Barnett (1998) 'Russian Hegemony and State Breakdown in the Periphery: Causes and Consequences of the Tajik Civil War in Tajikistan', in Barnett Rubin and Jack Snyder (eds) *Post-Soviet Political Order: Conflict and State-building*, London: Routledge, pp. 128–61.

Rubin, Barnett (2005) *Fragmentation of Afghanistan*, New Haven, CT: Yale University Press.

Rubin, Barnett and Snyder, Jack (eds) (1998) *Post-Soviet Political Order: Conflict and State-Building*, London: Routledge.

Ruffin, M. Holt and Waugh, Daniel C. (eds) (1999) *Civil Society in Central Asia*, Seattle: University of Washington Press.

Ruggie, John (1998*) Constructing the World Polity: Essays on International Institutionalization*, London: Routledge Press.

Russett, Bruce and Oneal, John (2001) *Triangulating Peace: Democracy, Interdependence, and International Organizations*, New York: W.W. Norton & Co.

Rustemova, Assel (2011) 'Political Economy of Central Asia: Initial Reflections on the Need for a New Approach', *Journal of Eurasian Studies*, 2, pp. 30–39.

Rustow, Dankwart (1970) 'Transitions to Democracy: Toward a Dynamic Model', *Comparative Politics*, 2, pp. 337–63.

Rybakovskii, L.L. (1996) 'Tsentral'naia Aziia i Rossiia: Mezhgosudarstvennyi Migrat-sionnyi Obmen', in Vitkovskaia G. (ed.) *Migratsiia Russkoiazychnogo Naseleniia iz Tsentral'noi Azii: Prichiny, Posledstviia, Perspektivy*, Moscow, Carnegie Endowment for International Peace, pp. 70–91.

Rywkin, Michael (ed.) (1988) *Russian Colonial Expansion to 1917*, London: Mansell.

Sabol, Steven (2003) 'Kazak Resistance to Russian Colonization: Interpreting the Kenesary Kasymov Revolt, 1837–1847', *Central Asian Survey*, 22(2), pp. 24–39.

Safronov, R. (1999) 'Tendentsii Razvitiya Islama v Tsentral'noi Azii', *Tsentral'naya Aziya i Kavkaz. Central Asia and the Caucasus: Journal of Social and Political Studies*.

Sahadeo, Jeff and Zanca, Russell (eds) (2007) *Everyday Life in Central Asia*, Bloomington, IN: Indiana University Press.

Said, Edward (2003) *Orientalism,* 3rd edn, London: Penguin.

Saidazimova, G. (2005) 'Kyrgyzstan: OSCE Election Observers Criticize Elections', *RFE/ RL*, February 28. Accessed 9 January 2011.

Sakwa, Richard (1989) *Soviet Politics: An Introduction,* London: Routledge.

Sandström, Björn (2004) *Nuclear Risk Assessment: Central Asia after Independence,* Stockholm: FOI: Swedish Defence Research Agency.

Sanghera, Balihar and Ilyasov, Aibek (2008) 'The Social Embeddedness of Professions in Kyrgyzstan: An Investigation into Professionalism, Institutions and Emotions', *Europe-Asia Studies*, 60(4), 643–61.

Sanghera, Balihar, Ablezova, Mehrigiul, and Botoeva, Aisalkyn (2010) 'Everyday Morality in Families and a Critique of Social Capital: An Investigation into Moral Judgements, Responsibilities and Sentiments in Kyrgyzstani Households', *Theory and Society*, 40(2), pp. 167–90.

Saray, Mehmet (1989) *The Turkmens in the Age of Imperialism: A Study of the Turkmen People and Their Incorporation into the Russian Empire*, Ankara: TTK.

Saroyan, Mark (1993) 'Rethinking Islam in the Soviet Union', in Susan Gross Solomon (ed.) *Beyond Sovietology: Essays in Politics and History*, Armonk, NY: M. E. Sharpe.

Saroyan, Mark and Walker, Edward (ed.) (1997) *Minorities, Mullahs, and Modernity: Reshaping Community in the Former Soviet Union*, Berkeley: University of California.

Satybaldieva, Elmira (2010) *The Nature of Local Politics in Rural Kyrgyzstan: A Study of Social Inequalities, Everyday Politics and Neo-liberalism* (unpublished PhD thesis, University of Kent).

Saunders, Robert A. (2010) *The Many Faces of Sacha Baron Cohen: Politics, Parody, and the Battle over Borat*, New York: Lexington Books Inc.

Savin, Igor (2003) 'Hizb Ut-Tahrir in Southern Kazakhstan: Social Makeup', *Central Asia and the Caucasus: Journal of Social and Political Studies*, 6(24). Available at: www. ca-c.org.ezproxy.st-andrews.ac.uk/online/2003/journal_eng/cac-06/08.saven.shtml (accessed 25 June 2008).

Schatz, Edward (2000) 'Framing Strategies and Non-Conflict in Multi-Ethnic Kazakhstan', *Nationalism and Ethnic Politics*, 6(2), pp. 70–92.

Schatz, Edward (2004) 'What Capital Cities Say about State and Nation Building', *Nationalism and Ethnic Politics*, 9(4), pp. 111–40.

Schatz, Edward (2005) *Modern Clan Politics and Beyond: The Power of 'Blood' in Kazakhstan*, Seattle, WA: University of Washington Press.

Schatz, Edward (2006) 'Access by Accident: Legitimacy Claims and Democracy Promotion in Authoritarian Central Asia', *International Political Science Review / Revue Internationale de Science Politique*, 27(3), pp. 263–84.

Schatz, Edward and Levine, Renan (2008) 'Framing, Diplomacy and Anti-americanism in Central Asia', Paper presented at the 2009 Annual Meeting of the American Political Science Association, Toronto, ON, Canada. Available at: http://works.bepress.com/ renan/15

Schlichte, Klaus (2005) *The Dynamics of the States: the Formation and Crises of State Domination*, Aldershot: Ashgate.

Schoeberlein, John (1994) *Identity in Central Asia: Construction and Contention in the Conceptions of "Özbek," "Tâjik," "Muslim," "Samarqandi" and other Groups*, Unpublished PhD Dissertation, Harvard University 1994.

Schoeberlein, John (1995) 'Conflict in Tajikistan and Central Asia: the myth of ethnic animosity', *Harvard Middle Eastern and Islamic Review*, 2(1), pp. 1–55.

Schoeberlein, John (2000) 'Between Two Worlds: Obstacles to Development and Prosperity', *Harvard International Review*, 22(1), pp. 56–61.

Schoeberlein, John (2002a) 'Setting the Stakes of a New Society', *Central Eurasian Studies Review*, 1(1), pp. 4–8.

Schoeberlein, John (2002b) 'The Role of Resources in Conflicts in Central Asia', in J. Verhoeven et al (eds) *Searching for Peace in Asia: An Overview of Conflict Prevention and Peacebuilding Activities*, Boulder, CO: Lynne Rienner.

Schulz, Michael, Söderbaum, Fredrik and Öjendal, Joakim (2001) (eds) *Regionalization in a Globalizing World: A Comparative Perspective on Forms, Actors and Processes*, London and New York: Zed Books.

Schweller, Randall L. (1998) *Deadly Imbalances: Tripolarity and Hitler's Strategy of World Conquest*, New York: Columbia University Press.

Schweller, Randall L. (2006) *Unanswered Threats: Political Constraints on the Balance of Power*, Princeton, NJ: Princeton University Press.

Seger, Alexander (1996) *Drugs and Development in the Central Asian Republics*, Bonn: Deutsche Gesellschaft fur Technische Zusammenarbeit.

Sestanovich, Stephan (2000/2001) 'Where does Russia Belong?' *The National Interest*. Available at: http://nationalinterest.org/article/where-does-russia-belong-629 (accessed 25 July 2008).

Seymor, Becker (1968) *Russian Protectorates in Central Asia: Bukhara and Khiva 1865–1924*, Cambridge, MA: Harvard University Press.

Seymor, Becker (1982) *Moscow's Muslim Challenge: Soviet Central Asia*, Armonk, NY: M.E. Sharpe.

Seymor, Becker (1995) 'The Creation of Soviet Central Asia: The 1924 National Delimitation', *Central Asian Survey*, 14(2), pp. 225–41.

Shahrani, M. Nazif (1984) 'From Tribe to Umma: Comments on the Dynamics of Identity in Muslim Soviet Central Asia', *Central Asian Survey*, 3(3), pp. 27–38.

Shambaugh, David (2003) China and the Korean Peninsula: Playing for the Long Term, *Washington Quarterly*, 26(2), pp. 43–56.

Sheives, Kevin (2006) 'China Turns West: Beijing's Contemporary Strategy Towards Central Asia', *Pacific Affairs*, 79(2), pp. 205–24.

Shelley, Louise (1999) 'Identifying, Counting, and Categorizing Transnational Organized Crime', *Transnational Organized Crime* 5, no. 1 (Spring 1999), pp. 1–18.

Shreeves, Rosamund (2002) 'Broadening the Concept of Privatization: Gender and Development in Rural Kazakhstan', in Ruth Mandel and Caroline Humphrey (eds) *Markets and Moralities: Ethnographies of Postsocialism*, Oxford: Berg, pp. 211–35.

Sievers, Eric (2003) *The Post-Soviet Decline of Central Asia: Sustainable Development and Comprehensive Capital*, London: Routledge.

Sinnott, Peter (1992) 'The Physical Geography of Soviet Central Asia and the Aral Sea Problem', in Robert A. Lewis (ed.) *Geographic Perspectives on Central Asia*, London and New York.

Sinor, Denis (1977) 'Modern Hungary', Bloomington, IN: Indiana University Press.

Sinor, Denis (1990) 'Introduction: The Concept of Inner Asia', in Denis Sinor (ed.) *The Cambridge History of Early Inner Asia*, Cambridge: Cambridge University Press, pp. 1–18.

Sinor, Denis (1997) *Studies in Medieval Inner Asia*, Aldershot: Ashgate Publishing.

Sjöberg, Fredrik M. (2011) *Competitive Elections in Authoritarian States*, Ph.D. Dissertation, Uppsala University.

Slezkine, Yuri (1994) 'The USSR as a Communal Apartment, or How a Socialist State Promoted Ethnic Particularism', *Slavic Review*, 53(2), pp. 414–52.

Smith, Graham (ed.) (1996) *The Nationalities Question in the Post-Soviet states*, 2nd edn, London and New York: Longman.

Smith, Jeremy (1997) 'The Education of National Minorities: The Early Soviet Experience', *The Slavonic and East European Review*, 75(2), pp. 281–307.

Smith, R. Grant (1999) 'Tajikistan: The Rocky Road to Peace', *Central Asian Survey*, 18(2), pp. 243–51.

Snyder, Jack (2000) *From Voting to Violence: Democratization and Nationalist Conflict*, New York: W.W. Norton.

Sokov, Nikolai (2005) 'The Not So Great Game in Central Asia', *Ponars Policy Memo Centre for Strategic and International Studies*, 403. Available at: http://csis.org/publication/ponars-policy-memo-403-not-so-great-game-central-asia (accessed 30 August 2009).

Soucek, Svat (2000) *A History of Inner Asia*, Cambridge, UK: Cambridge University Press.

Spechler, Martin C. (1999) 'Regional Cooperation in Central Asia: Promises and Reality', *Anthropology of East Europe Review*, 17(2), pp. 29–30.

Spechler, Martin C. (2002) 'Regional Cooperation in Central Asia', *Problems of Post-Communism*, 49(6), pp. 42–47.

Spechler, Martin C. (2007) 'Authoritarian Politics and Economic Reform in Uzbekistan: Past, Present and Prospects', *Central Asian Survey*, 26(2), pp. 185–202.

Spoor, Max (2007a) 'Cotton in Central Asia "Curse" or "Foundation of Development"', in Deniz Kandiyoti (ed.) *The Cotton Sector in Central Asia: Economic Policy and Development Challenges*, London: The School of Oriental and African Studies, pp. 54–74.

Spoor, Max (2007b) *Ten Propositions on Rural Poverty and Agrarian Transition in Central Eurasia*, Barcelona: IBEI Working Paper Series.

START (2011) 'Terrorist Organization Profile: United Tajik Opposition', *START: National Consortium for the Study of Terrorism and Responses to Terrorism*, University of Maryland. Available at: www.start.umd.edu/start/data_collections/tops/terrorist_organization_profile.asp?id=3688 (accessed 17 August 2010).

Suleimenov, Olzhas (1995) 'The Collapse of the Soviet Union is Tragedy to US', *Dagens Nyheter*, 28 April.

Sultanov, V.K. et al (2008) *SHOS v Poiskakh Novogo Ponimaniya Bezopasnosti: Mat. Mezhdura. Nauch. Konf. Almaty 4 October 2007*, Almaty: KISI.

Suny, Ronald Grigor (1993) *The Revenge of the Past*, Stanford, CA: Stanford University Press.

Suny, Ronald Grigor (1999) 'Provisional Stabilities: The Politics of Identities in Post-Soviet Eurasia', *International Security*, 24(3), pp. 139–78.

Sürücü, Cengiz (2002) 'Modernity, Nationalism, Resistance: Identity Politics in Post-Soviet Kazakhstan', *Central Asian Survey*, 21(4), pp. 385–402.

Suyarkulova, Mohira (2011) 'Reluctant Sovereigns: Central Asian States' Path to Independence' in Sally N. Cummings and Raymond Hinnebusch (eds) *Sovereignty after Empire: Comparing the Middle East and Central Asia* (Edinburgh: Edinburgh University Press), pp. 127–53.

Suyunbaev, Murat N. (2010) 'Estestvennye Osnovaniya Integratsii/Dezintegratsii Tsentral'noi Evrazii in *Sovremennye Vyzovy bezopasnosti Tsentral'noi Azii* Bishkek', pp. 143–9.

Svanberg, Ingvar (ed.) (1999) *Contemporary Kazakhs: Cultural and Social Perspectives*, London: St Martin's Press.

Swanström, Niklas (2005) 'China and Central Asia: A New Great Game or Traditional Vassal Relations?' *Journal of Contemporary China*, 14(45), pp. 569–84.

Swanström, Niklas (2010) 'Traditional and Non-traditional Security Threats in Central Asia: Connecting the New and the Old', *China and Eurasia Forum Quarterly*, 8(2), pp. 35–51.

Synovitz, Ron (2001) 'Central Asia: EBRD Says Reforms will Help Seize the Moment'. Available at www.rferl.org/nca/features/2001/11/20112001084505.asp (accessed 20 November 2001).

Tabyshalieva, Anara (1999) *The Challenge of Regional Cooperation in Central Asia: Preventing Ethnic Conflict in the Ferghana Valley*, Washington, DC: United States Institute of Peace.

Tabyshalieva, Anara (2000) *Post-Soviet Central Asia: Subregional Cooperation and Peace*, Peace and Security in Central Asia Occasional paper.

Tadjbaksh, Shahrbanou (1993) 'Causes and Consequences of the Civil War', *Central Asian Monitor*, 2, pp. 10–14.

Talbott, Strobe (1997) '"A Farewell to Flashman": American Policy in the Caucasus and Central Asia', speech delivered at the Central Asian Institute, Johns Hopkins University School of Advanced International Studies, Washington, DC, 21 July. Available at www.state.gov/www/regions/nis/970721talbott.html (accessed 29 August 2010).

Tazmini, Ghoncheh (2001) 'The Islamic Revival in Central Asia: A Potent Force or a Misconception?' *Central Asian Survey*, 20(1), pp. 63–83.

Teichmann, Christian (2007) 'Canals, Cotton, and the Limits of De-colonization in Soviet Uzbekistan, 1924–1941', *Central Asian Survey*, 26(4), pp. 499–519.

Terriff, Terry and Croft, Stuart (eds.) (2000) *Critical Reflections on Security and Change*, London: Routledge.

Thachuk, Kimberley L. (2001) 'Transnational Threats: Falling Through the Crack?' *Low Intensity Conflict & Law Enforcement*, 10(1), pp. 47–67.

Thoenes, Sander (1996) 'Kazakhstan's Sale of the Century', *Financial Times* (London), 25 October.

Thomas, Caroline (2000) *Global Governance, Development and Human Security*, London: Pluto Press.

Tishkov, Valerii (1992) *The Principal Problems and Prospects of the Development of National-territorial Entities in the Russian Federation*, Harvard University: John F. Kennedy School of Government.

Tolipov, Farkhod (2006) 'Central Asia is a Region of Five Stans', *Central Asia and the Caucasus: Journal of Social and Political Studies*, 2(38), pp. 17–26.

Trenin, Dmitri (2001) *The End of Eurasia: Russia on the Border between Geopolitics and Globalization*, Moscow: Carnegie Moscow Centre.

Trilling, D. (2010a) 'Kyrgyzstan: UN Head Chides Bakiyev as More Media Outlets Blocked', *EurasiaNet*, 4 April, available at: www.eurasianet.org/departments/civilsociety/articles/eav040510.shtml. Accessed on 17 September 2010.

Trilling, D. (2010b) 'Kyrgyzstan: Bishkek Hesitant as Otunbayeva Forms New Government', *EurasiaNet*, 8 April, available at: www.eurasianet.org/departments/insight/articles/eav040810a.shtml. Accessed on 17 August 2010.

Trisko, Jessica N. (2005) 'Coping with the Islamist Threat: Analysing Repression in Kazakhstan, Kyrgyzstan and Uzbekistan', *Central Asian Survey*, 24(4), pp. 373–89.

Tunçer-Kilavuz, İdil (2009a) 'Political and Social Networks in Tajikistan and Uzbekistan: "Clan", Region and Beyond', *Central Asian Survey*, 28(3), pp. 323–34.

Tunçer-Kilavuz, İdil (2009b) 'The Role of Networks in Tajikistan's Civil War: Network Activation and Violence Specialists', *Nationalities Papers: The Journal of Nationalism and Ethnicity*, 37(5), pp. 693–717.

Tunçer-Kilavuz, İdil (2011) 'Understanding Civil War: A Comparison of Tajikistan and Uzbekistan', *Europe-Asia Studies*, 63(2), pp. 263–90.

Turam, Berna (2004) 'A Bargain between the Secular State and Turkish Islam: Politics of Ethnicity in Central Asia', *Nations and Nationalism*, 10(3), pp. 353–74.

Ullman, Richard (1983) 'Redefining Security', *International Security*, 8(1), pp. 129–53.

Umarov, F.B. (2006) 'Rol' Shankhaiskoi Organizatsii Sotrudnichestva (SHOS) v Protsesse Regional'noi Globalizatsii', *Tadzhikistan I Sovremennyi mir*, 3(12), pp. 69–71.

UNESCO (1992) *History of Civilizations of Central Asia*, UNESCO, Paris, Vol. 1, pp. 477–80.

United Nations Human Development Report (1994) New York: Oxford University Press for the United Nations Development Program.

Ushakova, N.A. (2001) 'Tsentral' Noaziatskoe Ekonomicheskoe Soobshchestvo', *Protsessy Integratsii na Postsovetskom Prostranstve: Tendentsii i Protivorechiia*, Moscow: Rossiiskaia akademiia nauk, Institut mezhdunarodnykh ekonomicheskikh i politicheskikh issledovanii.

Ushakova, N.A. (2003) 'Central Asian Cooperation: Toward Transformation', *Central Asia and the Caucasus*, 21(3). Available at: www.ca-c.org.ezproxy.st-andrews.ac.uk/online/2003/journal_eng/cac-03/16.usaeng.shtml (accessed 15 February 2011).

Vakhabov, M.G. (1961) *Formirovanie Uzbekskoi Sotsialisticheskoi Natsii*, Tashkent.

Van der Heide, Nienke (2008) *Spirited Performance: The Manas Epic and Society in Kyrgyzstan*, Amsterdam: Dutch University Press.

Von Hagen, Mark (2004) 'Empires, Borderlands and Diasporas: Eurasia as Anti-Paradigm for the Post-Soviet Era', *The American Historical Review* 109(2), pp. 445–68. Available at: www.historycooperative.org/journals/ahr/109.2/hagen.html (accessed 23 February 2011).

Von Hellwald, Friedrich (1874) *The Russians in Central Asia: A Critical Examination Down to the Present Time of the Geography and History of Central Asia*, Translated by Lieut.-Col Theodore Wirgman, LL.B., London: Henry King & Co.

Wæver, Ole (1995) 'Securitization and Desecuritization', in Ronnie D. Lipschutz (ed.) *On Security*, New York: Columbia University Press, pp. 46–86.

Walker, Edward (2003) 'Islam, Islamism, and Political Order in Central Asia', *Journal of International Affairs*, pp. 247–71.

Walt, Stephen (2000) *Keeping the World "Off-balance"*: Self-restraint and U.S. Foreign Policy Research Programs, John F. Kennedy School of Government, Harvard University.

Waltz, Kenneth (1979) *Theory of International Politics*, New York: McGraw-Hill.

Walzer, Michael (1977) *Just and Unjust Wars*, New York: Basic Books.

Wardlaw, Grant (1982) *Political Terrorism: Theory, Tactics, and Counter-measures*, Cambridge, UK: Cambridge University Press.

Wegerich, Kai (2006) '"A Little Help from My Friend?" Analysis of Network Links on the Meso Level in Uzbekistan', *Central Asian Survey*, 25(1), pp. 115–28.

Wegren, S.K. (ed.) (1988) *Land Reform in the Former Soviet Union and Eastern Europe*, London: Routledge.

Weinthal, Erika (2002) *State Making and Environmental Cooperation: Linking Domestic and International Politics in Central Asia*, Cambridge, MA: MIT Press.

Weisbrode, Kenneth (2000) 'More to the World than Oil', *Foreign Affairs*, 79(2), pp. 183–4.

Weitz, Richard (2004) 'Storm Clouds over Central Asia: Revival of the Islamic Movement of Uzbekistan (IMU)?' *Studies in Conflict and Terrorism*, 27(6), pp. 505–30.

Welt, Cory and Bremmer, Ian (1995) 'Kazakhstan's Quandary', *Journal of Democracy*, 6(3), pp. 139–54.

Wendt, Alexander (1992) 'Anarchy is What States Make of It', *International Organization*, 46(2), pp. 391–425.

Wendt, Alexander (1999) *Social Theory of International Politics*, Cambridge: Cambridge University Press.

Werner, Cynthia (1998) 'Household Networks and the Security of Mutual Indebtedness in Rural Kazakhstan', *Central Asian Survey*, 17(4), pp. 597–612.

Werner, Cynthia (2009) 'Bride Abduction in Post-Soviet Central Asia: Marking a Shift Towards Patriarchy Through Local Discourses of Shame and Tradition', *Journal of Royal Anthropological Institute*, 15, pp. 314–31.

Wheeler, Geoffrey (1968) 'National and Religious Consciousness in Soviet Islam', *Survey*, January, pp. 29–47.

Williams, Phil (2001) 'Transnational Criminal Networks', in J. Arquilla and D. Ronfeldt (eds) *Networks and Netwars: The Future of Terror, Crime and Militancy*, Santa Monica, CA: RAND Corporation, pp. 61–97.

Winrow, Gareth (2001) *Turkey and the Caucasus*, Washington DC: Brookings Institute Press.

Wolfers, Arnold (1962) *Discord and Collaboration: Essays on International Politics*, Baltimore, MD: Johns Hopkins University Press.

Wood, D. (2010) 'Electricity Plays Key Role in Kyrgyzstan Uprising', World Resources Institute, 19 April. Available at: www.wri.org/stories/2010/04/electricity-plays-key-role-kyrgyzstan-uprising (accessed 17 August 2010).

Woodward. Susan L. (1995) *Balkan Tragedy: Chaos and Dissolution after the Cold War*, Washington DC: The Brookings Institution.

World Development Report: Conflict, Security and Development (2011) Washington, DC: World Bank Publications.

World Drug Report (2009) New York: United Nations Office on Drugs and Crime (UNODC).

Wright, R. and Tyson, A.S. (2005) 'U.S. Evicted from Air Base in Uzbekistan', *Washington Post*, 30 July.

Yapp, M. (1994) 'Tradition and Change in Central Asia', in Shirin Akiner (ed.) *Political and Economic Trends in Central Asia*, London: British Academic Press, pp. 1–10.

Yuldasheva, Guli (2002) 'Islam in Uzbekistan: Peculiarities and Perspectives for Development in the Context of Global Changes in Islam', *Central Asia and the Caucasus: Journal of Social and Political Studies*, 4(16).

Yuldasheva, Guli, Hashimova, Umida, Callahan, James (eds) (2010) 'Current Trends in Water Management in Central Asia', *Peace and Conflict Review*, 5(1), pp. 1–13.

Yurchak, Alexei (2006) *Everything was Forever, Until it was No More: The Last Soviet Generation*, Princeton, NJ: Princeton University Press.

Zacher, Mark W. and Matthew, Richard A. (1995) 'Liberal International Theory: Common Threads, Divergent Strands', in Charles Kegley (ed.) *Controversies in International Relations Theory: Realism and the Neo-liberal Challenge*, New York: St. Martin's Press, pp. 107–50.

Zanca, Russell (2004) 'Explaining Islam in Central Asia: An Anthropological Approach for Uzbekistan', *Journal of Muslim Minority Affairs*, 24(1), pp. 99–107.

Zhovtis, Evgenii (2008) 'Democratisation and Human Rights in Central Asia: Problems, Development Prospects and the Role of the International Community', *Engaging Central Asia: The European Union's Strategy in the Heart of Eurasia*, Brussels: Centre for European Policy Studies, pp. 20–42.

Zhusupov, Sabit (1998) 'Politicheskaya Elita Kazakhstana: Mekhanizmy Konsolidatsii I Rekrutirovaniia', paper presented at the Carnegie Foundation, Moscow.

Zhusupov, Sabit (2000) 'Democratic Reforms in the Republic of Kazakhstan: Reality and Prospects', *Central Asia and the Caucasus: Journal of Social and Political Studies*, 4. Available at: www.ca-c.org.ezproxy.st-andrews.ac.uk/online/2000/journal_eng/eng04_2000/04.zhus.shtml.

Zhusupov, Sabit (2008) *Politicheskaya Analitika Issledovaniya*, Almaty: Arna-b.

Zviagelskaia, Irina (1995) *The Russian Policy Debate on Central Asia*, London: The Royal Institute for International Affairs.

Index